JUST
ONE
YEAR

JUST ONE YEAR

A Global Treasury of Prayer and Worship

*Edited by*Timothy Radcliffe OP

ORBIS BOOKS
Maryknoll, New York 10545

Founded in 1970, Orbis Books endeavors to publish works that enlighten the mind, nourish the spirit, and challenge the conscience. The publishing arm of the Maryknoll Fathers and Brothers, Orbis seeks to explore the global dimensions of the Christian faith and mission, to invite dialogue with diverse cultures and religious traditions, and to serve the cause of reconciliation and peace. The books published reflect the views of their authors and do not represent the official position of the Maryknoll Society. To learn more about Maryknoll and Orbis Books, please visit our website at www.maryknoll.org.

First published in the United States in 2007 by
Orbis Books, Maryknoll, New York 10545-0308

First published in Great Britain in 2006 by
Darton, Longman & Todd, 1 Spencer Court, 140-142 Wandsworth High Street
London SW18 4JJ

CAFOD, Romero Close, Stockwell Road, London SW9 9TY

Christian Aid, 35 Lower Marsh, London SE1 7RL

Manufactured in the United States of America.

Library of Congress Cataloging-in-Publication Data

Just one year : a global treasury of prayer and worship / edited by Timothy Radcliffe.
    p. cm.
  Includes index.
  ISBN 978-1-57075-714-3 (pbk.)
  1. Poverty—Religious aspects—Christianity—Meditations. 2. Church work with the poor—Meditations. 3. Church year meditations. I. Radcliffe, Timothy.
  BV639.P6J87 2007
  242'.3--dc22

                                          2006101245

Contents

Preface

Through the seasons of the Christian year we remember, celebrate and enter more deeply into God's promises for the whole of creation. Every twelve months we live through the patient waiting of Advent and the birth of Jesus at Christmas, through the ashes of Lent and the darkness of Holy Week to the exhilaration of Easter, until finally at the end of the year we look forward to the coming of the Kingdom at the end of time.

The work of the overseas development agencies of our churches, CAFOD and Christian Aid, is not about generosity to needy people. It is about welcoming and using fully the gift of the new creation that is proclaimed throughout the Christian year. As Timothy Radcliffe writes, it is 'knitting together the human family in which we can all belong and discovering our shared humanity. It is healing the wounds of suffering and injustice that stop all human beings being fully alive.'

The prayers and reflections in *Just One Year* have been written by people engaged in the struggle for justice in many different situations around the world. Each of them expresses, in their own particular way and from out of their own personal experience, the urgency of God's demand for a renewal of creation. They are disturbing, moving and impossible to ignore. They are wonderful texts which will prove invaluable for both private and public worship. These prayers and reflections are more than 'resources'. When we gather in our churches and communities for worship, we enter into a yearly cycle not only of hearing the Word of God but of responding to it. In our Eucharists and Communions, as well as other weekly services of worship, in the gestures we make and in the words of anger and shame and yearning for a more just world that we proclaim, we share in the building of the Kingdom, welcoming a future that transcends all we can imagine.

Paula Clifford, Christian Aid
Linda Jones, CAFOD

The Christian Year: What Does It Mean to Celebrate It?

The Christian year tells a story. We begin with Advent, awaiting the birth of Christ, then make our way through Christmas, Lent, Holy Week, Easter, the Ascension and Pentecost, until we get to the end of the year, which looks forward to the end of time, the final coming of Christ and the Kingdom of God. We are invited to find ourselves inside this story. This book follows the evolution of this drama and offers material for us to celebrate its seasons.

What does it mean to live within this story? It tells us two things: who we are and what we hope for. First of all, then, who we are: one of the ways in which we understand ourselves is by telling stories about ourselves and other people. When we come home at night after a day's work, we tell stories of what we have done and whom we have seen. We tell stories of our childhood and of our friendships. We tell stories of our holidays and school days. All these stories explore and express our identity.

There are also stories that explore the identity that we share with larger groups, as members of a family, tribe or nation, as a supporter of a football club or a pupil of a school. I discover who I am by exploring who 'we' are. The only prize that I ever won at school was called, I think, *Little Arthur's History of England*. I was very proud of this prize, although I must admit that everyone in the class won a prize too! This history of England was intended to give me a sense of who we are as English people. It mainly told how we went around killing lots of other people, although I hardly noticed that at the time. But we carry with us lots of other stories: stories of our ancestors that tell us what it means to belong to this family, or stories of the wonderful victories of Newcastle United (founded by the Dominicans!), which tell us what it means to belong to the community of their supporters. Part of being a Dominican is that I learn stories about the foundation of the Order, and of what we have done through the centuries.

Every year, we live through the drama which is the Christian year, from waiting for Christ to be born, until we finish with the Feast of Christ the King. To live within this story is to express and explore an identity. On one level it is obvious that this is the identity of being Christian rather than, for example, Muslim. They celebrate Ramadan and we celebrate Lent. You can spot some Christians on Ash Wednesday by the smudge of ash on their foreheads. This shows that they are taking part in the annual cycle of feasts and fasts that belong to the Christian life. One used to be able to spot Catholics because we always had fish on Fridays.

But the Christian story is an odd one, because it is not fundamentally about being a Christian but about being human. The story that we re-enact each year points us not towards some cosy future in which all Christians will be gathered together around Christ, but towards the Kingdom in which all of humanity will be reconciled and united. To be a Christian is to claim that one's ultimate identity is to be found only in unity with the whole of the rest of humanity, when in Christ all divisions have been destroyed. He is the one in whom 'all the fullness of God was pleased to dwell, and through him God was pleased to reconcile to himself all things, whether on earth or in heaven, by making peace through the blood of his cross' (Colossians 1:19f). When, as a child, I became absorbed in *Little Arthur's History of England*, I was being initiated into an identity which marked me out from other people. I was English and so not French or German or American. But to live within the rhythm of the Christian story should not give me an identity which is exclusive – not Muslim or Buddhist. It invites me beyond all exclusive identities. It tells me that we cannot flourish fully and be properly ourselves outside the Kingdom, in which all injustice and suffering and inequality will be over. Herbert McCabe OP asserts that 'baptism is not the sacrament of membership of the Church, it *is* membership of the Church; it is the sacrament of membership of humanity.'

Stories tell us where we belong and what our home is like. Stories of England or India or Zimbabwe tell people that this is where they are at home. It is interesting that the story that we live every year as Christians has its roots in the Jewish story of the Exodus, which told of how the Hebrews were summoned by God out of slavery in Egypt to worship him in freedom on Mount Sinai. God then led them to the Promised Land, flowing with milk and honey. This was the story that Jesus remembered and celebrated with his disciples as they gathered together in the upper room on the night before he was brutally killed. They celebrated the Passover, the story of liberation and home-coming. But then Jesus took bread, blessed it and broke it and gave it to them saying, 'This is my body, given for you.' And so with the wine. This is the core of our Christian story, and tells of the home-coming of all humanity, the promise that in Christ all conflict and rivalry and hatred will be finished. So to be a Christian is to have an odd sort of identity. On one level, it is an exclusive identity. If one is a Christian then one is not an atheist or a Hindu. But on another level, it is an identity which points one beyond all exclusions, to a home which we cannot yet imagine or understand, as a citizen of the Kingdom.

The seed from which the Christian year grew, then, was the memory of the events which spanned Maundy Thursday and Easter Sunday. During the early centuries the story began to expand backwards and forwards to cover the whole year. In the early fourth century it spread backwards to include Lent, which was originally the time during which converts prepared themselves to enter the community by baptism during the Easter Vigil. And it spread forward, with the Easter season continuing until Pentecost. In this Easter time it was forbidden for Christians to kneel down or to fast. We had to stand up to show that God has raised us to our feet and will raise us up after death. And we feasted to celebrate our redemption. Then in the mid-fourth century we see the emergence of Christmas, with Advent being added in the sixth century. The story gradually evolved so as to explore more deeply who we are and what we hope for.

Each year we live through this long story. It stretches open our little identities, as English or Irish, as followers of this football team or that band, and points towards a larger identity which is beyond words, which is to be a member of the whole of humanity in Christ. No matter what is going on in our personal and family lives, Advent comes and we begin to wait for the birth of Christ. It has a rhythm that may not always chime in with what we are feeling at that moment. On some Good Fridays we may be filled with happiness for some reason: Newcastle United have won a match, the sun is shining and we shall be meeting someone we love at the end of the day. And yet this day in the year summons us to sorrow. On Easter Day the Church summons us to rejoice, but we may be feeling miserable. Notoriously Christmas is a time when millions of people feel depressed.

So what is the point of our lives being shaped by this Christian year, with its rhythm of anticipation and celebration, mourning and rejoicing? It reminds us that we belong with people who are different from us, whom we do not even know and yet who are our brothers and sisters in God. For some of the poorest, it is always Good Friday. Millions are crucified by debt and poverty. On Good Friday we share their desolation. For if they are dying then so are we, for they are flesh of our flesh. On Easter we are invited to rejoice, even if our lives are sad for some reason. We rejoice with the whole community which celebrates the conquest of death and injustice.

Following the story of Christ's life takes us through every possible emotion, from desolation to exultation. It stretches open our hearts and minds to identify with people who live all these moments now. Christ now is arrested unjustly and tortured by the police and soldiers all over the world. Christ today has his head covered with plastic bags and is beaten on his feet in torture cells everywhere. Christ is humiliated and mocked, and dies in millions of people. Christ today rises from the dead, in millions of small victories over injustice. Our story is his story. His story is ours. The Christian year stretches us open to all humanity, with its suffering and flourishing. By celebrating the drama every year our own personal and private stories are taken into the story of humanity.

The mission of Christian Aid and CAFOD is to work for a world in which poverty and injustice will be over and in which the dignity of every human being will be respected. This is about more than economics. It is about helping a world to emerge in which who we are and what it means to be human will be visible. If the humanity of any of our brothers and sisters on this planet is hidden or destroyed, then humanity itself is wounded. So making our way through the cycle of the Christian year, marking all its seasons, is a reaching out to discover who we are with each other in Christ.

We celebrate this year. The word 'celebrate' comes from the same root as 'celebrity'. To celebrate is to rejoice in, to pay honour to. We live in a culture of celebrity. Surveys have shown that the highest aspiration of the young in both Europe and the United States is to become a celebrity. To be a celebrity is of course, as it is often said, to be famous for being famous! But being famous is a sort of peak of existence. To be seen on the television is to really exist, to matter. This desire for fame has always existed. When St Augustine was a young man, he and his fellow young Africans longed 'to live for ever in the mouths of the people'. But celebrities are puffed up for a moment, and then deflated by the media that gave them existence. Most of the six billion people on this planet will not be known a few miles from where they are born and die. The vast majority of people live and die virtually in oblivion.

We celebrate the Christian year. And this means that we celebrate something deeper than celebrity. We celebrate the God whose memory embraces everyone and who never forgets. Inside this vast story sweeping from creation to the Kingdom, there is a space for all the little stories of the small people who are easily overlooked. In the Gospels we see Jesus meeting lepers, whom people wished to forget, and widows with their mites, whom they would never have noticed. We celebrate that you do not have to be a celebrity to matter, for in this story of God's friendship with humanity, no one is too insignificant for God. Jesus said, 'Whatever you do to the least of these, you do to me.'

This book is supposed to be a resource for the celebration of the Christian year. And one way that it does that is to include as often as possible the stories of those who are *often* unnoticed or ignored. The celebration of the Christian year honours those who are not famous, who have no adulation, and whose memories are not cherished. We hear their stories, and are offered the possibility of praying with their prayers. The book is full of their names, from all over the globe.

In Natal, one of my brethren, Philippe Denis, runs a project for AIDS orphans. Often these children lose both their parents. They grow up with no memories of their ancestors, and so no knowledge of who they are. Philippe helps them to make memory boxes for keeping photos, letters, bits of clothing: anything that preserves a memory of those who gave birth to them. This means that they have some sign of their identity, of their roots in the past. They have a sense of who they are, to which they can cling in this uncertain world. But humanity needs its memory boxes too, because those whom we forget are our brothers and sisters too. They have their part in the story of humanity that we celebrate. In this book we offer the prayers and reflections of people who come from all parts of the globe. When we prepare meetings or worship to celebrate the seasons of the Christian year, then we will be able to hear their voices too. Our own communities will be stretched open to hear the voices of our unknown brothers and sisters. We may be touched by a glimpse of the spaciousness of the Kingdom.

The second thing that this story of the Christian year does is to give us hope. Eight million people a year die of poverty; millions are suffering from malnutrition, AIDS and malaria. Unjust economic structures bring increasing wealth to some and poverty to others. Our planet is threatened by ecological disaster. The challenges are so great that we might feel tempted to give up and join the 'now generation': eat, drink and be merry for tomorrow we shall die.

We live in a time in which many people have lost hope for the future. This does not mean that they are miserable or depressed all the time. It is just that at the beginning of the third millennium we have fewer shared dreams for the future of humanity. Oliver Bennett of Warwick University wrote a book called *Cultural Pessimism: Narratives of Decline in the Postmodern World*.[1] He argues that with the increasing inequalities of our world, the spread of AIDS, growing violence in the inner city, the diffusion of criminal networks, we are suffering from a collective depression. Gone are the dreams of the 1960s, when everything seemed possible. Faced with the future, we have no good story to tell. Many people have ceased to dream of how we can make the world a better place for everyone, and tend to concentrate on what we can do for ourselves. Progress has been privatised.

There are today two stories that are often told about the future of humanity. The first is of ecological disaster and the second is of a war on terrorism. Neither of these promise anything for us and our children. The leaders of the rich nations, especially the United States, seem to lack the political will to confront pollution, and the war on terrorism seems to hold out the prospect of endless violence. What could ever count as winning it? Sir Martin Rees, the President of the Royal Society, recently published a book called *Our Final Century? Will the Human Race Survive the Twenty-first Century?*[2]

In the face of this temptation to despair, what is the hope that our Christian story offers? Does it tell us what is going to happen? Can we read the Bible and have a special knowledge of what is around the corner? I do not believe so. People have always tried to read the Book of Revelation as giving us hidden clues as to what is imminent, but it never turns out as they expect. In every generation people have examined the numbers and declared that 'the end is nigh', and they have always turned out to be wrong. I do not think that the Bible should be read as coded history. We do believe that God will be faithful to humanity, and that we shall ultimately find peace and flourishing in God. Human history will not turn out ultimately to be a dead end. The Christian story promises us the final triumph of meaning over absurdity, but it gives us no account of how this will happen. It is a story of hope, but it does not say how that hope will be realised in history.

The twentieth century was crucified by ideologies that knew the

1. Oliver Bennett, *Cultural Pessimism: Narratives of Decline in the Postmodern World* (Edinburgh University Press, 2001).
2. Martin Rees, *Our Final Century? Will the Human Race Survive the Twenty-first Century?* (Heinemann, 2003).

road map to Paradise. Fascism, Nazism, Communism, and even to a certain extent, raw neo-liberal Capitalism, knew the way to the future, and forced human beings to march towards it in accordance with their plans. They knew the story and wanted humanity to conform to it. And so tens of millions of people were sacrificed on the altars of their ideologies.

I cannot forget my visit to the Tuol Sleng genocide centre in Phnom Penh, Cambodia. Tens of thousands of people were brought here to be interrogated and killed. The walls are lined with thousands of photographs of those whose lives ended here. Some of them look at the camera with fear, some sullenly: some smile hesitantly, as if they hoped that a smile might earn a few more days of life. Those who ran the centre kept meticulous records which they had no time to destroy when the Pol Pot regime finally fell. There are signs which command silence. And everyone was silenced. This is what happens when one tries to force humanity to conform to a road map. The road leads to the Killing Fields. In July 2004, I visited Auschwitz for the first time. At the entrance there is a map with railway lines that covered the whole of Europe, from Vichy France to the Ukraine, from Norway to Greece. All the lines converged at the gas chambers. These were literally the end of the line. Human technological efficiency devoured the lives of millions, as it tried to force its Paradise on humanity.

As we begin this third millennium, we Christians have a story that does give us hope and which we re-enact every year. But it does not do this by presenting us with a road map. This is as well, since after the most destructive century in human history, we are naturally distrustful of anyone who proposes a plan for the future. How then does our story offer hope?

The nuclear seed of the Christian story, from which the whole story germinated, is that of the last three days of the life of Jesus. On the night before he died, he gathered his disciples together for the Last Supper. Already his death was plotted, and was on the way to being accomplished. As he celebrated the Last Supper, the soldiers were on their way. But at the table he made a sign. He took bread, blessed it, shared it with the disciples and said, 'This is my body, given for you.' And so with the wine, poured out for many.

The Last Supper is the time when the disciples lost any story to tell of the future. They had been sustained on their way to Jerusalem by stories of military victory, of Jesus being installed as Messiah, and no doubt they hoped that they would all get top jobs in the new regime. But on that night it was clear that all that they could see ahead of them was disaster, failure, a dead end. At that moment Jesus did not offer an alternative story of the future. He did not appeal to Plan B. He did not say, 'Well, crucifixion is just a temporary setback. On Easter Sunday, I will rise from the dead and we shall carry on as before.' He grasped this moment of defeat and made of it a sign of hope. The paradox at the heart of Christianity is that its founding story looks back to when there was no story to tell of the future. Its hope looks back to the moment when there was no hope. All we were given was a sign.

The Last Supper is the clash between two sorts of power. There is the power of the political and religious authorities. These are the strong and brutal power of money and armies, which will take Jesus captive and destroy him. In the face of their threat, Jesus does not reply with brutal force. He is the lamb who is taken away to be slaughtered. Instead he replies with a sign. He takes the Jewish sign of the Passover, of the exodus from bondage in Egypt, and makes of it a sign of our liberation from all that can imprison us and destroy us. This is a sign offered in the face of death. It does not tell us the story of what will happen afterwards, but it speaks of hope. When everything is falling apart, it speaks of our coming home.

I was in Rwanda during the early years leading up to the genocide, when violence was beginning to break out all over the country. One day four of us decided to go north to visit the Dominican sisters who were serving the refugees caught up in the midst of war. The soldiers had barricaded the road going north and warned us not to go any further because the country was on fire, but we did not realise how serious it was and set off. We were frequently stopped, hauled out of the car by groups of masked and armed rebels, and had to talk our way through. We visited a refugee camp with tens of thousands of people living in squalor under plastic sheets. We went to a hospital filled with young children whose limbs had been blown off. I shall for ever remember one young lad who had lost both his legs, an arm and an eye, and his father, who was sitting by the bed weeping. That evening we went back to the simple hut where our sisters lived. We celebrated the Eucharist. After the gospel, I was sure I was supposed to speak some encouraging words of hope. But what was there to say? But there was a sign that we had been given. This sign spoke of that for which we had no words. We had the memory of what Jesus had done in the face of death, when all had seemed without purpose.

The Christian year grows out of the seed of the story of those last three days. As I wrote above, it was extended backwards, to the birth of Jesus, to our waiting for that birth, and ultimately to the beginning of creation. It also reached forward to Pentecost, and ultimately to the coming of the Kingdom. The story was stretched backward and forward so that we could all find ourselves within its hope. The story was extended from those compact and dramatic last three days to take in all sorts of events. It made it a roomy story, with lots of space. We see Jesus meeting prostitutes, calling disciples, telling parables, healing the sick, arguing with Pharisees. We are taken back to Christ's birth and the expectant pregnancy of his mother. And it reaches forward to include our own time as we await the Kingdom. This was so that we can find all the dramas of our lives inside it, as children, as expectant parents, as sick and hurt, as curious and challenged by the words of this man. And our time too is embraced in the time between Pentecost and the end. Whatever pain or suffering or joy we may experience, it is somewhere there in that story. Whatever experiences we may have, they have their place in the drama of the Christian year. They are embraced and we are carried by the surge of the narrative onwards. For the now generation, any moment is absolute. If we are sorrowful, then the sorrow is absolute, because this is the only moment that there is. To live within this story is to find ourselves, whatever happens, moving towards the Kingdom. This story opens up a future in which things need not be as they are.

In *Animal Dreams* by Barbara Kingsolver,[3] we are told how to live in hope:

> 'Codi, here's what I have decided: the very least that you can do in your life is to figure out what you hope for. And the most that you can do is to live inside that hope. Not admire it from a distance but live right in it, under its roof … Right now I am living in that hope, running down its hallway and touching the walls on both sides. I can't tell you how good it feels.'

The Christian story is one inside which we can live, and run down its passages, touching the walls on both sides. Hope is not just for what is in the future. Our story makes it the atmosphere we breathe now. It remains a story that does not give us the false and dangerous assurance of a road map. It gives us hope but it does not tell us how that hope will be fulfilled. When we discuss debt relief, aid programmes, different economic theories, then as Christians we have no privileged information. We have to join in the debate with everyone else, arguing our corner. There is no special Christian political programme or economic theory. There are politics and economics that

---

3. Barbara Kingsolver, *Animal Dreams* (HarperPerennial, 2003).

we can reject as unchristian, but none which can claim our exclusive allegiance. We have to struggle with the facts and the argument, just like everyone else.

This Christian story embodies what is fundamental to our identity. We are citizens of the Kingdom. This is a more fundamental identity than any we could ever receive from any nation or city or ethnic group. But the gospel does not tell us how we are to bring about a society which realises that promised unity. The annual cycle of the liturgical year is a sign but not a manifesto. I can tell the story of England, which makes sense of what it means for me to be English. I cannot yet tell the story of humanity and know the fullness of what it means to be human. The story of the Christian year is a sort of sign of that. Its full meaning lies ahead.

We live that cycle every year. We triumphantly arrive at the end, with the Feast of Christ the King, awaiting Christ's coming at the end of time. But then we are taken right back to the beginning, and once again we are in Advent, waiting for Christ to come as a child. And we might be forgiven if sometimes we wonder whether it gets us any-where. It may seem like a sort of liturgical snakes and ladders. Just when we are attaining the goal, then we slide back down to the beginning again. Might we not be tempted to think that this endless repetition means that we are going around in circles, wandering around in the desert for year after year, like the Israelites after the escape from Egypt? What is the point of beginning yet again?

We celebrate the Christian year. And celebration is more than just attending meetings or fulfilling rituals. Celebration implies song and joy; these look beyond the present moment to give us a tiny glimpse of the Kingdom already. I was in Kinshasa, in the Democratic Republic of the Congo, when the rebels surrounded the city. It looked as if the city might fall at any moment. The tension was terrible. And then we went to celebrate the Eucharist, and in Africa one sees what celebration really means. Before we even arrived at the altar everyone was dancing. We might have been in the midst of war but for a moment there was a glimpse of God's promise, the joy of the Kingdom. Celebration gives us hope.

The earliest prayers in our tradition are the Psalms and these are songs. In these songs the Israelites recounted everything: their vic-tories and their defeats, their anguish and fear, their sorrow and their joys. Everything that is human can be found in these songs, even violence and neurosis, and yet nearly every psalm makes its way beyond the darkness into the light. And this is right because song and music are perhaps the ultimate expression of hope. Music is strong enough to carry within itself even despair, and transcend it. Karl Barth said of Mozart's music that it was a great 'no' embraced by a resounding 'yes'. The Psalms reach beyond all that is destructive in human beings towards a hope which is beyond words, and sustained only by music and metaphor. In Psalm 57, for example, the psalmist is obviously having a tough time. Everyone is out to get him or her: 'I lie in the midst of lions that greedily devour the sons of men; their teeth are spears and arrows, their tongues sharp swords.' But all this pain is transformed into music that overcomes the night: 'I will sing and make melody. Awake my soul! Awake, O harp and lyre! I will awake the dawn.'

Faced with the suffering and injustice of this world, we are sustained in our hope by songs that speak a hope which is beyond words. It is a hope that, as Zechariah sings, gives 'light to those who sit in darkness and in the shadow of death' (Luke 1:79). We celebrate the Christian year, rather than just recounting it, because it is a celebration that embodies hope. And so this book contains songs too, for every season, to carry us onwards through its narrative of liberation, even when no future is in sight. It is to help you celebrate.

The cycle of the Christian year has sometimes in the past been a source of division between Christians. Some denominations at the time of the Reformation banned the celebration of even Christmas and Easter because they were considered to be superstitious. During the centuries, we can give thanks that these hostilities have been largely overcome. And it is a sign of hope that this book brings together, for the celebration of the liturgical seasons, Christians from every Church. If we can hear each other's hope and love, each other's songs, then we shall be drawn together and Christianity will better fulfil its vocation, to be a sign of the unity of all humanity in the Kingdom.

Practical Advice on Creating a Liturgy

Linda Jones

Worship is like a conversation – it is our response to God's revelation. And at its best, worship engages all our senses and sends us out into the world, refreshed and ready to serve. For this to happen, a service of worship must be carefully designed. It needs shape and movement and its content needs clarity and vision.

Work together with your parish priest/minister/worship leader/ musicians to create vibrant worship which people enjoy and remember. This may sound daunting, but don't be put off. The key is forward planning, careful preparation and shared creativity. Working in groups shares the load and you can exchange ideas.

Global justice in worship – some preliminary ideas
How can we make a focus on poverty and global justice more apparent in our services?

- *Intercessory prayers.* Ask whoever is preparing these to include praying for a global issue, such as peace, international debt or trade.
- *Hymns and songs.* Choose music with meaning – the words of songs can really help people to understand and take on board these issues.
- *Bible readings.* Try to choose a Sunday when the readings are particularly relevant to the issue you want to focus on – you may be surprised how many there are!
- *Talks/sermons.* Ask the preacher to link the sermon with poverty/ justice issues. Many lectionary Bible passages are concerned with these so it probably won't be a false connection. Alternatively, ask if you can give a two-minute talk in the service, or invite a speaker from CAFOD, Christian Aid or a similar organisation.

- *Be more adventurous.* Even if you don't have an adventurous con-gregation, try drama, movement or dance to illustrate the issues you are tackling. Or create a PowerPoint™ presentation to accom-pany a reading or a prayer – include photos as well as words. Members of your youth group are likely to have the skills to do this.
- *Visual impact.* Create a display and put it where all can see it. Include leaflets, cards or additional information so that people can find out more at their leisure. Ask CAFOD or Christian Aid for resources, such as prayer leaflets and cards, posters, action post-cards – these are all free.
- *Different age groups.* Think about the children or young people's groups. How could you involve them both in preparation and in delivery? They are likely to be interested as questions of 'fairness' are highly important at this age.

The aim is to help people to understand how action, reflection and prayer on issues of global justice are part of their faith life – but be sensitive. Try not to harangue, lecture or offend people. Encourage them and offer them opportunities to get involved. Inspire them to recognise the significance of putting their faith into action.

Planning worship: getting started
In the early stages of planning there are a number of key questions:

- Are we working within the parameters of a set order of service or are we creating an alternative order of service?
- Which liturgical season are we in? Is this significant?
- (*For some*) Will the worship fall on a fast or feast day?
- What will be the overall theme?
- Who is the service for? Adults, children, all ages?
- How long will it last?
- What is its message?
- How can we make the best use of the available worship space?
- What musical resources are available?
- How much preparation time is there?

Writing a skeleton plan
If you are working with a set order of service, the bare bones will already be there. If you are creating your own, the next stage of plan-ning is to write an outline keeping the above questions in mind. Remember that worship is a conversation with God. For example:

- A call to worship
- Hymn/music – our response to God in praise
- Prayer of confession – as we realise that we are not all that we should be
- Reading – we listen to God
- Hymn/music – our response to what we have heard from the Scriptures
- Talk/drama/musical piece – we listen again as we are enabled to understand God's word
- Silence/time for reflection or prayer – our response to what we have heard
- Symbolic action – another means of responding to what we have heard
- Prayers of intercession – we respond by praying for God's world
- Hymn – our response again, probably preparation to go into the world
- Dismissal – we are sent out to serve God

At this point, check the service for movement, balance and variety, and be careful not to overload it. As far as you are able, estimate how long each item will last. Don't forget to leave room for silence and reflection.

Choosing the readings and music
When you choose the music (hymns, chants and so on), make sure it reflects the theme and mood of the liturgy and serves the purpose you intend. For example, the first hymn often praises God or acts as a call to worship, so the words and music should reflect this. A hymn at the end of the service usually acts as a dismissal; its purpose is to send us out into the world.

Readings (biblical, poems or prose) are the most obvious way to communicate the theme and message, so pick them carefully. If you choose a biblical reading, look at different translations before deciding which one to use. Ask yourself questions such as, 'Does it read well out loud?' 'Is the language inclusive?' 'Is it suitable for children?'

Leading the worship
Bear in mind that what a congregation sees helps to form their ideas about God and informs their faith. If we believe in a God who values people irrespective of their gender, race, colour, sexuality or ability, then as far as possible, those involved in leading the worship need to reflect this diversity.

Sometimes, making worship inclusive means allowing extra time to train and rehearse people who would not normally take a lead. But avoid tokenism. Rota people in and be open to new talent.

Practice and rehearsing
It is a worthwhile exercise for worship leaders to walk through an unfamiliar order of service beforehand to check for any unforeseen hitches.

Readers need to be rehearsed – watch out for speed and audibility – and music needs to be practised. If you are singing unfamiliar hymns or tunes, a run-through with the congregation before the service makes for better worship.

Printed materials
Where possible, a simple order of service, which is clear and easy to read and with good directions, will help worshippers to relax into the service. Juggling several books and pieces of paper can be off-putting.

Preparing the worship area
Look at the size and shape of the worship space, and decide how best to use it.

If the service is to be held in a conventional church setting, try to use the space creatively. Use light and dark to best effect. Arrange flowers or other displays to complement your theme. If possible, arrange the pews or chairs in a way that brings the congregation together, and make imaginative use of symbols (see below).

In a less conventional setting, you can experiment more easily. Perhaps you could dispense with seating altogether and create your own focal point. Take a few risks and see how they work.

Using symbols
Symbols – objects, actions or words that represent, recall or communicate a reality larger than ourselves – are used in worship to express our feelings and beliefs about God. They also help to focus our thoughts and create atmosphere.

Everyday symbols
The most obvious example of a Christian symbol is the cross. Many other symbols are less specific. Their richness lies in the fact that they are everyday objects with a multitude of associations; for example, bread, wine, water and light. They are full of meaning. The bread and wine remind us of food (spiritual and physical), work, celebration,

sacrifice and so on. Water, as the baptism service reminds us, is associated both with life (refreshment and liberation) and death (the deep waters of destruction). Light, too, is rich in meaning, for its presence brings truth, warmth, growth and health.

Symbolic action

Symbols are not only helpful as visual aids, but can also be used in symbolic actions. For example, lighting a candle as we intercede keeps the prayer 'burning'; laying down a stone as we ask God for help or forgiveness allows us to let go of the burden we are carrying; placing a flower in a vase as we pray can be an expression of thanksgiving, and so on.

Sometimes an object can be used to help us get in touch with a particular experience. For example, a bowl of sand can symbolise the desert and can be used to recall the Israelites' wilderness experience, or the temptations of Jesus. It can also put us in touch with our own internal wanderings and can help us to focus on our spiritual journey. So long as a symbol has appropriate meaning and aids worship, use it.

Symbolic movement

We tend to associate churches with stillness and services with sitting still. While stillness has an important part to play in worship, so has movement. A procession can be used to symbolise a journey, spiritual or otherwise. Different attitudes of prayer – bowing, kneeling, prostrating – can symbolise our inner attitudes towards God. Mime and dance can often convey what words cannot express.

Using our senses to express the symbolic

Very often we limit the way we worship by only engaging two of our senses – sight and hearing. By employing all our senses we engage our whole selves in worship. For example, the smell of incense reminds us of God's presence; the scent of flowers makes us think of the richness of God's creation; the aroma of freshly baked bread reminds us of Christ, the bread of life.

Our sense of touch can also be employed in symbolic actions. For example, sharing the peace symbolises our oneness as a body; standing with arms outstretched expresses our openness to God. Less obvious ways of using touch are no less effective. For example, handling a nail can be a useful aid to help us meditate on the crucifixion, or feeling a stone can remind us of our hardness of heart.

Even our sense of taste can contribute to a better understanding of our faith: bitter herbs, such as horseradish, can remind us of the bitterness of the wilderness experience; honey can remind us of the 'sweetness' of God's word; while an *Agape* (a shared meal in the manner of the early Christians) can symbolise solidarity, togetherness and celebration.

Using music in worship

Music has an important part to play in the liturgy. It is integral to worship and carries enormous power.

- *Music is creative*. It can build an atmosphere of celebration, of stillness and reflection, of questioning or commitment.
- *Music is participative*. People can sing, clap, play instruments, read words over music, hum the chorus, dance or meditate. Music reaches people; it moves them and it makes them move.

Choosing music

Music is central to the worship and cannot be an add-on. It needs to be included in the initial stages of all thinking and planning.

First check whether the day of the service is a feast day or a day set aside for special prayers, say for peace or homelessness. Then look at the biblical readings and choose songs and music to reflect their message. If possible, plan together with the priest or whoever is leading the service.

Choose music to serve the right purpose within the liturgy. For example, the first hymn usually acts as a call to worship, so the words and music need to reflect this.

Finding performers

You do not need to be an expert to make music. It is usually possible to find at least one instrumentalist. They do not have to be an organist or a pianist. You could try a single guitar or a recorder; or ask someone with a strong, clear singing voice, which they can keep in tune, to lead. If none of this is possible, then use a CD player.

Think, too, about the balance of instruments you use. Some songs suit trumpets and drums, others a flute and guitar. Not everyone has to play for every hymn. Children learning to play should be encouraged and welcomed. If they make more mistakes than the more experienced players, so what? Music should be inclusive. It should be as good as possible, but it does not have to be perfect every time.

Working with a choir

If you have a choir and/or an instrumental group in your parish or community, you have a wonderful opportunity. But you also have a built-in danger. Many congregations heave a subconscious sigh of relief at the sight of a choir. They feel that it lets them off the hook – they don't have to join in. The role of a choir is to switch people on to music so that they feel inspired to join in – not to switch them off!

A good cantor can be a wonderful asset. She or he can lead the singing, sing the difficult bits and inspire the congregation. However, some get carried away and think they're on the West End stage! This should be gently discouraged, as no one else will join in. Such a person could be pointed in the direction of a training course. Training for cantors and choir leaders is available from many dioceses and church organisations.

Encouraging the congregation

Make sure the congregation knows which parts of the service they are expected to sing, and which parts of the service will be led by the choir or musicians.

Teach them anything new before the service – but introduce only one new piece at a time, and use it at regular intervals so that it is not forgotten. Praise their efforts – but don't patronise them.

Music is a great responsibility, but it is also fun. In one way or another everybody can join in and feel part of something special. Good music is worship.

Designing a school assembly

An assembly that is well thought out, well rehearsed, and which carries a pertinent message will hold young people's attention and provide them with food for thought. At best it will awaken a pupil's spirituality by tapping into the heart of issues relevant to his or her world and relating them to a wider social and spiritual context.

Planning

The key to an effective school assembly is planning and preparation.

- Decide well in advance when and where the assembly will take place.
- Give time to thinking through structure, content and presentation.
- Ensure that the venue is booked and check that no one else is using it directly before or after you.

Choosing a subject

Often a subject that the pupils have been studying will suggest an assembly theme – for example, environmental or citizenship issues, human geography, climate changes, health care, food technology and so on. Sometimes local issues will provide a focus: for example, the closing down of a refugee hostel or the start of a homelessness project. A situation that is on the news may also suggest a subject – though you will have less preparation time if you want to keep it of the moment.

Preparation

A clear beginning and a clear end – perhaps marked with a communal prayer to help people move in and out of worship – is essential, as is a level of humour to lighten potentially heavy subjects. Before rehearsals begin, make sure that everything hangs together and that the overall message is clear and focused. Check that the assembly is not overloaded and that there is time for reflection.

Involving the children

Try to use people's talents imaginatively. Everyone will have something to offer. Build enough time into the preparation schedule to allow the children not only to develop their ideas, but to experiment and to build up enough confidence to produce results. Pupils need to feel involved from the start, so that they can own the finished product and take pride in their work.

If a large number of pupils are involved (for example, a class), it may be helpful to set up small working groups to take responsibility for different parts of the assembly. Each group would need to be well briefed and to understand its role.

It may be that an initial working party will need to map out the shape and form of the assembly, ensuring that it has balance and variety. The remit of other working parties might be as follows:

• Music
• Prayers
• Dance
• Setting up the worship area

Remember that an assembly in a church school may be very different from one in a local authority school. A state school does not require its pupils to have a common faith background, so remember that although Christian prayers and songs may be available for all to listen to, you must not assume that the pupils will participate in them. Check what is appropriate with the Head or responsible teacher.

Rehearsals
- Practice is important
- Readers need to be rehearsed
- Singers need to be heard
- Musicians need to be taken through their music

Ask someone to watch rehearsals, to offer constructive criticism and to time everything – a paragraph takes longer to read out than one might think! Preferably, spoken parts should be either very simple or so well rehearsed that a script is not needed.

On the day
Request that any school notices be kept to a minimum and dealt with at the beginning of the assembly. Giving priority to the assembly is important. Before the assembly itself, allow time for quiet. A sense of the occasion – an act of worship – needs to be realised.

Those leading the assembly need to feel confident and relaxed, not fraught and anxious. Afterwards they may need time to debrief. It is always valuable to assess what things worked and what could have been done better.

CAFOD/Christian Aid and the school assembly
Bringing in help from outside the school is often valuable. Use any contacts that the pupils and staff may have with people or organisations linked to the developing world. Agencies like CAFOD/Christian Aid are always happy to provide information and material. Many have their own schools department and sometimes can offer guest speakers.

Each fast day CAFOD produces special assemblies for both primary and secondary schools. Christian Aid regularly produces assembly material for use with different age groups.

Contact the CAFOD/Christian Aid schools sections for resources, help and advice on how to include a global justice theme.

Advent

In October 2004, a plane crashed in Canada. The pilots had been flying for almost twenty-four hours. They were carrying fresh vegetables from Africa to Western markets. Consumers want to eat their mange tout, asparagus and sugar snap peas all year round. They do not wish to wait until the due season for their fruit and vegetables to arrive. They want them now. In order to provide them at competitive prices, the supermarkets buy them from companies that fly old planes which have not been properly serviced, registered in countries whose safety standards are not high, in this case in Ghana. The pilots fly for dangerously long hours. This is the fourth time a plane owned by this company has crashed since 1992. The founder of the company said that it is not the fault of the supermarkets. They are merely responding to market demand.

One of the differences between the rich and the poor is that the rich are, as far as possible, freed from waiting for their desires to be satisfied. As Zygmunt Bauman wrote, they have taken 'the waiting out of wanting'.[1] But the poor must wait. In agricultural communities, they must wait for the land to produce its fruit. They must wait in queues to buy what is available, and if there are shortages, then they may wait in vain. They wait for jobs. Above all they wait for justice. Anyone who has travelled in Africa or India will have seen the immense patience of the poor. Oliver Tambo was asked what sustained him through all those years of imprisonment on Robben Island for his opposition to apartheid. He replied: 'Patience and faith'.

Advent is a time when we are invited to learn how to wait for the Lord who comes. The temptation is to eliminate Advent and move directly to Christmas. The moment that the Nativity draws near, it is time to begin partying. Christmas lights are turned on in our shopping malls and people greet each other with 'Happy Christmas' long

1. Zygmunt Bauman, *Liquid Modernity* (Polity Press, 2000), p. 76.

before the Lord is born. We cannot wait. This is my excuse for not
sending Christmas cards. Before the feast I consider it too early, and
after the feast everyone else considers it too late! Why must we wait?
I am an impatient person, and I become very irritated waiting in
queues, in shops, to check in at airports, or to board planes. On the
eve of the Millennium, I was due to catch a plane from the Ivory
Coast to Angola. When I tried to check in I was told that it would be
a little late. 'How late?' 'Three days late.'

What can Advent teach us about waiting? First of all, we who are
rich must open our eyes to the poor who have no option but to wait.
We must share their patient vigil as they wait for a more just world,
and their struggle to bring it about. We must try to liberate ourselves
from the imperious desires of the rich, who sacrifice everyone for the
instant satisfaction of their wishes. In Psalm 70, the poor cry out: 'But
I am poor and needy; hasten to me, O God! You are my help and my
deliverer. O Lord, do not delay.' We struggle to diminish the length of
their waiting.

Why does the Lord delay? Why do the poor still have to go on crying out for justice two thousand years after the coming of Christ?
Why does not God bring about a world in which all of humanity may
flourish now? Ever since Christ people have wandered around proclaiming that 'The end is nigh', and they have been proved wrong
every time. Why must millions of people die of hunger in Darfur,
suffer the impact of unjust trade and unpayable debt, and still the
Lord tarries?

We do not know the answer to that but at the very least we must
live with the urgency of the question. Any answer that looks like an
explanation of vast suffering is likely to appear horrible, even blas-
phemous, as if so much human misery could be part of some
monstrous divine plan. All that we can do in Advent is share in that
clamouring of the poor for a better world and do all that we can to
hasten its coming.

Perhaps one tiny element of a response is in deepening our understanding of how God comes. One reason why our God takes so much
time is because he is not a god. Our God is not a powerful, celestial
superman, a sort of invisible President Bush on a cosmic scale, who
might come from the outside. The coming of God is not like the
cavalry galloping to our rescue. God comes from within, in our
deepest interiority. He is, as St Augustine said, closer to us than we
are to ourselves. Or as it says in the Qur'an, God is closer to us than
our jugular vein. God says in Jeremiah, 'In those days and at that time
I will cause a righteous branch to spring forth for David' (23:5). God

comes in our fertility and that cannot be forced. Pregnancy takes time.

During Advent, we practise patience as we wait and watch for the coming of the Lord. Like midwives gathered around the bed, we await the birth. But God's coming was not just the birth of a child; it was the coming of a word. One might even say that it was the coming of a language.

It needed hundreds of years for English to evolve to the point at which Shakespeare might write *Hamlet*. The language had to be formed by poets and lawyers, preachers, philosophers and peasants, by nurses and grave diggers, before it was ready. English society had undergone a profound transformation before English could be fertile with Shakespeare's words.

In a similar way it needed thousands of years before there was a language in which God's Word could be spoken in the form of Jesus. We needed all those experiences of liberation and exile, of the building and demolition of kingdoms. We needed innumerable prophets and scribes and poets struggling to find words before Jesus could be born as the Word. The Word of God does not come down from heaven like a celestial Esperanto. It wells up from within human language.

One of my Dominican brethren, a rugged Scot called Anthony Ross, was a famous preacher until he was struck down by a stroke that left him wordless. The specialist who came to see him told him that he would never be able to utter a word again, to which he replied, 'Thank you, doctor.' That left the doctor speechless! Anthony could never say much, but every word that he struggled to bring out was the fruit of that awful suffering and victory. People would come hundreds of miles just to hear him say a single word. You had to wait for it. Before I left for Rome he gave me a single word, 'Courage'. And it was food for me for a long time. Similarly God's Word takes time to gestate within us.

Waiting for the coming of God is not then mere passivity. We do not only wait with the poor, we share their struggle. Also we must try to find ways of talking which are hospitable to the lives of the poor. We must evolve a consciousness, a way of seeing things, which does not shut them out. We must be attentive to the experience of the poor, so that together we gestate a language in which their hopes may find expression. Then indeed we may have words into which the Word of God may come and find a home.

Reflections

1. Mothers together

'Blessed is she who has believed that what the Lord has said to her will be accomplished!'
                    (Luke 1:45)

Here is a scene familiar throughout history. Two expectant mothers greeting each other, sharing the excitement of their pregnancies and dreaming dreams together. It is a scene so easy to imagine. Yet Mary and Elizabeth were two very special 'expectant' mothers; their expectancy was shared by a wider world. All creation was waiting for these two babies, the first to herald the coming of the second. Two extraordinary births followed by extraordinary lives.

Luke's very human account of the meeting of Mary and Elizabeth reveals just a hint of their breathless, bewildered comprehension of the uniqueness of their friendship, and the awesome privilege of God's calling on their lives. Did they also dare to anticipate the pain and anguish that awaited them in years to come as God their Saviour worked out his plan? Mary certainly recognises in the song of praise that follows that salvation has *already come* with the presence of each child in the womb. She must have known, too, that both she and Elizabeth had been called to mother 'against the odds': that alongside the joy there would be pain; alongside nurture, loss.

The world over, mothers still mother against the odds. They wave photographs of 'lost' sons in front of TV cameras and keep vigil in sparsely equipped hospitals alongside war-wounded children. We watch helplessly as a malnourished mother struggles to breast-feed her dying baby, her grip on hope as desperate as her child's on her empty breast. This is indeed mothering against the odds. It is daring to go on believing in the impossible, hoping against hope, loving beyond belief because of the calling of motherhood.

Mary must often have recalled the words the angel Gabriel had given her, as she struggled to keep an eternal perspective on the pain of her son's journey to the cross. But could she have begun to understand how God would turn the world upside down through the salvation given by the life, death and resurrection of her son?

Yet Mary believed that what the Lord had said to her would be accomplished. 'I am the Lord's servant,' she declared, and with those words she surrendered her parenting into the hands of the God she trusted, and was blessed. Mothers – fathers – among us will all too often be called to do the same.

Wendy Bray

2. Reconciliation

... they shall beat their swords into ploughshares, and their spears into pruning hooks ...
(Isaiah 2:4)

Alienation and division are as old as humankind itself but so too is the desire for reconciliation and unity. The prophets proclaimed this fact. Isaiah said they 'will hammer their swords into ploughshares, their spears into sickles. Nation will not lift sword against nation, there will be no more training for war' (Isaiah 2:4 – reading for the first Sunday of Advent). Reconciliation is the renewing of relationships; it is a return to friendship among persons, families, social groups and nations. Jesus singled out those who worked for reconciliation for special blessing: 'Happy the peacemakers: they shall be called the children of God' (Matthew 5:9).

The Old Testament contains many passages which show the need for, and the process of, reconciliation. The relationship between Yahweh and the people was strained and broken many times in the history of the Chosen People. With each return to friendship the covenant is renewed and strengthened and the reconciliation is celebrated.

An awareness that the people were constantly straining this relationship and so needed a formal return to Yahweh led to the annual celebration of the great Day of Atonement (at-one-ment). A number of rites were combined in this ceremony to signify the admission by both priests and people of their failures which they wanted expelled from their midst (symbolised by the scapegoat) and their desire to be at-one with Yahweh again (Leviticus 16:1–34).

Isaiah prophesying about the Messiah referred to him as the 'Prince of Peace' (Isaiah 9:6). The Gospels record many incidents where Jesus worked for reconciliation. He saw that there could be no reconciliation without forgiveness, so forgiveness became a major theme in his preaching. He outlined the ideal of forgiveness and the resultant reconciliation in some of his parables. After a graphic description of the shepherd who goes into the wilderness in search of the lost sheep and having found it returns with joy to celebrate, Jesus adds a note of reassurance: 'there will be more rejoicing in heaven over one repentant sinner than over ninety-nine virtuous men who have no need of repentance'. This theme is repeated in the parable of the Prodigal Son.

This theme gives us hope. God is a concerned shepherd, a loving father, anxious to restore personal relationships with each individual every time they 'break away'. But Jesus emphasises that it is not just relationships between individuals and God that matter. So too does a person's relationship with the community, with the wider society and with the environment. Building right relationships between nations is particularly important at this time in human history. We should challenge, support and encourage our leaders in this endeavour. Building right relationships is what the Good News is all about. It is what justice entails. It is the challenge we all face every day of our lives.

Sean Healy SMA
Ireland

3. *Let justice descend, O heavens, like dew from above,*
    like gentle rain let the skies drop it down.
                                            (Isaiah 45:8)

Advent has always been a time in-between, a time between now and the end time. Then the reign of God will come in its fullness, that great and perfect *shalom* (peace) of many Advent readings, especially Isaiah. It reminds me of times as a teenager when groups of antsy adolescents used to loiter at street corners in our Aotearoa/New Zealand suburb. Looking at the 'scenery' (girls) was an important part of growing up. It consumed much time, a 'dream-time' when possibilities were mulled over – voiced with great bravado, if inwardly more tentatively. It was a time of waiting.

Presently I am living in the Solomon Islands, where the people are beginning to recover a positive sense of a similar Advent longing. They are slowly overcoming the despair that accompanied the 'tensions' of the civil war that exploded in 2001. Then their dream of better things died. People were scattered, whole districts burned down and precious government infrastructure destroyed. Much of that remains to be rebuilt. Only now, with the intervention of an Australian-led force from neighbouring Pacific countries, called the

Regional Assistance Mission to the Solomon Islands (RAMSI), has the dream begun to grow again. Listening to stories of 2001 terror and sensing hope of greater stability brings a longing that the Solomons will again be a centre of God's great *shalom*. That a shattered sense of law and order will be restored. That organs of government will work – without corruption and fairly among all ethnic groups. Stories of a bright future are freely bandied about, with lots of humour. But one can sense a reserve, with some people preaching caution. Have the causes of the 'tension' been resolved? Has reconciliation truly been effected between the peoples of Guadalcanal and Malaita, from among whom the principal militants and causes of trouble came? Is the old 'dream' alive? Does a better 'dream' exist? We are still waiting.

The people of the Solomons are waiting to take a rightful share in the riches of those neighbours who still exploit them (for logs and fish mainly), knowing that only the good, bounteous, Creator God can ultimately fill their need – to live the 'dreamtime' of God's *shalom* in the way that only God can give. Isn't that Christmas?

Kevin Toomey OP
Solomon Islands

4. The daily dance

... The flocking birds wheel and turn above Baghdad buildings.
Sunlight glints white on their wings.
In the morning sun, their wings flash like light; in the evening, like
 blood.
I do not know why they dance like this.
I think it is simply for joy of the wind.

... In Kerbala, during a visit to the hospital, I met dozens of bombing
 victims
injured in a pre-Christmas suicide blast.
Faces swathed in bandages; skulls stitched together.
Ahmed, age 32. Khalid, age 13.
Students, porters, taxi drivers.
And Simah, a 6-year-old shepherd girl
whose legs were torn to pieces by gunfire.

... Elections. Everyone is talking about them
or trying to avoid the topic.
'Will you vote?' I asked all my friends.

'No,' said Um Bushra, a Sunni widow who lives with her daughter
in a servant's shack in the backyard of an abandoned house.
'I will not vote, I am too afraid of explosions.'

'Of course we will vote, both myself and Noor,' said Abu Zayneb.
'Sayyid Sistani told all the Shi'a people that we must take courage
and let our voices be heard.'

'This will not be a perfect election,' said Emad, a Chaldean Christian.
'In fact, it will be the worst.
But it is step one.
I have never had the right to vote before,
so of course I will use it.'

'It is ridiculous,' says Abdullah, a Sunni from western Iraq.
'The election is a joke, a tool of the Americans.'

In Kerbala, the schools will be used as voting centres.
Every day, children go through checkpoints and searches
before they enter their school.
Many parents are keeping their children at home these days,
so frightening is this ordeal and so grim the prospect of sabotage
    bombing.

'Even Iraqis do not go out much.' Plenty of people say this.
But I am tired, tired, of the same old street, the same old building.
Tired of walking up and down the stairs
but rarely out across city blocks.
Every time I get in the car and ride across Baghdad,
I feel great relief, but also as if I am risking my life.
'Will there be a car bomb now?'

To survive, I sit on the roof and watch the birds' daily dance.
And remember my Iraqi family mom who said through the phone,
'I miss you. Please come,'
and then sent her daughters to visit me and continue the dance.

                                                          Sheila Provender
                                                          Dominica

5. Compassionate prayer

When we come before God with the needs of the world, then the healing love of God which touches us touches all those whom we bring

before him with the same power. This experience of God's healing love can become so real, so immediate, that at times we can even sense God's healing grace in the lives of others, although they may be far away physically, mentally, or spiritually.

Thus, compassionate prayer does not encourage us to flee from people and their concrete problems into a self-serving individualism. By deepening our awareness of our common suffering, it draws us all closer together in the healing presence of God. It reaches out not only to those whom we love and admire, but also to those whom we consider our enemies.

Prayer cannot exist together with hostile feelings. The fruit of prayer is always love. In prayer, even the unprincipled dictator and the vicious torturer can no longer remain the objects of our fear, hatred, and revenge, because when we pray, we stand at the centre of the great mystery of divine compassion.

Henri Nouwen

6. God is near

There is a way to know if God is near us or far away: everyone who is concerned about the hungry, about the naked, about the poor, about the disappeared, about the tortured, about the prisoner, about all the flesh that is suffering, will find God near.

'Call out to the Lord and he will hear you.' Religion is not praying a great deal. Religion involves this guarantee of having my God near because I do good to my brothers and sisters. The proof of my prayer is not to say a great many words, the proof of my plea is easy to see: how do I act toward the poor? Because God is there.

Oscar Romero

Prayers

7. *'Here am I, the servant of the Lord.'*

(Luke 1:38)

Father God,
Turn our hearts and minds to those who mother 'against the odds' across our broken world.
Help us to uphold motherhood as part of your mission and, as we do

so, to trust you for our children and believe in our hearts that 'nothing is impossible with God'.
Amen.

Wendy Bray

8. '*Let it be to me according to your word.*'
(Luke 1:38b)

Thank you, God, for all those Gabriels who delight and astound us with your good news. We praise you for the richness and complexity of the world in which surprise and joy constantly await us.
For we, too, have found favour with God.

Too often we close our minds to new or fresh starts. Too often we bring your kingdom down to our level. Too often we fail to grasp how much you cherish us.
For we, too, have found favour with God.

We pray for those who live in conditions of such want, exclusion, fear or bigotry that they have little chance of being surprised or of living in hope. We pray for ourselves when we are crabby or feel sorry for ourselves.
For we, too, have found favour with God.

We resolve to take nothing for granted, to see nothing as immutable; not people, not systems, not your Kingdom. Give us a passion for your Gospel and a vision of your Kingdom in which all are included.
For we, too, have found favour with God.

Gray Featherstone

9. *The light shines in the darkness and the darkness did not overcome it.*
(John 1:5)

Advent God,
meet us as we face the darkness of our world,
that we may embrace you in the shadows and move out to greet your light.
**Dispel our fears,
increase our hope.**
Enlighten us as we search for truth amongst the clamour of war,

that we may have the courage to proclaim peace and determination
to seek justice.
Dispel our fears,
increase our hope.
Embolden us to cry out in the wilderness,
that we may find a voice to disarm power and a way to challenge
prejudice.
Dispel our fears,
increase our hope.
Guide us as we seek to make straight your paths,
that we may guard against self-righteousness and look to you for
help.
Dispel our fears,
increase our hope.
Move us as we reach out to those in need,
that we may respond with urgency and wait with patience.
Dispel our fears,
increase our hope.
Challenge us with your promise of salvation,
that we may put aside all fear and proclaim the hope of liberation.
Dispel our fears,
increase our hope.
and grant us peace.
Amen.

Annabel Shilson-Thomas

10. *But those who do what is true come to the light …*

(John 3:21)

Longing for light, we wait in darkness.
Longing for truth, we turn to you.
Make us your own, your holy people,
light for the world to see.

Chorus
Christ, be our light!
Shine in our hearts.
Shine through the darkness.
Christ, be our light!
Shine in your church
gathered today.

Longing for peace, our world is troubled.
Longing for hope, many despair.
Your word alone has power to save us.
Make us your living voice.

Longing for food, many are hungry.
Longing for water, many still thirst.
Make us your bread, broken for others,
shared until all are fed.

Longing for shelter, many are homeless.
Longing for warmth, many are cold.
Make us your building, sheltering others,
walls made of living stone.

Many the gifts, many the people,
many the hearts that yearn to belong.
Let us be servants to one another,
making your Kingdom come.

Bernadette Farrell

11. *'Comfort, O comfort my people,' says your God.*

(Isaiah 40:1)

LEADER: As we acknowledge our successes and our failures, what
we have done,
and what we have been unable to do,
we turn to God, in prayer:

READER: Lord, comfort your people
and clothe us with your strength.

ALL: **Comfort your people, God of power and compassion.**

READER: Calm our anxieties, soothe our anguish
and light the darkness that surrounds us.

ALL: **Comfort your people, God of power and compassion.**

READER: Compel us with your courage
and enable us with your wisdom.

ALL: **Comfort your people, God of power and compassion.**

READER: Hear our voices and our hearts
as we wait and watch together.

ALL: **Comfort your people, God of power and compassion.**

READER: Surround us with your love

and anoint us with your peace.

ALL: **Comfort your people, God of power and compassion.**

Linda Jones

12. *When Elizabeth heard Mary's greeting, the child leaped in her womb.*
(Luke 1:41)

Compassionate God,
as we look to you for judgement, hold out your hand of compassion
that we may be chastened by your show of mercy and reach out to
others in reconciliation.
Lord, we look to you
in whom we hope.
As we contemplate our end, make us mindful of your promise of a
new beginning
that we may share your promise of life and bring hope to those who
sit in darkness.
Lord, we look to you
in whom we hope.
As we remember Elizabeth in her barrenness, fill us with longing for
the birth of a new creation
that we too may be surprised by joy, and labour with those who seek
to make all things new.
Lord, we look to you
in whom we hope.
As John leapt in his mother's womb, help us so to recognise Christ in
friend and stranger
that we may respond in love, and learn to serve our neighbour with
generosity, not judgement.
Lord, we look to you
in whom we hope.
As Mary and Elizabeth sought each other, grant us the wisdom to
recognise our needs
that we too may seek each other in solidarity and offer
strength/power to the powerless.
Lord, we look to you
in whom we hope.
As Mary proclaimed the salvation of the Lord, give us courage to
stand alongside the downtrodden
that we may sing of their hopes and join hands to realise their dreams.
Lord, we look to you

in whom we hope.
and long to see.
Amen.

Annabel Shilson-Thomas

13. *... and all who heard it were amazed ...*

(Luke 2:18)

Almighty God, during this Advent season, we who live in a world of political deceit, turmoil, anxiety and war, once again come before your throne of grace, for there is no other to whom we may go.

We come in humility, and in faith cry out to you that there is no peace in our world because there is no justice.

We come in humility, and praise you that you have given us peace and justice in Jesus Christ, your Son, our Lord and Saviour.

We come in humility, and praise you that despite the hardships and storms of life that we experience daily you are with us, assuring and reassuring us that you will never leave us nor forsake us.

We come in humility, and praise you that in our weakness you have given us strength; in our hopelessness, you have given us hope; in our voiceless state, you have given us your Word incarnate; in our deepest sorrow, you have given us comfort beyond comparison; in the nakedness of our humiliation, while chained and grounded to the evils of terror, you liberated us and clothed us with your love, mercy and compassion.

We thank you that in your Son, our Lord and Saviour, Jesus Christ, and through the power of the Holy Spirit each of us can live in the dignity of being truly human. We thank you that we can experience peace in spite of calls for war and that we can experience justice in a world that is riddled with injustice. We thank you that you have made it possible for us to live life to the fullest, to joyfully serve and always rejoice. So, we rejoice in the tribulations and afflictions of our time, for our crosses are never greater than we can bear.
Amen.

Lesley G. Anderson

14. *... and they went out together from Ur of the Chaldeans ...*

(Genesis 11:31)

Lord of hope and compassion, Friend of Abraham,
who called our father in faith to journey to a new future,

we remember before you all the peoples of the Middle East who honour him as father:
> those who guard and celebrate the Torah,
> those for whom the Word has walked on earth and lived among us
> those who follow their prophet, who listened for the word in the
> > desert
> and shaped a community after what he heard.

Lord of reconciliation, God of the painful sacrifice uniting
humankind,
We long for the day when you will provide for all nations of the earth
your blessing of peace.
Help us to recognise in one another a family likeness, our inheritance
from our one father Abraham.
In times of strife, fear and tension, preserve within us a generous spirit
which recognises in both foe and friend a common humanity.
This we ask in the name of the one who came to offer us the costly gift
of abundant life.
Amen.

*(In Arabic Abraham is often called El Khalilâ which means the Friend
[of God]. Ur and Haran, the cities from which, according to Genesis,
Abraham was summoned by God, both lie within the territory of
modern Iraq.)*

Alan and Clare Amos

15. *The grass withers, the flower fades, but the word of our God will
stand for ever.*
(Isaiah 40:8)

She stands tall in the desert
a lone figure
without a shadow
the sun high above her head

dignity holds her back straight
the inevitable her eyes fixed
loss her arms empty

bright cloth surrounds
her swollen belly

her fragile limbs
there are none to see her
so only she sees
the blade of grass
standing tall
beside her
one shoot in unforgiving soil
lush green in brutal earth

together they move in the sudden breeze
the word of comfort
blown in on the wind
comfort my people

a sip of water becomes a well
a growing shoot becomes plenty
a whisper becomes a cry

my people are not alone
comfort, comfort my people

Marjory Macaskill

16. ... *make straight in the desert a highway for our God.*
(Isaiah 40:3)

From the hungry
comes the message
that all will be filled.

Make straight the road.
Prepare the way of the Lord.

From the thirsty
comes the news
that all will be satisfied.

Make straight the road.
Prepare the way of the Lord.

From the lame
comes the dance
that all will perform.

Make straight the road.
Prepare the way of the Lord.

From the blind
comes the vision
that all will follow.

Make straight the road.
Prepare the way of the Lord.

From the poor
comes the wealth
that all will share.

Make straight the road.
Prepare the way of the Lord.

From the oppressed
comes the freedom
that all will know.

Make straight the road.
Prepare the way of the Lord.

Out of the wilderness
joy.

Out of the earth
water.

Out of the darkness
light.

Out of the shadows
vision.

Out of the suffering
life.

Out of the woman
child.

Make straight the road.
Prepare the way of the Lord.

For a child comes to lead his people
and all creation will know it together.

Make straight the road.
Prepare the way of the Lord.

Marjory Macaskill

17. *... and they shall name him Emmanuel ...*
(Matthew 1:23)

God of all ages,
maker of time,
mark of the alpha and
point to omega,
Creator, sustainer of everything living,
touching us all who hold a hope
with a vision that breaks through boundaries
to grasp the blurred horizon.

You gave your promise,
a blessing of joy
to those who've not lost their faith in you.

Now time is poised with renewed expectation
of *Emmanuel*, God with us.

To know our time
of proclaimed favour
we make again the pledge you ask:

'Share justly, the good things I give you.
Reconcile with peace the rule of abuse.
Give courage to those who voice the words
of lives that have been silenced.'

Send us to carry your good news
to those burdened with debt.
Transform their chains into clasps of love,

of prayer, concern and then action.

Aware of your Spirit always among us
we sustain your purpose with passions.
Increase our endeavour to do what you ask,
of 'Where there are wrongs, they be righted.'

Now is the time.
It will be achieved.
In acting justly,
in loving tenderly
and in walking closely with you, our God.

Lala Winkley

18. *... for the day of the Lord is near ...*
(Isaiah 13:6)

Waiting breathless, in the blackness;
watching, hoping earth will change:
change its driven, self-deluding,
status-seeking search for gain.
Now's the time for holy anger,
time to challenge all that's wrong:
time for conscience, time for justice,
time to sing our Saviour's song.

Light was promised, love is present,
judgement's given in God's name;
hope was dormant, now it's dawning:
human life can't be the same.
Jesus' coming's all that matters –
God is breaking into time:
counter-culture, other acting,
he'll turn water into wine.

Yahweh is our-Saving-Justice:
poor are welcomed, proud brought low;
people mourning sing in gladness,
cursed are blessed, oppressed say, 'No!'
A child is changing earth's perspective,
wealth is shared by all, not some;

peace is flowering, bells are ringing,
waiting's over: 'Come, Lord, come!'
> *(Tune: Suo Gân [traditional Welsh folk song];*
> *Calon Lân; Hyfrydol)*
> Pamela Turner

19. *'She will bear a son, and you are to name him Jesus, for he will save his people from their sins.'*
> (Matthew 1:21)

God of hope,
As we light the Advent candles in preparation for our celebration of the birth of your Son, may the fire of your love burn away the dusts of our complacency.
May we be able to see the world as it really is and light anew the flame of our passion for justice.

> Linda Jones

20. *... he will bring forth justice to the nations.*
> (Isaiah 42:1)

Lord, we wait with eager expectation for the coming of your Kingdom when the humble will be exalted and the hungry fed.
Your Kingdom come,
your will be done.
Lord, we prepare for your advent with searching minds and contrite hearts,
trusting in your healing spirit and redemptive love.
Your Kingdom come,
your will be done.
Lord, we watch with those who wait and weep,
longing to see the rule of justice and the reign of peace.
Your Kingdom come,
your will be done.
Lord, we seek you amongst the despised and rejected,
knowing that there we will find your light shining in the dark.
Your Kingdom come,
your will be done.
Lord, we proclaim sight to the blind and liberty to the oppressed,
trusting in your tender mercy and passion for justice.

Your Kingdom come,
your will be done.
Lord, we work with CAFOD/Christian Aid to proclaim your truth,
challenging the mighty and raising the meek.
Your Kingdom come,
your will be done.
Lord, we wrestle with our hopes and our fears, our struggles and our
    joys
labouring with creation to come to new birth.
Your Kingdom come,
your will be done
on earth as it is in heaven.

Annabel Shilson-Thomas

21. *... she has served her term ... her penalty is paid.*

(Isaiah 40:2)

God of our desire and longing,
we await your coming with eager expectation
and with joyful hope.
Strengthen our hearts and minds
with the beckoning light of your redeeming love
that we may earnestly work for the coming of your Kingdom
and be ever ready to receive you in those we meet.
Amen.

Annabel Shilson-Thomas

22. *... that he may teach us his way and that we may walk in his paths.*

(Isaiah 2:3)

Generous loving God,
As we begin this season of preparation and hope, teach us how to live
in love. Show us how to walk in your ways, ready to learn and ready
to change. Help us always to hold in our hearts and minds all those
who go hungry. Give us the courage and compassion, tenderness and
strength to work for an end to the scandal of poverty, and to fight, in
peace, for justice.
Amen.

Linda Jones

23. Swords into ploughshares

... and they shall beat their swords into ploughshares and their spears into pruning hooks ...

(Isaiah 2:4)

God of the dispossessed,
as we prepare to greet your saving light,
give us grace to watch with those who weep
and endurance to stand with those who wait
for a safe place to rest,
a return to home
and the fulfilment of hope,
that together we may beat swords into ploughshares
and make straight the paths that lead to peace.
Amen.

Annabel Shilson-Thomas

24. Make us aware

'Keep awake, therefore, for you do not know on what day your Lord is coming.'

(Matthew 24:42)

Merciful God, forgive
that we fall asleep
when you call us to watch and pray.
We fail to see the signs of your coming.

Christ our Saviour, forgive
that we are not watchful
we do not choose hope
or plant the seeds of hopefulness.
We fail to see the signs of your coming.

Forgiving Spirit, forgive
that in the rush of the Christmas season
we forget to stop and listen for the sound of angel voices
we forget to stop and look for a star
to guide us to Christ.
We fail to see the signs of God's presence.

God over all
Christ within us

Spirit around us
hear our prayer
and send your messenger
of peace to us and to your sleeping world.

Kate McIlhagga

25. A prayer for trust
... but those who act faithfully are his delight.

(Proverbs 12:22)

Creator God,
you made us for your delight,
you took risks to give us freedom,
you weep when we hurt or ignore one another.

Restore in us your way of seeing,
give us the vision to look beyond our fears and suspicion to your way
    of love.
Strengthen our wills to come closer to one another,
grant us a wisdom that perceives the difference between good and
    evil,
and to trust as you trust us.

Through Jesus Christ our Lord.
Amen.

Grace Sheppard

26. God who comes to us
*A shoot shall come out from the stump of Jesse, and a branch shall
grow out of his roots. The spirit of the Lord shall rest on him ...*

(Isaiah 11:1–2)

Lord, I think of your first coming, heralded by angels,
attended by shepherds,
visited by travellers from afar.
Born for us in poverty,
coming to us as a refugee,
you filled the stable with your light.
I think of you journeying with your disciples,
not knowing where the next meal was coming from,
rubbing wheat between your hands,

watching the widow putting her everything into the treasury.
'Blessed are the poor,' you said, 'for the Kingdom of heaven
    is theirs.'

I think of the thief on the cross, the one who turned to you
in his last moments.
What a coming of joy he found with you,
harvested into Paradise!

I think then of the first Easter morning,
the stone rolled away,
the amazement, the fear – and the gift of hope.
Did you not reach down to the depths
to pull up Adam and Eve from the darkness?*
So you rescue us too, from our private hells
from the prisons others make for us
or we build for ourselves.
You set the captives free!

I think of that day in Bethlehem,
some years ago,
when I had to bend low to enter the place
where you were born,
crouching down to get through the stone doorway,
then down the steps to wonder at a star set in the floorspace,
surrounded by candles.
Lord, help me to be ready to bow down
to cross the threshold into the place where there is need,
where words will not nourish, but where love is all.

And you will come again, to be our Judge.
To be judged by love, could we stand the pain?
To be judged by how much we loved,
how much we gave?
Lord, have mercy!

*(*Adam and Eve – the reference is to the Icon of the Resurrection of the Orthodox
Church, where Christ descends to the under-world, breaks down the gates of hell,
and raises up Adam and Eve, grasping their hands with his own and pulling them
up out of the darkness.)*

Clare Amos

27. Creed of hope

He came as a witness to testify to the light, so that all might believe through him.
(John 1:7)

I believe in God.
The God of all creeds, with all their truths.
But, above all, in the God
who rises from the dead words
to become part of life.
I believe in God who accompanies me along
every step of my path on this earth,
many times walking behind me, watching me and suffering with my
    mistakes,
other times walking beside me, talking to me and teaching me,
and other times walking ahead of me, guiding and marking my pace.
I believe in the God of flesh and blood, Jesus Christ,
the God who lived in my skin and tried on my shoes,
the God who walked in my ways, and knows of lights and shadows.
The God who ate and starved,
who had a home and suffered loneliness,
who was praised and condemned, kissed and spat on, loved and
    hated.
The God who went to parties and funerals,
the God who laughed and cried.
I believe in the God who is attentive today, who looks at the world
and sees the hatred that segregates, divides,
sets people aside, hurts and kills,
who sees the bullets piercing the flesh,
and the blood of innocent people flowing on the earth,
who sees the hand that dips into another's pocket,
stealing what somebody needs to eat,
who sees the judge that favours the highest bidder,
the truth and justice of hypocrites,
who sees the dirty rivers and the dead fish,
the toxic substances destroying the earth
and piercing the sky,
who sees the future mortgaged and
man's debt growing.
I believe in God who sees all this ...
and keeps on crying.

But I also believe in God
who sees a mother giving birth – a life born from pain,
who sees two children playing – a seed growing,
who sees a flower blooming out of the debris – a new beginning,
who sees three crazy women clamouring for justice – an illusion that
      doesn't die,
who sees the sun rising every morning – a time of opportunities.
I believe in God who sees all this ...
and laughs,
because,
in spite of it all,
there is hope.

Gerardo Oberman
Argentina

28. We bring before you, O Lord,
    the troubles and perils of peoples and nations,
    the frustrations of prisoners and captives,
    the anguish of the bereaved,
    the needs of refugees,
    the helplessness of the weak,
    the despondency of the weary,
    the failing powers of the aged and the hopelessness of the starving.
    O Lord, draw near to each,
    for the sake of Jesus Christ our Lord.

After St Anselm (1033–1109)

29. **The just ruler**
    God, endow the king with your own justice,
    his royal person with your righteousness,
    that he may govern your people rightly
    and deal justly with your oppressed ones.

    May hills and mountains provide your people
    with prosperity in righteousness.
    May he give judgement for the oppressed among the people
    and help to the needy;
    may he crush the oppressor.

May he fear you as long as the sun endures,
and as the moon throughout the ages.
May he be like rain falling on early crops,
like showers watering the earth.

In his days may righteousness flourish,
prosperity abound until the moon is no more.
For he will rescue the needy who appeal for help,
the distressed who have no protector.

He will have pity on the poor and the needy,
and deliver the needy from death;
he will redeem them from oppression and violence
and their blood will be precious in his eyes.

*Blessed be he who in his love stooped to redeem mankind! Blessed be
the King who made himself poor to enrich the needy! Blessed be he
who came to fulfil the types and emblems of the prophets! Blessed
be he who made creation to rejoice with the wealth and treasure of
his Father!*

Ephraem the Syrian (*c.* 306–73)

30. Grant us your light, O Lord,
that the darkness in our hearts being wholly passed away,
we may come at last to the light that is Christ.
For Christ is the morning star,
who when the night of this world is past,
brings to his saints the promised light of life,
and opens to them eternal day.
Amen.

Bede

31. O thou who art love, and who seest all the suffering, injustice and
misery, which are in this world: have pity, we implore thee, on thy
children. Look mercifully upon the poor, the oppressed, and all who
are heavy laden with error, labour or sorrow. Fill our hearts with deep
compassion for those who suffer and hasten the coming of thy
Kingdom of justice, truth, and love. Through Jesus Christ our Lord.
Amen.

Author unknown

32. I dream of a community
where justice is practised
and leaders are not dictated
where human rights are observed
where tribalism does not exist
where leaders are honest and able
where politicians listen in silence.
I dream a lot more
and I still believe God will provide.
Amen.

Clementina Naita
Kenya

Christmas and Epiphany

In those days a decree went out from Caesar Augustus that all the world should be enrolled. This was the first enrolment, when Quirinius was governor of Syria. And all went to be enrolled, each to his own city. And Joseph also went up from Galilee, from the city of Nazareth, to Judea, to the city of David, which is called Bethlehem, because he was of the house and lineage of David, to be enrolled with Mary, his betrothed, who was with child. (Luke 2:1–5)

Mary and Joseph are brought to Bethlehem by the command of the emperor. Like everyone else, they must be registered. They must submit to the power that ruled their world, and which counted and taxed everyone. Their journey was a sign of their powerlessness faced with the greatest superpower that the West had known until then. But meanwhile God was working in the tangle of history, bringing the pregnant mother to the place where the Christ must be born. The bureaucrats were unknowingly serving not Caesar but God.

This does not mean to say that God had a great plan that was imposed on history and that we have no free will. Rather it is that God is like a judo fighter, who uses our strength and freedom to achieve his purpose. God is creatively present, invisibly opening doors to the future even when we close them.

The last century saw the rise of a culture of government control, where everyone must be registered, identified, taxed. Its crazy climax was in the technological efficiency of the Nazi death camps. Primo Levi wrote of his arrival at Auschwitz in 1944, 'Nothing belongs to us anymore; they have taken away our clothes, our shoes, even our hair; if we speak they will not listen to us, and if they listen, they will not understand. They have even taken away our names ... My number is 174517; we have been baptised, we will carry the tattoo on our left arm until we die.'

Today we are faced with global control. Our world, like that of Jesus, is dominated by one great superpower, whose interests and security may not be questioned by anyone. And then there are international organisations, like the World Trade Organisation, that impose their trade barriers and tariffs. There are the multinationals, calculating profit and loss, measuring and assessing, largely unchecked by government. In the face of all this power, those who long for a just and free world may be tempted to despair. What can we achieve, faced with these vast forces? Our Christmas faith is that God has not deserted us, that somehow God's irrepressible freedom is at work, bringing Christ to birth among us still today.

The real drama is not that of the Emperor and his court who decree that all should be enrolled. It is announced by the uncountable host of heaven. Angels do not appear on any census form. There is a glorious extravagance in the scene. One angel appears to make the announcement of the birth of the Christ. Why send more? Surely one angel is enough. But 'suddenly there was with the angel a multitude of the heavenly host praising God and saying: "glory to God in the highest, and on earth peace among those with whom he is pleased"' (Luke 2:14).

And the witnesses are the shepherds. They were considered disreputable people, who lived on the edge of society, not to be trusted. They probably never made it onto the census either. They were often the invisible people, who just survive on the margins. They probably were not counted, and they certainly did not count. So it is the uncountable host of heaven who announce the birth of the Saviour to those who do not count. Angels and shepherds were both way off the bureaucratic map.

If we wish to hear angelic announcement now, then we need to be with the shepherds, those on the edge, and we shall hear that a Saviour is born for us. During the military dictatorship in Brazil, a whole community of Dominicans was arrested on suspicion of collaboration with the enemies of the regime. One of them, Frei Betto, wrote:

> Christmas night in prison ... Now the whole prison is singing, as if our song alone, happy and free, must sound throughout the world. The women are singing over in their section, and we

applaud ... Everyone here knows that it's Christmas, that someone is being reborn. And with our song we testify that we too
have been reborn to fight for a world without tears, hatred or
oppression. It's quite something to see these young faces pressed
against the bars and singing their love. Unforgettable. It's not a
sight for our judges, or the public prosecutor, or the police who
arrested us. They would find the beauty of this night intolerable.
Torturers fear a smile, even a weak one.

We may feel suffocated by a culture of control that, paradoxically,
often appears unable to achieve its end. We cannot easily see how our
struggle for a just world will bear fruit. But at Christmas we remember the uncalculating extravagance of God, who said to a lonely and
barren old couple, Abraham and Sarah, 'Look towards heaven and
number the stars, if you are able to count them ... So shall your
descendants be' (Genesis 15:5). This is the God who gives each elm
tree six million leaves! And if that God counts the hairs of our head,
an ever easier task in my case, then it is a sign of infinite tenderness,
like a mother caring for her child.

On Boxing Day 2004, the tsunami struck. The numbers of dead
rose hour by hour. The death of one person is unimaginable, and so
how could we get our minds around these horrifying statistics of
death and destruction? The number of those who were bereaved and
whose lives were torn apart is beyond calculation. We were heartened
by the rising millions of dollars given spontaneously by people from
all around the world. For the first time ever, there was a global
response of humanity to this disaster.

Where is God in all this? The angel says to the shepherds, 'And this
will be a sign for you: you will find a babe wrapped in swaddling
clothes and lying in a manger.' A child is always a sign of hope, of a
future which we cannot guess. Fatalism tempts us to think that we
know what must be and that nothing can be done. Every child
contradicts that certainty. Its life has infinite possibilities, beyond all
calculation. The first time I went to Rwanda was during the terrible
genocide. I visited a Canadian priest who was in tears. He had lost all
of his friends. For years he had worked for reconciliation and peace.
Now all seemed destroyed. But the next Christmas he sent me a
picture of himself holding two fat Rwandan babies, and on it he
wrote, 'Africa has a future.'

Every Christmas Christians remember the birth of Jesus and we
say, 'Humanity has a future.' There are children being born after the
tsunami, and in all the other forgotten places of the world. We cherish

our Saviour in cherishing them and their future. Every child is a sign of hope. If we can struggle to give hope and a future to these children, they offer hope and a future to us.

Reflections

33. Justice will be seen to be done!
'*I cannot dance, Oh, Lord, unless Thou lead me!*'
(Mechtild of Magdeburg [1212–83])

He dances in front of us,
he dances before us,
he dances in around us,
in the improvised tent
we call Church,
    where we have to get in step,
    with him,
    but also with all our sisters and brothers
    together with the whole of creation,
    the sun and the moon, the water and the earth,
        one step to the right,
        one step to the left,
        one step forward,
        one step backward,
looking up at the tent lines,
and to the sky
through a hole in the roof,
down to the earth,
out of the tent opening
to the far off sky of a new city.
        Tables are set up,
        name tags distributed,
        committees formed,
        bread is broken,
        wine is shared,
        now and then there is a hush
        as if all are in prayer,
        and then the rehearsals veer off again
            one step to the right,
            one step to the left,
            one step forward,
            one step backward,

groups are formed,
circles opened,
blessings shared,
oil and water splashed around
anointings and baptisms,
> a trumpet blast,
> the sound of instruments tuned,
> directives are given,
> maps laid out,
> and marked are the roads
> leading to our destiny
> the home of God self.
Remaining ourselves,
but more and more together
in ever growing ecstasy,
> we are taken up in the swirling movement,
> of the dance that is already moving around and ahead,
>> one step to the right,
>> one step to the left,
>> one step forward,
>> one step backward,
> we are still trying
> to catch his rhythm,
> and the words of the song,
> He sings and pipes
> in our midst.
> Others are joining,
> balancing gifts on the top of their heads,
> playing their drums and trumpets,
> adding to a cacophony,
> that sounds more and more like a symphony
> the longer it lasts.
It is almost dawn,
> the rucksacks are packed,
> the children awake,
> ready to dance into the dawn of a new day,
> and we,
> we are on our way
> and justice will be seen
> to be done!

Joseph Donders
USA

34. *'Arise, take the child and his mother and flee into Egypt.'*

(Matthew 2:13)

In Matthew's stories surrounding Jesus' birth, the human suffering caused by Herod's cruelty appals and saddens. However, the full import of the story comes to us in this sublime proclamation in the Gospel of John: 'The Word became flesh and dwelt amongst us.' Jesus, we hear, is indeed Emmanuel, God-with-us. So it is God-with-us who in Matthew's story escapes death by flight from Herod's insecure but brutal power, banished to share his human ancestors' bitter experience of exile. In the beginning, as at the end, the 'kingdom of this world' had no room for Emmanuel.

Today, the bitter experience of exile is shared by millions of refugees in flight from the loss or abuse of their human dignity and rights. Their very lives are at the mercy of prosperous nations who control and enjoy so much of the world's God-given resources. Why are so many of them knocking in vain at the doors of nations claiming to honour human rights? Or nations whose cultural heritage has been shaped in part by the Christian ideal: 'Love the Lord your God ... and love your neighbour as yourself'?

In my prosperous country, fear of 'the other' seems to have hardened into an attitude which regards any group that may disturb our comfortable status quo as a threat, a potential burden, an enemy to be kept at bay. Directed to refugees, such an attitude breeds indifference to both their suffering and their rights and condones policies of self-interested exclusion, short-sightedly claimed to be 'in the national interest'. Are we, in a strange paradox, in flight from the refugee whose plight challenges us to be truly human? For the Christian the challenge cuts even deeper. If in flight from our human brothers and sisters in dire need, are we not in flight from Emmanuel, God-with-us? 'As often as you did it to one of these, you did it to me' (Matthew 25:40).

In sharp contrast to national policy in 2004, a public sign outside a parish school in Sydney proclaimed that Gospel message: 'We welcome Christ who comes to us in the refugee.'

Mary Britt OP
Australia

35. *'Glory to God in highest heaven and on earth peace among those he favours.'*
        (Luke 2:14)

Some of our people ask how can we celebrate Christmas
with all the closures and checkpoints,
with all the injustice and oppression,
with all the violations of human rights,
with the presence of a wall that separates families and friends,
and a multitude of hardships that the occupation imposes to make
people's lives miserable,
how can we speak of love, peace and joy when most of our people
and millions of others around the world do not experience liberty and
peace?

The questions are legitimate. Yet Christmas and New Year must be a
time of renewal, of hope and anticipation, of determination and zeal
to work for a better world where people can experience these essential qualities of life. Therefore, wherever empire exists and the powers that be are in control through domination, there is a greater
responsibility for all of us to take a stand against all that dehumanis-
es people and to work for their liberation.

The Christmas story is a story of a liberating God who comes to
join an oppressed people in the work of liberation. God's message
through the angels is a message of defiance. In spite of the presence
of empire, human arrogance and oppression, God is announcing
peace and goodwill. This is God's agenda. Glory belongs to God and
not to the emperor nor to the powers. Once that is genuinely
acknowledged, peace is not far away.

It is in the midst of the Roman occupation that the Incarnation took
place;
it is in spite of the occupation that Mary and Joseph found joy and
love in the birth of Jesus;
it is in spite of the occupation and in the midst of economic hardships
that the shepherds came to visit a family of modest means and discov-
ered great joy and peace;
it is in spite of the occupation that the Magi came to offer their gifts
to the child.

We celebrate in the midst of the occupation and in spite of it. Through
our celebration

we defy the occupation;
we defy the injustice;
we defy the oppressors;
we defy the powers.

They do not possess the last word,
they can build high walls, but they cannot take away our hope,
they can put us in jail, but they cannot take away our joy,
they can prevent us from visiting family, but they cannot take away
    our love,
they can stop us at checkpoints and impose all kinds of restrictions,
    but they cannot take away our pursuit of freedom and liberation,
they can prevent us from going to Bethlehem, but they cannot prevent
    the spirit of Bethlehem from reaching us,
they can treat us as non-humans, but they cannot crush our spirit nor
    can they take away our God-given human worth and dignity,
they can act with hate and disgust but, by the grace of God, we can
    always refuse to stoop to the level of hate and maintain our love of
    God and neighbour that includes them.

Therefore Christmas makes us defiant.
We defy the evildoers because we believe in the goodness which they
    are capable of doing,
we defy hate because we believe in the power of love and forgiveness,
we defy despair because we believe in life and hope,
we defy violence and terror – both state and individual – because we
    believe in the power of peace and non-violence,
we defy war and the occupation of other people's lands because we
    believe in the power of peaceful methods based on international
    law and legitimacy,
we defy and challenge those who humiliate and degrade others
    because we believe in the dignity of every human being.

The Incarnation took place when God took on our humanity, when
the Word became flesh and dwelt among us. This happened in
Palestine under Roman occupation. Then as now and in spite of all
the hardships, we celebrate Christ's birth, Emmanuel, God with us,
giving us hope, joy, peace and love.

We are defiant. We are full of hope. We will continue to work for
peace through justice.

Naim Ateek
Sabeel, Jerusalem

36. The story of Christmas as told by a football obsessive

The **goal** of the first Christmas was to end the **division** between humans and God.

Now it came to **pass** that God sent an angel to a girl called Mary. He said, 'You have been **marked** by the Holy Spirit. You will give birth to a baby and his name will be Jesus. He will be in a different **league**, for he will be God's own son.'

Mary and Joseph travelled **away** from **home**. Bethlehem was crowded, and the result was that they were **sent off** to find **cover** in the **corner** of a **Dyer** stable. That is where Jesus was born.

Shepherds on a hillside saw a **squad** of **wingers**, singing at a high **pitch**, 'Your Saviour is born. Glory to God!' The shepherds were **Keane** to see the baby. They **Beckhamed** to each other: 'Let's **Rush** to visit the child even though we are only sheep **Shearers**.' When they saw Jesus they were overjoyed. 'We have **Neville** seen anything so wonderful. We're having a **ball**!'

They went **forward** praising God and telling everyone what had happened. God and humankind could now be **United**. Men, women and children could be **friendly**. Sin was going to meet its **match**. At peace with God, humans would **transfer** to heaven. What a **result**!

Christian Aid

37. There is nothing we can do but love

What we would like to do is change the world – make it a little simpler for people to feed, clothe and shelter themselves as God intended them to do. And to a certain extent, by fighting for better conditions, by crying out unceasingly for the rights of the workers, of the poor, of the destitute – the rights of the worthy and the unworthy poor, in other words – we can to a certain extent change the world; we can work for the oasis, the little cell of joy and peace in a harried world. We can throw our pebble in the pond and be confident that its ever-widening circle will reach around the world.

We repeat, there is nothing that we can do but love, and dear God – please enlarge our hearts to love each other, to love our neighbour, to love our enemy as well as our friend.

Dorothy Day
USA

Prayers

38. *In the beginning was the Word ...*

(John 1:1)

He who comes
comes to us now

in the silence
in the darkness
in the confusion
in the loneliness

as Word and
as Light
as Truth and
as Love

Emmanuel
God-with-us
now.

Harry Wiggett
South Africa

39. *And the Word became flesh and lived among us ...*

(John 1:14a)

The Word became the hungry child with empty eyes and swollen belly. We are his hope that one day his belly will be filled with good things and the rich sent away empty.
Lord, give us grace to see
and faith to respond.
The Word became the poor who live amongst the garbage the rich throw away. We are their hope that one day justice will prevail and equality will be born.
Lord, give us grace to see
and faith to respond.
The Word became the war widow fleeing her savaged country with six children and six plastic bags. We are her hope that one day the

mighty will be put down from their thrones and her home will be rebuilt.

Lord, give us grace to see
and faith to respond.

The Word became the skeletal man, wracked by AIDS and shunned by all. We are his hope that one day treatment will be given and he will be understood..

Lord, give us grace to see
and faith to respond.

The Word became the young girl prostituting her body to keep her baby alive. We are her hope that one day the good news of great joy will mean she can feed and clothe her child.

Lord, give us grace to see
and faith to respond.

The Word became the orphan boy, bewildered and confused. We are his hope that one day war will be no more and peace will be won.

Lord, give us grace to see,
faith to respond
and wisdom to receive from those to whom we give.

                                              Annabel Shilson-Thomas

40. Canterbury rap

And the Word became flesh ...
                    (John 1:14)

In the beginning was the Word.

God spoke his Word through
          Abraham and Moses,
          Deborah and Hannah,
          Samuel and David,
          Isaiah, Zechariah.
It is written   it is written.

And the Word became   flesh.

God spoke his Word through
          Mary and Elizabeth,
          Simeon and Anna,
          Peter and Paul,
          Matthew and Johanna.
It is written   it is written.

God speaks his Word in
      Urdu and Tamil,
      Xhosa and Hausa,
      Spanish and English,
      Mandarin and Maori.
It is read   it is read.

In the beginning was the Word
And the Word became   flesh.

It is written   it is read.
It is old   it is new.
It is God's   it is true.

Graham Kings

41. Protection and comfort

Joseph also went ... to be registered with Mary ... who was expecting a child.
     (Luke 2:4–5)

As we journey with the Holy Family to Bethlehem, we pray for all who make forced journeys. Give them strength to carry on and courage to walk the road ahead.
Wake up, little baby God
and hear our cry.
As we hear the innkeeper say there is no room, we pray for refugees for whom there is no country. Gather them to yourself and keep them free from harm.
Wake up, little baby God
and hear our cry.
As we contemplate that first Christmas night, we pray for those with nowhere to lay their head. Comfort them in their need and uphold them in their plight.
Wake up, little baby God
and hear our cry.
As we listen to the cry of the infant king, we pray for children everywhere born into poverty. Wrap them in your love and uphold them in your tender mercy.
Wake up, little baby God
and hear our cry.

As we remember the fear of the shepherds in the presence of the
angels, we pray for all who are afraid to look ahead. Reassure them
with your presence and embolden them to face the future.
Wake up, little baby God
and hear our cry.
As we recall the flight of the Holy Family into Egypt, we pray for all
who flee from danger. Enfold them in your care and challenge us to
offer our protection.
Wake up, little baby God
and hear our cry
that justice may be born.

                                        Annabel Shilson-Thomas

42. *And she ... laid him in a manger.*
                    (Luke 2:7)

I lift my grateful heart to the Christ child,
who set aside the riches of heaven
to be laid in a manger, helpless and among strangers.

I lift my celebrating voice to the Christ child,
thankful for the food and the colour and excitement,
and wanting the good things I enjoy to be shared fairly throughout
    the world.

I lift my heartfelt prayers to the Christ child,
from the comfort of my home this Christmas,
for the children growing up in poverty, without the education or
    healthcare they need.

I lift my hopes and fears to the Christ child,
longing for a world in which violence is at an end,
and pleading for those who have known nothing but brutality all
    their lives.

To the Christ child of Bethlehem I pray:
out of the injustice, out of warfare, out of fear,
lift every human heart this Christmas.
Amen.

                                        Christian Aid

43. A prayer for others

... because there was no place for them in the inn.

(Luke 2:7)

How can we break bread
    and not remember those
        who have no bread?
How can we meet together
    and not remember those
        separated from their families and friends?
How can we shelter here
    and not remember those
        whose only shelter is a refugee camp or cardboard box?
How can we speak of peace
    and not remember those
        whose peace is shattered by constant fear and the rattle of guns?
How can we sing our hymns
    and not remember those
        who cannot openly express their religious beliefs?
How can we offer our gifts
    and not remember those
        who are caught in the never-ending cycle of poverty and debt?
How can we pour wine
    and not remember those
        who are imprisoned by addiction to bottle, needles or pills?
How can we celebrate
    and not remember those
        who suffer from depression, mental illness or grief?

God of human experience,
    born in a stable in Bethlehem,
Spirit alive in us today,
    present in community,
in our worship and in our reflecting,
    may we look outwards to the suffering of our world,
        remembering the hope of your shalom.
Amen.

Clare McBeath

44. *And she gave birth to her firstborn son ...*
(Luke 2:7)

Christ child, thrust from the warmth and security
of your mother's womb
into the bitter cold of the night
and the stark reality of the world;

in your vulnerability, demanding instant attention;
kicking and screaming for your mother,
for reassurance and for food;
making your presence felt.

You began your life like many a child, in poverty,
facing an uncertain future.
Yet – you were no ordinary child
for you were born the Son of God.

Christ child, Son of God, born to be King
and rule over your Kingdom
of love, justice and peace;
coming the long-awaited,
long-promised Saviour;

striding through the world,
gathering to you the weak,
the oppressed and the vulnerable;
still making your presence felt.
Christ child, son of Mary, Son of God,
we celebrate your coming.

Jan Grimwood

45. Welcome
... because there was no place for them in the inn.
(Luke 2:7)

Jesus, born in poverty,
your shelter inadequate,
shut out, a stranger.

You found no welcome.

Bethlehem life went on
as usual that morning.

**Today, once again, we are too busy
to notice you,
alive amongst us.
Forgive us.**

But despite the coldness of our welcome,
you are the one who welcomes us,
each one, to the feast of heaven,
to share the bread of life,
to taste the coming kingdom.

Jesus, you invite us today
to share in the feast that you have prepared for us.

**We accept with thanks.
We will come at once.
Thanks be to you, O God.**

Fiona Liddell

46. *'For my eyes have seen your salvation.'*
(Luke 2:30)

Thank you, God, that the time of waiting is now over, that with Simeon we can bless you for the coming of Jesus into the world. We praise you for a new intimacy you invite us to share with you.
We, too, are inspired by your Spirit.

We confess that many times we fail to see your purpose, your presence, in what lies before us. We confess closed minds and stunted expectations, spurning the creativity and spirit with which you have entrusted us.
We, too, are inspired by your Spirit.

We pray for millions of people today who, in material terms can afford very little to honour the birth of Jesus. We pray that you will constantly move us to stand alongside our sisters and brothers in need.
We, too, are inspired by your Spirit.

Direct what we think, say or do that we may be transformed by your new beginning in Jesus Christ, our Lord and Salvation. Give us a passion for your Gospel and a vision of your kingdom in which all are included.
We, too, are inspired by your Spirit.

Gray Featherstone

47. '*Blessed be the Lord God of Israel, for he has looked favourably on his people and redeemed them.*'
(Luke 1:68)

Open our mouths, O God, as you opened the mouth of Zechariah.
Open our mouths to proclaim your praise and glory.
We lift the Christ child out from his crib, and hold him high,
that all might see his vulnerability and marvel at your tender mercy.
In darkening shadows, in fragile candle light,
on the cusp of Christmas joy;
we pray
for
peace,
for
justice,
for
redemption.

We are often afraid to speak out; forgive us our lack of courage,
our struggles with integrity.
Open our mouths, O God, as you opened the mouth of Zechariah
that we might praise your holy name.
Amen.

Vivienne Lassetter

48. *... and laid him in a manger ...*
(Luke 2:7)

In Nazareth, on Christmas night, a baby was born in a stable.
He wasn't the first.
He won't be the last.
For the poor will always be with us.

Mary wrapped her precious child; relieved they'd both survived.
No bows,
no balloons, to celebrate;
Just dirt and straw and tiredness.

Until we change our hearts and minds,
Until we thirst for justice,

Until we live the words we sing
And act the words we pray
Our joy is hollow on Christmas day
for the poor will always be with us.
Amen.

Vivienne Lassetter

49. *In that region there were shepherds living in the fields, keeping watch over their flock by night.*
(Luke 2:8)

On a cold, dark night, in a world full of dreams,
every home lay still, heavy with sleep;
but the poor kept watch and they heard of a birth,
and they came with hope, bringing their sheep,
to greet the Lord of the Earth.

On a cold, dark night, in a world full of dreams,
all the rich slept warm under their fur,
but the wise kept watch and they heard of a birth,
and they came with gold, incense and myrrh,
to greet the Lord of the Earth,
the new-born Lord of the Earth!

Maranatha! Maranatha!
In a waiting world, Lord, we long for your birth.
Maranatha! Maranatha!
And we want to bring you a gift to honour your birth,
O Lord of the Earth!

On a cold, dark night, in a world full of dreams,
every gift lies wrapped, shiny and new,
but if we keep watch, we will hear of a birth,

and our hearts will know what we can do,
to greet the Lord of the Earth,
the new-born Lord of the Earth!

Maranatha! Maranatha! ...
We can give new hope to the poor of the world,
and the chains of debt we can release.
We can give new seeds and the water of life,
and with hand in hand, travel in peace,
to greet the Lord of the Earth,
the new-born Lord of the Earth!
Maranatha! Maranatha! ...

> *('Maranatha' is Aramaic for the 'The Lord is coming'.)*
> Peter Rose and Anne Conlon

50. Unadorned King

*... on entering the house, they saw the child with Mary his mother;
and they knelt down and paid him homage.*

(Matthew 2:11)

In the star we see the cross;
its points, the thorns,
the azure ring, his robe.
The light which shines on all
the arms which embrace all.
And this despite their mockery,
mock majesty, pageant pantomime and pomp.
All human conceptions of kingship
border on the vaudeville
verge on the burlesque.
Kings in a stable
out of proportion
distorted, like the body on the cross.
Our attempt to nail down Divinity
racked and disjointed,
still suffering our mock homage.
Cast crowns, cast lots, cast off your
tawdry kind of kingship –
so much dressing up –
Christ rides triumphant over cast-down cloaks
every inch a king with none of the apparel.

His crown, the star
the cross, his throne where he
invests the cosmos with his gift of Love, unadorned.

Laurentia Johns OSB

51. '*... for Herod is about to search for the child, to destroy him.*'

(Matthew 2:13)

Faithful God,
we pray for all families who have been forced from their homes
by war, or flood, or the need to find food.
Grant them courage as they travel,
safety as they seek refuge,
and hope for a secure future.
And may we, who have been given so much,
learn to be generous and welcoming to those who,
fearful and needy,
seek shelter among us.
Amen.

Christian Aid

52. '*... take the child and his mother, and flee to Egypt ...* '

(Matthew 2:13)

Almighty God,
you whose son had to flee the evil plans of King Herod
and seek refuge in a strange land,
we bring before you the needs of the many refugees throughout the
world.
We pray for those known personally to us
whom we now name before you ...
We pray for those in their need for necessities of life –
for shelter and food.
Grant that they may have the skills and equipment
to build shelters and grow food.

South African Council of Churches (adapted)

53. '*Get up, take the young child and his mother, and flee ...* '

(Matthew 2:13)

We pray for all those who are far away from home.
Hold them in your love.

That those sick in homes and hospitals
may know their value as whole people, mind, body and spirit.
Lord, we pray,
hold them in your love.

That those in prisons and detention centres
may know that they are not written off or forgotten by society.
Lord, we pray,
hold them in your love.

That those who flee violence, oppression and injustice
may know that hatred does not have to have the last word.
Lord, we pray,
hold them in your love.

That those who have no home or resting-place
may know that identity does not depend on having an address.
Lord, we pray,
hold them in your love.

That those who seek their home in your heart
may know that they are cherished and beloved.
Lord, we pray,
hold them in your love.

And for ourselves we pray.
Lord God, by the love we have seen in Jesus,
hold us, nurture us and sustain us,
that in your name, we may draw others to you.
Amen.

                                                    Mary Cotes

54. A prayer for refugees

'Get up, take the young child and his mother, and flee ... '
                                                    (Matthew 2:13)

Lord, you bid us feed the hungry, aid the oppressed, shelter the
homeless.

You tell us to seek God's justice for your world.
We pray for all those in fear of their lives within their own
  countries.
We give thanks for the work of all agencies combating oppression,
but chiefly on this day when we recall our Lord's flight into a less
  hostile land,
we remember all those whose desperation has driven them to our
  shores.
May our doors be wide and our hearts be generous to all who face
  extermination in their home countries,
knowing that we too are strangers and pilgrims
on the road to heaven.
Amen.

Stephen J. Brown

55. Merry Christmas
A voice was heard in Ramah ... Rachel weeping for her children ...
(Matthew 2:18)

At the heart of Christmas there was
pain, bleeding and crying;
love was with difficulty brought to birth.
Not to a sanitised stable did God come,
but to a world that needed mucking out;
his birth no tidy affair, but through
a single parent, in bed and breakfast
shelter; an inconvenience, not welcomed
by bureaucrats with important business;
acknowledged mainly by low-paid workers,
foreign visitors, and animals.
The sequel: attempted murder, exile.

People wounded by indifference
struggle to give love birth in the
cold comfort of charity, largely
unrecognised by those with power.
At the heart of Christmas, still there's
pain, bleeding and crying,
a sword piercing the heart of God,
opening the wounds of love.

Could we be midwives for the love of God,
cradling that strength born in fragility,
delivering healing to the crying world?

Ann Lewin

56. *The peace of God, which passes all understanding, will keep your*
hearts and minds in Christ Jesus.
(Philippians 4:7)

Gracious and loving God, you have given us the gift of Christmas
peace – your Son, the Prince of Peace. In him we have experienced the
fulfilment of all the promises of his grace. In him we are rich. In him
we have salvation. In him we have liberation. In him we have
deliverance. In him we have forgiveness. In him we have new life. In
him we have everlasting life. In him we have faith, hope and love.
In him we have that peace which passes all understanding.
O Lord our God:
Grant us peace and justice in Jesus Christ, our newborn Saviour!

Gracious and loving God, you have given us the gift of Christmas
peace – your Son, the Prince of Peace. We confess that we have not
loved you with all our heart, mind, body, soul and strength. We confess that we have not loved our neighbours as we love ourselves. We
confess that we have been engaged in war rather than peace. We confess that we have not reached out to those in need: the hungry are still
hungry; the thirsty are still thirsty; the poor are now the suffering
poor; and, the helpless are now hopelessly helpless. We pray for a
change in our way of behaving and cold-hearted apathy.
O Lord our God:
Grant us peace and justice in Jesus Christ, our newborn Saviour!

Gracious and loving God, you have given us the gift of Christmas
peace – your Son, the Prince of Peace. Renew within us a right spirit
of heart and mind. Restore within us the joy of our salvation.
Strengthen within us the gifts of smiling and laughter. Rekindle within us the flame of unceasing love for others. Overflow within us the
outstanding quality of faith. Fortify within us the courage to embrace
peace. Confirm within us the spirit of hope. Inspire within us genuine
undertakings of justice. Resonate within us the announcement of the
Good News of Jesus.
O Lord our God:

Grant us peace and justice in Jesus Christ, our newborn Saviour!

Gracious and loving God, you have given us the gift of Christmas peace – your Son, the Prince of Peace. We pray that through him and the power of the Holy Spirit, the numerous acts of violence, the murders of innocent people, the ill-treatment of women, the aggression against police officers, the abuse and misuse of children, the seeds of destruction against the environment, the cruelty meted out to blood-stained students, the unwarranted imprisonment of some political leaders and the painful experiences we bear daily, may all be transformed into doves of peace and fruits of justice.
O Lord our God, may peace and justice reign in the name of the Prince of Peace.
Amen!

Lesley G. Anderson

57. How ancient and lovely (What star shall we follow?)
'For we observed his star at its rising ... '
(Matthew 2:2)

How ancient and lovely this news of a star,
a baby, a mother, the kings from afar.
Come close now, Lord Jesus, we ask you to stay
and show us your face in your people today.

What star shall we follow but one that leads here
to a baby born homeless and a fam'ly in fear?
What heav'n shall we long for but one that starts there
for all the world's children in your tender care?

We thank you, Lord Jesus, for coming to earth;
for the lights in the darkness that shone at your birth,
for life in its fullness that you promise today,
and the hope in a baby asleep on the hay.

Rebecca Dudley

58. He came amid the turmoil (Liberating Lord)

He came amid the turmoil of thousands heading home,
complying with the census decreed by Caesar's Rome;
but no one is a number to Christ the Lord of grace;
to him each one is special: a name, a heart, a face.

His coming breached the darkness of Herod's brutal reign,
and hopes of Israel's glory were kindled once again;
yet Jesus offers freedoms no politics can give,
and by his mortal anguish invites us now to live.

He came within a household of poverty so raw
they scarcely found the off'rings demanded by the Law;
yet through such bitter hardships he meets our ev'ry need:
he gives eternal treasures and makes us rich indeed.

We thank you, Christ, for coming to set your people free:
you opened up the windows of hope and dignity!
Inspired by your example and by your love restored,
How glad we are to serve you, our liberating Lord!

Martin E. Leckebusch

59. Bridges of reconciliation

'... and on earth peace among those whom he favours.'
(Luke 2:14)

Prince of Peace,
you were born into a world
where terror reigned and fear ruled
and live today in a world crucified by war.
Fill us with your passion for justice
that wherever we see evil abound
we may live to disturb its path
and strive to build bridges of reconciliation.
In the darkness, beckon us with your kindly light
that we never lose sight of your vision of peace
in which the lion lies down with the lamb.
Amen.

Annabel Shilson-Thomas

60. Light through darkness

'... the dawn from on high will break upon us, to give light to those who sit in darkness ...'
(Luke 1:78)

God, our dayspring and our dawn,
we turn to you when we fear the dark

and all around us weep.
We pray you greet us with your shining light
that we may spread your warm embrace
and kindle the hope of Christmas
in all whose lives remain in shadow.
Come and be our strength
O Lord, our hope and our salvation.
Amen.

Annabel Shilson-Thomas

61. Vision of a world made whole

'... and he is named Wonderful Counsellor, Mighty God, Everlasting
Father, Prince of Peace.'
(Isaiah 9:6)

Wonderful Counsellor, grant insight and wisdom to those in authority that they may listen to the cries of the afflicted and work unceasingly to alleviate their plight.
Shine light on those who walk in darkness,
grant peace to those who long for justice.

Mighty God, shake those who trample on the defenceless that they may turn away from evil and learn to seek the way of peace.
Shine light on those who walk in darkness,
grant peace to those who long for justice.

Everlasting Father, look with compassion on those who dwell in lands of deep darkness that their peoples may look beyond their fear and be upheld by a vision of your love.
Shine light on those who walk in darkness,
grant peace to those who long for justice.

Prince of Peace, inspire those who work in your name that they may be ready to challenge injustice and to actively pursue reconciliation.
Shine light on those who walk in darkness,
grant peace to those who long for justice.

Child of God, hold the hands of the vulnerable that they may be comforted by your touch and guided to follow in your path.
Shine light on those who walk in darkness,
grant peace to those who long for justice.

Emmanuel, Son of God, be with us in our pain and in our joy that we
may know your presence and be upheld by a vision of a world made
whole.
Shine light on those who walk in darkness,
grant peace to those who long for justice,
and of your government let there be no end.

Annabel Shilson-Thomas

62. Candlemas prayer

He came as a witness to testify to the light, so that all might believe
through him.
        (John 1:7)

I left my candle burning. Lit from light
borrowed from another, it stood there
witness to Christ, Light of the world;
prayer that light would overcome darkness.
As I left, another lit a candle from my light,
dispelling gloom with added strength.
Who knows how many joined their light to those,
or drew fresh courage from their company;
who knows how many took a step, drawn by the
light of Christ from darkness to new life?

Lord Christ, set me on fire.
Burn from me all that dims your light,
kindle an answering flame in lives around;
that darkness may be driven back into this world,
transforming it with love.
Amen.

Ann Lewin

Jesus
Begins
His
Ministry

Ordinary Time 1

Much of the liturgical year focuses on dramatic moments in the story of our faith: Jesus' birth, the coming of the Magi, his last days in Jerusalem, humiliation and death, resurrection and ascension, the coming of the Holy Spirit at Pentecost, and our final hope of the Kingdom. Between these are two slabs of what is called 'ordinary time'. Nothing much seems to happen. It sounds boring, something to be got through before the next exciting thing happens.

But the word 'ordinary' here refers to something basic to our humanity. We can only be human because we are ordered, meaning pointed, away from ourselves. We are ordered towards each other, and we are ordered towards God. Ordinary time is when we grow in the ways that we belong to each other and to the Kingdom.

This first block of ordinary time, between celebrating the birth of Christ and beginning Lent, is largely about how we are ordered towards each other. The second slab of ordinary time, between Pentecost and the end of the year, is more about how we are ordered towards the Kingdom. In this first bit of ordinary time Jesus calls the disciples; he reaches out to those on the edge; he eats and drinks with prostitutes and the most disreputable people of all, the tax collectors. He touches lepers. Jesus summons us to belong to each other. Bishops are called 'ordinaries' not because they are boring but because they are charged with creating communities in which everyone belongs. In the eighteenth century the word was also used for people who delivered messages, the early equivalent of postmen.

In Western society, we tend to have a very individualistic under-standing of being human. I seek for my own private good, for my happiness, for my freedom, for my life. But we cannot flourish as soli-tary beings. One of the joys of my time in Africa was being reminded constantly that to be human is to belong to other people. There is an African expression: 'I am because we are.' I can only find myself and be fully human in daring to belong.

It was this sense of our shared lives that was at the centre of Nelson Mandela's commitment to justice. He had to explain to his own children why he was often away, and for years in prison:

> In that way my commitment to my people, to the millions of South Africans I would never know or meet, was at the expense of the people I knew best and loved most. It was as simple and incomprehensible as the moment a small child asks her father, 'Why can you not be with us?' And the father must utter the ter-rible words: 'There are other children like you, a great many of them … ' and then one's voice trails off … I found that I could not even enjoy the poor and limited freedom I was allowed when I knew that my people were not free. Freedom is indivisible; the chains on any one of my people were the chains on all of them, the chains on all of my people were the chains on me.[1]

The work of Christian Aid and CAFOD is not about being gener-ous to needy people. It is about knitting together the human family in which we can all belong and discover our shared humanity. It is about healing the wounds of suffering and injustice that stop all human beings from being fully alive. In the Middle Ages 'charity' was not something that you gave. It was what you lived, the shared life of the community. In the seventeenth century the meaning of the word began to change. It came to mean money which rich people give to the deserving poor. That sort of charity is condescending and patron-ising. Christian Aid and CAFOD are charities in the older sense, of serving the evolution of a world in which human beings belong to each other, and in which the gross and ugly inequalities of wealth are abolished so that we can flourish together.

1. Nelson Mandela, *Long Walk to Freedom* (Abacus, 1995), p. 750.

Because we are incomplete without each other, in ordinary time we learn to delight in and cherish all those who are considered just ordinary. In a world obsessed with celebrity, and in which some people are famous just for being famous, we learn to value ordinariness. When I leave my community and walk up the street, I go past a notice on the meeting place of another religious group which says 'The world can be changed by ordinary people like you.' I am embarrassed to admit that this used to irritate me. How do they know that I am ordinary? They have not even met me! But I am wrong, because when God became human, then he embraced us in our ordinariness and that is enough.

Thomas Merton, the Cistercian monk, wrote after walking in the streets of his local town after seventeen years in the monastery:

> It is a glorious destiny to be a member of the human race, though it is a race dedicated to many absurdities and one which makes terrible mistakes: yet, with all that, God himself glorified in becoming a member of the human race. A member of the human race! To think that such a common-place realisation should suddenly seem like news that one holds the winning ticket in a cosmic sweepstake. There is no way of telling people that they are all walking around shining like the sun ... There are no strangers ... If only we could see each other [as we really are] all the time. There would be no more war, no more hatred, no more cruelty, no more greed ... I suppose the big problem would be that we would fall down and worship each other ... the gate of heaven is everywhere.

It is in ordinary time that Jesus and his disciples walk towards Jerusalem, where dramatic events will take place. They are filled with expectation. James and John, the sons of Zebedee, ask Jesus, 'Grant us to sit, one at your right hand and one at your left, in your glory' (Mark 10:37). They wish to be stars, top apostles. But Jesus tells them that this is not his to grant: it is for those for whom it has been prepared. In fact it will be two ordinary and unnamed people, robbers, who are on his left and right when he is enthroned in glory on the cross. We hope for and hasten towards a world in which the glory of all the forgotten or excluded will shine forth.

Reflections

63. Jesus begins his ministry
Then Jesus came from Galilee to John at the Jordan to be baptised by him.
  (Matthew 3:13)

When one of us wants to set up a new enterprise – a company, an organisation, a project – we try to put it from the start on a secure and credible basis. Do I have the relevant qualifications? Do I have the funds for a proper launch? Do I have the names of well-known people as backers?

It is not wrong to do this. Yet as Jesus begins his ministry, he shows us another way, which breaks all the rules and gives hope to those who cannot follow the usual recommended practices because they do not have the resources. Instead of getting qualifications, he presents himself to John the Baptist for baptism, as though he were a sinner. It is a sort of anti-qualification, which Jesus insists on despite John's protests.

Then instead of looking for a bank loan, Jesus goes away for forty days of elected poverty, with neither shelter nor food. Why? Jesus knows that it is the poor, the hungry and the homeless whose ears are most sharply attuned to God's promises and go straight to the point. In the faces of South American *campesinos* who have nothing, sometimes not even teeth, we see tranquillity, gratitude and faith, while those from the richer countries often get held up in distracting critiques. While Europeans were disputing over the film *The Passion of the Christ*, the *campesinos* who saw it simply wept for sorrow.

In his month of fasting, free of other distractions, the ultimate options of life are spread out clearly before Jesus: What am I here for? What really matters? What are my priorities? He comes back with a clear and simple message: the Christ has come for the poor and the captives, the blind and the oppressed (Luke 4:18).

He puts that into practice, working not through institutions, but independently and in the open air. It is what happens in poor countries today, where houses are small and meetings of base communities take place outside rather than inside. From the start, Jesus' ministry is a new enterprise and an option for the poor.

Margaret Hebblethwaite
Paraguay

64. '*Blessed are those who mourn, for they shall be comforted.*'
(Matthew 5:4)

Jesus' beatitudes are all paradoxical, and none more so than this one. We can just about imagine how the poor or the hungry might be 'blessed' – provided they are not so very poor, and not hungry for too long. You can be short of money, and even of food, and still remain light-hearted. But those who mourn can never have lightness of heart. Wherever there is grief, there is pain; and while time and distractions may bring a kind of relief, such comfort will not restore what death has taken away.

Perhaps we need to take a step back, and ask what mourning involves. In order to be bereaved we need first to have loved another person. Grief is a fundamental part of our lives only because we were made to love. That is why, all the world over, we weep for such similar things. Other people's laughter might irritate or baffle or shock us, but we always understand their tears.

It is because of this that we can grieve for each other's grief. There were many terrible images on our television screens in the days after Boxing Day 2004, but the one that stuck in my mind was inspiring rather than harrowing. It was of a packed Old Trafford, with 60,000 normally rowdy people united in intense and absolute stillness in tribute to those who had died in the tsunami. What overwhelmed me was the thought that almost none of those fans knew anyone directly involved, or had ever even been to the Indian Ocean. They shared in this appalling sorrow simply because they too were human.

To suffer because others suffer is one of our deepest human instincts. In the passion and resurrection of Christ this instinct is taken up by God and transformed into something divine: the weakness of compassion becomes the power of new life. Blessed are those who mourn, because their grief is the fruit of love. Blessed are those who mourn, because love, in Christ, has already proved stronger than death.

Margaret Atkins

65. Letter to Dominic and Gregory, July 2005

Dear Dom and Greg,

It is 10:00pm and I am watching your crumpled, warm bodies slumbering so peacefully. I realise what joy you have brought to me and your mother. But that contentment is pierced tonight by a shaft of anxiety that I haven't felt for a long time.

Today brought the news that the terrorist attacks in London last week were almost certainly suicide bombings. You are too young to understand what it might mean to strap explosives to your body, to detonate a bomb that kills you and those around you, in the name of religion – as if by binding Semtex to your body you are fulfilling the Latin derivation of the word religion – meaning 'to bind'. What must it be like for the family of one of these suspected suicide bombers? They had contacted the police because their son was missing. For days they had no news, suffering the unbearable anxiety of not knowing his whereabouts. They had perhaps prepared themselves that he might have been a victim, only to discover he was a perpetrator of this madness. How could any parent cope with the knowledge that one they had fed and nurtured, loved and cajoled into life had chosen death, together with so many others, to make a political and religious statement?

You sharpened my anxiety when you asked at bedtime why I was a priest. I suspect the question came because my work has, of late, taken me away from home, something you do not like. Several things ran through my head by way of response. The most prominent was a quotation from the Book of Deuteronomy that was thudding its way around my brain tonight: 'Today I set before you life and death, blessing and curse. Choose life.'

Your question helped me realise that I hear my calling in helping others to choose not pathways of destruction but life in abundance, one that means awareness of both the glory and the pain of human experience. That, to me, is what a priest must be. But I didn't know how to say that to you, aged six and five!

That's why we read together the story of Jesus calling his first disciples. I had remembered that your Bible contained a wonderful illustration of the Sea of Galilee. It would enable me to explain that Jesus calling those first disciples out of the sea was a powerful symbol of a God who calls people out of places of hopelessness, chaos and death (people feared the sea at that time) onto dry land where they would encounter something much more hopeful, as they listened to Jesus' teaching and tried to live by it. This would give them the confidence to venture back, to cast their net upon the waters, in the knowledge that an enormous catch – the greatest riches in fact – would emerge from the whirlpool.

Unsurprisingly, I wasn't able to convey all this to you! So I tried to explain it instead by giving you a flavour of a film called *The Wooden Camera*, set in Cape Town – where you spent your earliest years.

You'll remember the big township, Khayelitsha, because you used to talk about its shacks. Two young boys, Madiba and Sipho, are playing one day by the railway line which runs through the township, when a body is pushed from the train, landing feet away from them. The man – who is dead – is clutching a briefcase. In their curiosity, they open it. Inside are two objects: a gun and a video camera. Sipho takes the gun, Madiba, the camera. This decision is to have huge consequences for their lives.

Sipho, his status enhanced by gun ownership, becomes a gang leader. Madiba makes a wooden toy camera, inside which he hides the real camera, lest it be stolen. Sipho's delusions of power lead him to terrorise his neighbours, but Madiba gains real power – the sort that comes from imagination and insight – as he films the township community. Alcohol, drugs, thinners, glue – the trappings of Cape Town's petty-gangster world – debilitate Sipho's ability to discern right from wrong, and his life spirals out of control. Madiba keeps in touch, but at a distance – through the lens of his camera. He can only watch Sipho's descent into the abyss. He cannot stop it. It is no surprise that Sipho commits a hold-up, shoots someone, and is later himself shot dead.

For Madiba things are very different. Through his lens he sees reality: the horrors of Sipho's gangster world but also the great beauty beyond – the fun and laughter of township life, the exuberant joy of neighbours and friends. As a budding cameraman, Madiba achieves a different angle and perspective on things. When he ventures into Cape Town he notices details: the play of light on a street corner, a plastic bag with its contents, a pavement walk which through his lens becomes the journey to Samarkand. He observes the signs of a community awakening to the possibilities of post-apartheid South Africa. He becomes caught up in these when he sees a young white girl, Estelle, stealing a book, who notices that he is filming her theft. They subsequently become the closest of friends.

Much of the film deals with the tensions and the possibilities of this iconic friendship across communities, formerly estranged and now struggling to understand each other. Estelle's cello teacher encourages Madiba in his creativity behind the lens. Madiba's alcoholic father, like many victims of apartheid, cannot break out of a cycle which makes the abused into abusers. He eventually finds Madiba's camera and sells it, presumably for a few bottles of beer. Estelle's father cannot break out of victimhood either. His racism leads him to forbid Estelle to see Madiba but their friendship somehow flourishes. They emerge as the victors over their circumstances, riding on the back of a train, if not into the sunset then at least into a more discernably hopeful future.

Which is, dear Dom and Greg, what I hope will be the case for you. Though I believe my calling as a priest is to support the Siphos and Madibas of this world in making the best possible choices, my biggest responsibility is as a parent to you. As you sleep so serenely, and as I think of all the kindnesses you shower on us – the way you, Dominic, stroke our faces in the morning to express your affection (and to wake us up!); the way you, Gregory, mouth softly but so genuinely the words every human being needs to hear, 'I love you' – I pray that you will always follow your noblest, gentlest instincts, as I also pray that I can – together with your mother and the whole community – support you to face a world of blessing and curse, life and death, in such a way that you always choose life.

                                                                Chris Chivers

66. *'Love your enemies and pray for those who persecute you.'*
                                                            (Matthew 5:44)

If this instruction of Jesus were to be taken seriously, there would be a radical change in the world as we know it today. If all those involved in conflicts, however big or small, were to look at their enemy and see, instead of 'enemy', a fellow human being: a man or woman who is part of a loving family, who desires peace, who want a place to live and daily sustenance. If only …

I live in South Africa, a country where 'if only' has, to a large degree, become reality; where sworn enemies now sit down together and debate legislation for the common good; where they walk hand in hand down church aisles, sing together in church choirs, and let their children go to school together.

For those of us who lived through the 'miracle' it is hard to be blasé about the changes that have occurred. Things are very far from perfect. Racism and discrimination still exist. Negative attitudes about the 'new' South Africa are often strongly expressed. But who can deny that the winds of change have swept through the hearts of many; sometimes as a gentle breeze to lightly prod the conscience and at other times as a forceful gale, to blow into disarray old thought patterns.

Love of enemy is not just a blind acceptance that someone has changed sides and now agrees with you. It is about finding a common space, beyond the conflict, where neither is right or wrong, and beginning to dialogue about mutual interests, values and goals. It is about discovering shared hopes and dreams for a peaceful world. It is about a willingness to put aside selfish rights and talk about shared responsibilities.

This is something that happens at every level of our lives, from personal relationships to international affairs. Learning to love our enemies is about personal growth and development. It is about seeing the broader picture and recognising that we are a part of the whole and that our immediate world is not the centre of all existence. It is about being willing to sacrifice and compromise so that everybody wins.

Imelda Davidson
South Africa

Prayers

67. The gift
Then Jesus came from Galilee to John at the Jordan to be baptised by him.
(Matthew 3:13)

Jesus, out of love for us
you were baptised in the River Jordan.
We thank you for the gift of water
to cleanse us and revive us.
We thank you
that through the waters of the Red Sea
you led your people out of slavery
to freedom in the Promised Land.
We thank you
that you passed through the deep waters of death
and rose again in triumph.
Have mercy on us
who seek profit from what you offer so freely.
Confront us

who turn the sacrament of liberation
into the material of oppression.
And as water flows from your side on the cross
pierce our consciences
and convert us again to your ways.
Amen.

Adapted from the service of Baptism,
Common Worship

68. Water
And when Jesus had been baptised ...
(Matthew 3:16)

In my heat
of anguish
and fear
I am refreshed
by the sprinkling
of your
cool, refreshing water.
In my filth
and dirtiness
I am washed
by your
pure and cleansing
water.
In my weariness
and
directionless life
I am swept along
by the strong current
of your
water.
In my half-heartedness
half-giving
half-loving
half-living
help me
to be immersed
fully
in your water
and cross

Jordan
to the
promised land.

From the Maranatha Community

69. *Then the devil left him ...*
(Matthew 4:11)

Lord,
you were tempted by the devil,
and yet you managed to see his empty promises for what they were.
Be with me as I face the daily temptations of life.
Let your victory over Satan inspire me to remain faithful to you and
your ways.
Amen.

Imelda Davidson
South Africa

70. *In those days Jesus came from Nazareth ...*
(Mark 1:9)

Hands strengthened to learn a trade;
hands stretched out to help a need;
hands lifted to rejoice in a new start;
hands clasped to celebrate a partnership:
we lift high the hopes of the world's poorest people
to our God, who has the whole world in his hands.
Amen.

Christian Aid

71. Rejection and resurrection
He unrolled the scroll and found the place ...
(Luke 4:17)

Jesus of Nazareth,

You returned to the place where you were brought up.
People in the synagogue approved
with astonishment as you interpreted
the prophecy of Isaiah.

Although they heard you
        they failed to listen.
They heard only what they
        wanted to hear.
The truth hurt them.
You made them feel uncomfortable,
        and they rejected you.

For our world today there remain some uncomfortable truths:
        the good news has still to reach the afflicted;
        captives still await liberation;
        sight has still to be restored to the blind;
        the oppressed have still to go free;
        and proclaiming a year of favour has been missed,
        and millions of people have plunged further into the mire
        of despair and poverty.

Even now you are being rejected
        because people refuse to listen.
Our fellow humans suffer rejection:
        they are dying because they are victims
        of oppression, imprisoned for their beliefs;
        of discrimination, driven down by the world's trading rules;
        of prejudice, condemned by their colour or gender;
        of poverty, enslaved by unjust economics.

Walking through the hostile crowd,
        you began your journey towards the cross.
It was a journey taking you beyond death
        towards triumph and resurrection.
We want to walk with you
        at the risk of ourselves being rejected.
We want to champion the rights of the weak,
        the despised and the under-privileged.

Show us how we may seek your Kingdom
        and help to bring peace to a troubled world.
Grant us the courage to campaign for justice;
        and, above all, make us immune to hostility and rejection.
Only by walking with you will we come to understand
        the joy of resurrection.

                                        Tony Singleton

72. Sent by the Lord

'The Spirit of the Lord is upon me, because he has anointed me to bring good news to the poor.'

(Luke 4:18)

Sent by the Lord am I; my hands are ready now
to make this earth a place in which the Kingdom comes.
(*repeat*)

The angels cannot change a world of hurt and pain
into a world of love, of justice and of peace.
The task is mine to do, to set it really free.
Oh help me to obey, help me to do your will.

Hunger and Justice

73. A prayer of approach

'The Spirit of the Lord is upon me.'

(Luke 4:18)

Jesus our friend, may we be prepared to listen.
Let the Spirit be on us as we hear your word.
Jesus our neighbour, may we be prepared to speak.
Let the good news of liberation be announced among us.
Jesus our Saviour, may we be prepared to act.
Let the signs of shalom be seen even here in this place.

Terry Oakley

74. Lord of the Universe

look in love upon your people.
Pour the healing oil of your compassion
on a world that is wounded and dying.
Send us out in search of the lost,
to comfort the afflicted,
to bind up the broken,
and to free those trapped
under the rubble of their fallen dream.

Sheila Cassidy

75. A prayer for the tortured – and for those who cause their pain

'*... to proclaim release to the captives ... to let the oppressed go free.*'
(Luke 4:18)

Lord Jesus Christ, you proclaimed liberty to the captives, freedom to
the oppressed.
We pray for all whose minds and bodies have been damaged by
torture;
all who are enduring torture at this moment;
all who live in dread that they will be tortured again;
all who are plagued by guilt because of what they revealed under
torture.
End their torment. Heal their wounds. Bring peace to their troubled
souls.

We pray for all who are responsible for torture:
those who break people out of a sense of duty, and those who cause
pain for their own pleasure;
those who abuse their calling to heal by helping to inflict hurt;
those who order torture to protect themselves;
those who know the truth but keep silent because they are afraid;
and all who believe that torture is none of their business because they
cannot see it.
Melt hard hearts. Open eyes kept wilfully blind. Grant your courage
and your compassion.

We pray for those who give themselves to exposing torture, fighting
for its victims, seeking to mend broken lives. Sustain them in their
struggle. Keep before us the vision of a world without torture, and
grant us grace to work for its coming.

Roy Jenkins

76. *And he said to them, 'Follow me ...*
(Matthew 4:19)

Living Jesus, by your word of power and actions of love, call us to be
your disciples. Remind us constantly of your love for all people. Send
us out in your name to tell people that you are alive, and to make sure

that, in this rich and fertile world, everyone has access to the food
they need.
Amen.

Janet Wootton

77. Answering the call
'Follow me and I will make you fish for people.'
(Matthew 4:19)

You call us, Lord, to share your life,
to follow where you lead,
to live as you live, to love as you love,
to preach the good news of God's Kingdom
of justice and joy, of peace and hope.

If we're to share your life, Lord,
then we have to invite you to share ours,
to be part of all we do and say.
We can't share your life if we're not prepared
to let you into ours.

Come into our lives, Lord,
open our hearts,
broaden our minds,
strengthen our convictions,
lead us the way you want us to go,
so we, too, may be
your disciples in the world.

Jan Grimwood

78. *'You are the salt of the earth ... '*
(Matthew 5:13)

Lord, you placed us in the world to be its salt. Give us now your
strength to confront the structures of injustice, the institutions, laws
and practices that keep poor people disempowered.
In your mercy,
Lord, hear our prayer.

Lord, you placed us in the world to be its light. Give us now your

strength to demand accountability, honesty and transparency in international law, governance, trade and aid.
In your mercy,
Lord, hear our prayer.

Lord, you came to proclaim recovery of sight to the blind, to open the eyes of the oppressed and oppressors. Give us now your strength to work in solidarity with the poor and the courage to open our eyes to the injustices of our own lifestyles.
In your mercy,
Lord, hear our prayer.

Lord, you came to bring good news to the poor, to speak against injustice. Give us now the strength to support the oppressed as they speak out and challenge their rulers and the international community.
In your mercy,
Lord, hear our prayer.

Lord, you came to proclaim release to the captives and to set the oppressed free. Help us together, to break the chains that bind us, and transform them into a chain of solidarity.
Amen.

CAFOD

79. Blest are the poor (Amen, amen, it shall be so!)
'Blessed are the poor in spirit … '
(Matthew 5:3)

Blest are the poor in spirit, the kingdom of heav'n is theirs.
Amen, amen it shall be so! Amen, alleluia!

Blest are the sorrowful, the sorrowful,
they shall be comforted.

Blest are the gentle, the gentle,
the earth shall be their own.

Blest are the hungry for justice,
they shall be satisfied.

Blest are the merciful, the merciful,
they shall find mercy shown.

Blest are the pure in heart,
for they shall see their God.

Blest are the earth's peacemakers,
each one shall be God's child.

Blest are those victimised for doing good,
the kingdom of heav'n is theirs.

John Bell

80. Teach us how to walk in your footsteps
'My steps have held fast to your paths; my feet have not slipped.
(Psalm 17:5)

Teach us how to walk in your footsteps, Jesus,
teach us how to walk in your way.
Teach us how to show your love to our neighbour,
teach us how to do it today.

Chorus
And we will dance, dance, dance, dance on injustice,
we will stand, stand, stand, stand with the poor
and we will sing, sing, sing songs of freedom
with Jesus the servant whose love is over all.

Teach us how to see through your eyes, Jesus,
and teach us how to love the poor.
Give us your heart as you see the hungry
and teach us to love them more.

Teach us how to see through your eyes, Jesus,
to stand with the refugee.
And those whose land has been taken from them
the forgotten ones we fail to see.

Teach us how to break the walls of injustice,
teach us how to make a stand.

Teach us how to build a community of peace
where love has the upper hand.

We dance today to thank you, Jesus,
you give us hope to sing.
You dance beside us in the battle for justice
and justice is going to win.

Hunger and Justice

81. Intercessory prayer
Pray without ceasing.
(1 Thessalonians 5:17)

We hold in the light of Christ's love each person here,
and the circle of lives linked to each one at home and at work;
that with these immediate contacts we may open the way for God to
    act
by becoming channels of his peace and his redemptive love.
**May our prayers rise like incense and our hands like an evening
    offering.**

Loving God,
you show yourself in those who are vulnerable,
and make your home with the poor and weak of this world;
warm our hearts with the fire of your Spirit.
Help us to accept the challenge of HIV and AIDS.
We pray for those who have to contend with illness as well as drought
    and famine
and we pray too for the many orphans who are left behind by those
    who have died from AIDS.
**May our prayers rise like incense and our hands like an evening
    offering.**

Protect the healthy, calm the frightened,
give courage to those in pain,
comfort the dying and give to the dead eternal life;
console the bereaved, strengthen those who care for the sick.
**May our prayers rise like incense and our hands like an evening
    offering.**

Into your hands, O Lord,

we place all who are victims of prejudice, oppression, or neglect,
especially the frail and unwanted.
May everyone be cherished from conception to the grave.
**May our prayers rise like incense and our hands like an evening
offering.**

May we your people, using our energy and imagination,
and trusting in your steadfast love,
be united with one another in conquering all disease and fear.
**We make this prayer in the name of the one who has borne all our
wounds**
and whose Spirit strengthens and guides us,
now and for ever.
Amen.

Diakonia Council of Churches
South Africa

82. We want to celebrate life
'I am the resurrection and the life.'
(John 11:25)

God of all we pray to you.
We are young people, we want to celebrate life!
We cry out against all that kills life:
hunger, poverty, unemployment, sickness, repression,
individualism, injustice.
We want to announce the fullness of life:
work, education, health, housing, bread for all.
We want communion, a world renewed.
We hope against hope.
With the Lord of history we want to make all things new.

Brazilian youth group

83. *God chose what is weak in the world to shame the strong.*
(1 Corinthians 1:27)

Holy God,
if the world insists that the weak need the strong,
remind us that in your Kingdom
the strong also need the weak.

If the world tells us that the fate of the poor must be dictated by the
rich,
remind us that in your Kingdom
the rich are transformed by the poor.

If the world declares that peace is made by violence,
remind us that in your Kingdom
peace joins hands with justice.

If the world believes that there is nothing more to hope for,
remind us that your Kingdom is built
by those who expect their God to come.
Amen.

                                                              Mary Cotes

84. A prayer for justice
   '*... to let the oppressed go free.*'
                                       (Luke 4:18)

(This prayer could be read by three voices.)

God of the nations, so many of your children are crying out,
worn down by the burden of debt,
brought to their knees by unfair trade.
We pray for justice,
and look for a world where all shall have life in its fullness.
Help us in the decisions we make daily to remember those who are
      poor,
and to act where we can to bring hope and healing for others.
            In Nazareth, Jesus, you read the Scriptures,
            telling that you had been anointed to bring good news to the
                  poor,
            recovery of sight to the blind, and to let captives go free.
            Make us the bearers of good news, help us bring sight and
                  liberation to people oppressed by an unjust world.
Holy Spirit, you fill us with love, with faith and hope.
Make us active servants and followers,
ready always to pray and pray again
that justice may be done, and that your Kingdom may come
on this earth, as in heaven.

Like the waters, may your justice flow,
like everlasting streams, may your righteousness flood the earth.
Help us to dig new channels for your refreshing goodness
so that those who thirst from despair may drink,
and those who are soiled by life's woes may be made clean.
Come among us, God of love, come we pray.
Amen.

Timothy Woods

85. WOMEN: Where children walk without fear, heads held high;

    MEN: where knowledge for all youth is free;

    WOMEN: where society has not been broken into fragments by
           narrow domestic walls;

    MEN: where the words of teachers and politicians spring out from
           the depths of truth;

    WOMEN: where the tireless striving of social reformers stretches its
           arms towards perfection;

    MEN: where the clear stream of creative culture has not lost its
           way into the desert sand of dead habit;

    WOMEN: where the minds of leaders, scientists and writers are led
           forward by thee into ever-widening thought and action;
           into that divinely given freedom, Father of all, let our
           country awake.

Adapted from Rabindranath Tagore's prayer
for true freedom

86. In the midst of hatred that divides people of different nations, ethnic
    groups, classes, religions and gender,
    God, forgive us.
    In the midst of our difficulty in accepting each other and in respect-
    ing our differences,
    God, forgive us.
    In the midst of the covetous desires of the people and nations to pos-
    sess what is not their own,
    God, forgive us.
    In the midst of the greediness which exploits the work of human
    hands and lays waste the earth,
    God, forgive us.
    In the midst of our envy of the welfare and happiness of others,
    God, forgive us.

In the midst of our indifference to the plight of the imprisoned, the homeless, the refugees and the migrant workers,
God, forgive us.
In the midst of the lust that dishonours the bodies of men, women and children,
God, forgive us.
In the midst of pride which leads us to trust in ourselves and not in God,
God, forgive us.
Lord, have mercy on us.
Amen.

Christian Conference of Asia

87. Five prayers specially written for World Debt Day

The Church has the right and the duty to play a full part in the creation of a just society, using all the means at our disposition and in union with other believers. We pray that we, as disciples of Jesus, may know how to commit ourselves, at all levels and through concrete action, to the changing of unjust structures which imprison people in permanent oppression.
Hear us, Lord of Justice.
Lord of Justice and of Peace, hear our prayer.

Let us pray for rulers and heads of governments and of all international organisations, that they might strive ever more for a worldwide solidarity which assures the dignity due to people and peoples, attacking the very roots of injustice and suffering; and that they might implement effective measures to lighten the crushing debt of poorer nations.
Hear us, Lord of Justice.
Lord of Justice and of Peace, hear our prayer.

For poor countries suffering from widespread corruption, often caused by exterior interests but exacerbated by dishonest politicians; we pray that through a renewal of conscience they might achieve a harmonious and transparent management of their affairs.
Hear us, Lord of Justice.
Lord of Justice and of Peace, hear our prayer.

We pray, too, for rich countries. May they be more aware of their duty to support the efforts of poorer neighbours to escape from

poverty and misery; this is the only way to ensure the conditions necessary for a stable peace and a lasting spirit of harmony.
Hear us, Lord of Justice.
Lord of Justice and of Peace, hear our prayer.

We pray for all those who struggle today for a just and truly human standard of life for everyone. May the Lord help them in their commitment, and may they never be discouraged by the difficulties they face.
Hear us, Lord of Justice.
Lord of Justice and of Peace, hear our prayer.

White Fathers of the Sahara

88. God,
The image of your son is not visible
in the pages of our newspapers
in the faces of our leaders
in the deployment of our weapons
in the violence of our actions.

Christ,
take our words,
our world
our weapons
our work
and transform them in your image.

So we may see your face
in truth where news is reported
in justice where power is abused
in peace where war is threatened
in reconciliation where deeds foster hatred.
Open our eyes, Lord!

World Council of Churches

89. **Litany for peace**

ONE: From words and deeds that provoke discord, prejudice and hatred,
ALL: **O God, deliver us.**

ONE: From suspicions and fears that stand in the way of reconciliation,
ALL: **O God, deliver us.**

ONE: From believing and speaking lies about other peoples or nations,
ALL: **O God, deliver us.**

ONE: From cruel indifference to the cries of the hungry and homeless,
ALL: **O God, deliver us.**

ONE: From all that prevents us from fulfilling your promise of peace,
ALL: **O God, deliver us.**

ONE: Deliver us from our brokenness, we pray, O God,
ALL: **and by your grace and healing presence deliver us to you.**

ONE: To still waters and green pastures,
ALL: **O Creating God, deliver us.**

ONE: To the freedom and forgiveness we find in you,
ALL: **O Risen Christ, deliver us.**

ONE: To the tough task of loving our enemies,
ALL: **O Jesus, deliver us.**

ONE: To joyful service in your name,
ALL: **O Servant of All, deliver us.**

ONE: To the promise of a new heaven and a new earth,
    to the wholeness of justice,
    to the power of your peace,
ALL: **O Holy Spirit, deliver us now and in the days to come.**
World Council of Churches

90. Lord God, you humble me before the poor.
    The more I have the more I want to cling to.
    Jesus didn't grasp at divine equality but laid aside his glory,
    stripping himself of privilege and security
    to live a life under the conditions we live under.
    He was a vulnerable child, unprotected from
    Herod's wrath, a refugee:
    he was found alongside the lowest, the least, the lost.

He gave all, even life itself.
Yet I hesitate to give some of my abundance.
Lord God, you humble me before the poor
who when they have little to eat, share it,
who, having nothing, yet seem to possess so much.
I cringe away from the sacrifice Jesus asked of the rich young man.
But I also believe I am not called to part with my possessions as he was.
Or am I? Search my heart; you know my innermost thoughts.
Teach me to handle the possessions you have entrusted to me
that whatsoever is asked of me,
they will be treated as yours, not as my own.
Teach me grace to give whatever you require of me,
and grace to refuse any false guilt.
Teach me to fight unjust systems which rob people
of their share of your provision;
teach me to be alert to how I justify these systems to myself.
Teach me not to want to keep the poor in poverty.
Teach me to want your daily bread for everyone.
Teach me to want your Kingdom come.
We ask all of this in Jesus' mighty name.
Amen.

Anonymous

91. We have been given ...

We have been given

Eyes   to see and ears to listen

Tongues   to speak for the innocent ... and the guilty
            to praise, encourage and support
            to proclaim, in season and out, the news that is good
                news ...

Hands   to reach out and to strengthen the fearful
            to protect the weak and lift up the fallen
            to embrace the dying
            to share burdens and wipe away tears ...
            to build up, not tear down,
            to fan the embers, not quench the smouldering wick
            to bless, not strike
            to give, not to withhold ...

Minds   to judge ... ourselves, not others
                situations, not motives
           to seek solutions, not excuses
                justice, not expediency
           to discern the essential from the merely desirable
                the good from the less good and the less good from the
                bad ...

Hearts   to feel
           to interpret the hidden meanings beneath the words spoken
           to open doors closed by despair
           to discover the best in others and set it free
           to understand and forgive ... or simply to forgive
           to comfort the sorrowful
           to love and thereby heal scars ...

All   these things God has given us that people around us
           may neither doubt nor forget his presence among them
           that in our touch, our words, our actions
           he may touch and speak and act and they, in turn, may
                sense his presence
           when we pass by and, seeing us, know with little effort
           that they catch a glimpse of God.

                                                        A prayer from Zimbabwe

92. We beg you, Lord, to help and defend us. Deliver the oppressed, pity
    the insignificant, raise the fallen, show yourself to the needy, heal the
    sick, bring back those who have gone astray, feed the hungry, lift up
    the weak, take off the prisoners' chains. May every nation come to
    know that you alone are God, that Jesus Christ is your Child, that we
    are your people, the sheep that you pasture.
    Amen.

                                                        Clement of Rome (*c.* AD 100)

93. Lord Jesus Christ, the way, the truth and the life;
        let us not stray from you who are the way,
        not distrust you who are the truth,
        nor rest in any other but you who are the life.
        Teach us by your Holy Spirit
        what to believe, what to do and say,

and in what to take our rest.
We ask this for your name's sake.
Amen.

Erasmus

94. O God who art peace everlasting, whose chosen reward is the gift of peace, and who hast taught us that the peace-makers are thy children, pour thy peace into our souls, that everything discordant may utterly vanish, and all that makes for peace be sweet to us for ever.
Amen.

Mozarabic Sacramentary (before AD 700)

95. Thou who art love, and who seest all the suffering, injustice and misery which reign in this world, have pity, we implore thee, on the work of thy hands. Look mercifully upon the poor, the oppressed, and all who are heavy laden with error, labour and sorrow. Fill our hearts with deep compassion for those who suffer, and hasten the coming of thy Kingdom of justice and truth.
Amen.

Eugene Bersier (1831–89)

96. O God, the father of the forsaken, the help of the weak, the supplier of the needy, who has diffused and proportioned thy gifts to body and soul, in such sort that all may acknowledge and perform the joyous duty of mutual service; who teachest us that love towards the race of man is the bond of perfectness, and the imitation of thy blessed self; open our eyes and touch our hearts, that we may see and do, both for this world and for that which is to come, the things which belong unto our peace. Strengthen me in the work I have undertaken; give me counsel and wisdom, perseverance, faith and zeal, and in thine own good time, and according to thy pleasure, prosper the issue. Pour into me a spirit of humility; let nothing be done but in devout obedience to thy will, thankfulness for thine unspeakable mercies, and love to thine adorable Son Christ Jesus.
Amen.

Antony Ashley Cooper, Earl of Shaftesbury
(1801–1885)

Lent

Lent is our forty-day preparation for the Feast of Easter. It looks back to Jesus' forty-day fast in the wilderness before he began his mission. Lent was observed in all the Christian Churches from the fourth century onwards. Christians practised penance and ate only one meal a day after Vespers, abstaining from meat, fish and even dairy products. For most of Christian history it was as demanding as Ramadan is for Muslims today. Faced with tensions between religions all over the world, it would be wonderful if we were to share fasts together with Muslims and people of other faiths as a sign of a shared longing for peace. In France, Christians often share part of the Ramadan fast with Muslims to show solidarity, and Muslims fast during part of Lent too. It is also a time when many Christians fast as a sign of solidarity with the hungry throughout the world.

Penance and fasting sound grim and world-denying. But in the Catholic liturgy it is called 'this joyful season'. The word 'Lent' just meant 'Spring' until the thirteenth century. It was a time of renewal and rejuvenation, as we prepared for the explosion of new life at Easter. By abstaining from things that we want – alcohol, chocolate or whatever – we are brought back to our deepest desires, for peace and justice, for the fullness of life, and ultimately for God.

Lent is a time to reconnect with the fundamental hunger at the core of our being, for the one in whom we find all happiness. The forty days Jesus spent in the desert suggest one of the ways in which we may do so, by coming to have a mature relationship with power. Let us glance at Matthew's account (Matthew 4:1–11). This episode is often called 'the temptations of Jesus'. But that is not very accurate. Jesus may have been tempted to turn the stones into bread (Matthew describes him as very hungry). But it is hard to believe that he was tempted to do such a daft thing as to throw himself off the Temple, and certainly not that he considered for a moment worshipping the devil. A better word is 'testing'. When Ellen MacArthur sailed around the world, it tested her mettle. It took her to the limits of endurance and showed us who she is, a remarkably courageous woman. No doubt she had temptations: to give up half way around or to gobble down all her provisions in one go. But temptations are only a small part of testing. Temptations are about what one does, but testings show who one is. These testings of Jesus also show what it meant for him to be the Son of God. Twice the devil says to him, 'If you are the Son of God, do this.' Above all, these tests reveal Jesus' relationship to power.

The struggle for a just world, in which the dignity of every person is respected, demands of us a good relationship with power. We will sometimes have to struggle with the powers that be, and at other times collaborate with them. We will have to fight if the powerless are to be liberated into strength. We will not be able to do this unless we have a mature relationship with power, the powers of this world, our personal power and with those who are excluded from power.

This is the first test: 'If you are the Son of God, command these stones to become loaves of bread.' If you are the Son of God, then you can do anything. You can turn these stones into bread if you are hungry, or into armchairs if you are fed up with sitting on stones. As Herod says in *Jesus Christ Superstar*, if you are God, you can do anything: 'Prove to me that you're divine. Change my water into wine.'

Few of us may feel tempted to turn stones into bread, but Western culture is deeply impregnated with the lure of dominating power, the desire to do what we wish, and to impose our will on reality. Robert Suskind was told by an aide of President Bush that the Democrats belong to 'the reality-based community', those who 'believe that solutions emerge from your judicious study of discernible reality'. But the aide insisted, 'that's not the way the world really works any more. We're an Empire now, and when we act we create our own reality. We're history's actors and you, all of you, will be left to just study what we do.'[1] If they decide that stones are bread or guns for that matter, then so be it. This is the temptation to think that the power of the children of God is absolute dominion over creation. This attitude lies behind the rape of creation which is destroying our little planetary home.

This testing takes place in the desert, which in the Bible is seen as the place of demons, where God seems absent. For many people in our society, God seems to have disappeared, gone into hiding, or

1. Michael Northcote, referring to an article in *The New York Times Magazine* in 'The Triumph of Imperial politics', *The Tablet* (6 November 2004), p. 4.

perhaps just never to have existed. In such a world, whether one is a believer or not, the temptation is to take God's place, and claim God's power. God spoke a word and the world came to be, and so now too I can do what I want with creation. But Jesus replies that we live from every word that comes from the mouth of God. God is always the one who is the giver of good things.

The second testing transports Jesus to a radically different location. He is snatched away from the place of God's absence to the holy city, Jerusalem, and to that most holy place, the Temple. Here we are offered the opposite misunderstanding of the power of the children of God, which is irresponsibility. The devil is saying to Jesus, if you are God's Son, then just let your celestial daddy look after you. You can cast aside all responsibility, throw yourself in the air, and God will make sure that everything is OK. Faced with the suffering and injustice of this world, with the pollution of the planet, then we do not need to worry. God will have a plan up his divine sleeve and sort it all out. This also justifies me not having to seek justice, since my daddy in the sky will take care of the poor. But Jesus replies to the devil: 'Don't bet on it.' We must not test God.

The final testing on the mountain is a vicious combination of the two, and they do often coalesce. The devil shows him the kingdoms of the world and says, 'All of these I will give you, if you fall down and worship me.' It combines megalomania and infantilism. If you degrade yourself, then I will give you absolute power. If you wish to be the absolute Master, then you must grovel.

Jesus does not grovel before the devil. He does not even bow down before his Father, his Abba. Worship of the true God does not demand our humiliation. After human beings have humiliated Jesus on Good Friday, his Father raises him up on Easter Sunday. That is why when we sing the 'Our Father' at Mass, we all stand. We worship and adore the one God, who lifts us to our feet.

Relationships between parents and children grow by being tested, and these will often involve little power struggles. But we, as God's children, are not in a competitive relationship with God. In Lent, we are called to worship the one true God, who makes us stand upright. Lent is a time for us to grow into Christian maturity. Thus we can face issues of power, seeking neither domination nor flight from responsibility, but confident that God empowers all with strength and grace and freedom. If we have a mature relationship with power, having been tested ourselves, then we can empower others, unafraid and unthreatened by their flourishing.

Reflections

97. The beggar

Lazarus (was) covered with sores and longing to eat what fell from the rich man's table.
                (Luke 16:19–31)

Jesus tells a story about a rich man and a poor man. Like several parables, and despite the view of the great Bible critics of an earlier day, it is a story with more than one point. But it is at least a story about denying food to the poor. Put your money where your mouth is. Put your money where his mouth is. The dangers of wealth is such a characteristic theme for Luke.

Over the last few years a biblical idea of jubilee has inspired the churches and others together to demand the cancellation of unre-payable debt. The relations between the world's rich and the world's poor are judged by a story Jesus told about a rich man and a poor man: and by the past and present determination of those of us who are rich to grab all we can, and more, from the mouths of the poor.

The suffering of the poor – that is what Christian aid agencies are about. Relieving the suffering of the poor, putting a stop to their suffering.

Overwhelmingly, prison populations are made up of poor people. Compared with the population as a whole, prisoners are five times more likely to have no educational qualification, twelve times more likely to have experienced long-term unemployment, thirty times more likely to be homeless. The story about the rich man and Lazarus is a story about how invisible poor people are. By definition, the poor people who are in prison are completely invisible, but that does not mean they are to be ignored or forgotten. Of course, they can be ignored or forgotten: but Jesus told this story so that those who are his friends might learn.

As Holy Week approaches and the sufferings of Jesus are spread wide on the cross, it is right to remember his strong words – among the hardest recorded in the Gospels – about the sufferings of the poor. He was one of them himself, and their sufferings are his sufferings still. The Son of Man must undergo great suffering.

Let me weep today with the poor.

With those in our great cities where the happiness of so many homes is fragile.

With the poor of a hungry world, where endless labour brings no riches.

Let me weep and work and pray for the day when God will wipe away every tear.

Amen.

Andrew McLellan

98. Ash Wednesday – how to become human

' ... *but when you fast, put oil on your head and wash your face* ... '
(Matthew 6:17)

In today's world we celebrate many events: Independence Day, Mothers' Day and many other special occasions. However, has no one ever thought of celebrating 'Conversion Day'? These days we need to be converted, not only to be Christian, but simply to be human. Have not even the massacres in Rwanda, nor the poverty of three thousand million human beings, brought home the need for change in each and every one of us?

God thinks differently. He tells us: 'Rend your hearts.' Throughout the ages our Christian Churches have rarely welcomed the word of God. After all, it puts demands on them as well. At least the Churches have not dared to silence it, and every year, during Lent, they offer us time to think about conversion.

We have to be thankful for that, given that we live in a world of injustice and cruelty, where the seven richest men have enough wealth to wipe out poverty within a few years. A world where a footballer, a boxer or a singer earns more than entire towns and villages in Asia, Africa or Latin America and in which they are better known and more admired than the countless martyrs who have given their lives for love.

We live in a world where existence has been trivialised, where the tragedies of injustice are covered up. It is as if nothing serious ever happened in our lives, as if being human didn't have much to do with honesty, with seeing things as they are.

Joel (2:12), Jesus and the martyred archbishop Oscar Romero are all right, despite the little attention paid them by Wall Street or the United Nations Security Council. We have to start by accepting that we have hearts of stone and ask for them to be made flesh.

Ignacio Ellacuria, the rector of the University of Central America in San Salvador who was murdered along with five other Jesuits, was right in the last speech he gave. In Barcelona in November 1989, a week before his death, he said: 'We have to turn history around.' In words that few would dare speak he said: 'Today's civilisation of abundance must become a civilisation of poverty.'

Jon Sobrino SJ
El Salvador

99. From the Orthodox tradition

'We waited, and at last our expectations were fulfilled,' writes the Serbian Bishop St Nikolai of Ochrid, describing the Easter service at Jerusalem:

> When the Patriarch sang 'Christ is risen,' a heavy burden fell from our souls. We felt as if we also had been raised from the dead. All at once, from all around, the same cry resounded like the noise of many waters. 'Christ is risen,' sang the Greeks, the Russians, the Arabs, the Serbs, the Copts, the Armenians, the Ethiopians – one after another, each in his own tongue, in his own melody ... Coming out from the service at dawn, we began to regard everything in the light of the glory of Christ's resurrection, and all appeared different from what it had yesterday; everything seemed better, more expressive, more glorious. Only in the light of the resurrection does life receive meaning.[2]

This sense of resurrection joy, so vividly described by Bishop Nikolai, forms the foundation of all the worship of the Orthodox Church; it is the one and only basis for our Christian life and hope. Yet, in order to experience the full power of this Paschal rejoicing, each of us needs to pass through a time of preparation. 'We *waited*', says Bishop Nikolai, 'and at last our expectations were fulfilled.' Without this waiting, without this expectant preparation, the deeper meaning of the Easter celebration will be lost.

So it is that before the festival of Easter there has developed a long preparatory season of repentance and fasting ... there follows after Easter a corresponding season ... of thanksgiving, concluding with Pentecost ...

2. Bishop Nikolai (Velimirovich), *Missionary Letters* (Serbian Bible Institute).

Those who fast, so far from repudiating material things, are on the contrary assisting in their redemption. They are filling the vocation assigned to the 'sons of God' by St Paul:

> The created universe waits with eager longing for the revealing of the sons of God ... The creation will be set free from its bondage to decay and will obtain the glorious liberty of the children of God. We know that the whole creation has been groaning in travail until now. (Romans 8:19–22)

By means of our Lenten abstinence, we seek with God's help to exercise this calling as priests of the creation, restoring all things to their primal splendour. Ascetic self-discipline, then, signifies a rejection of the world only in so far as it is corrupted by the Fall; of the body only in so far as it is dominated by sinful passions. Lust excludes love: so long as we lust after other persons or other things, we cannot truly love them. By delivering us from lust, the fast renders us capable of genuine love. No longer ruled by the selfish desire to grasp and exploit, we begin to see the world with the eyes of Adam in Paradise. Our self-denial is the path that leads to our self-affirmation; it is our means of entry into the cosmic liturgy whereby all things visible and invisible ascribe glory to their Creator.

Bishop Kallistos of Diokleia

The Prayer of St Ephrem
O Lord and Master of my life, give me not a spirit of sloth, despondency, lust for power and idle talk.
But a spirit of chastity, humility, patience and love give to me thy servant.
O Lord and King, grant me to see my own faults and not to judge my brother or sister for blessed art thou to the ages of ages.
Amen.

100. A lone voice
John replied in the words of Isaiah the prophet, 'I am the voice of one calling in the desert, "Make straight the way for the Lord."'

(John 1:23)

This is the starting point of revolution. The lone voice, the clear-eyed one, who suddenly sees that something is wrong, that all is not right with the world, and starts shouting about it, being difficult and troublesome, rocking the boat. Other people find it embarrassing, accuse you of being extreme, even mad, exaggerating, and sometimes you even have doubts yourself.

John the Baptist must have seemed all of these things. He delivered his message of radical justice in the most uncompromising way, haranguing his listeners as a 'brood of vipers', denouncing their way of life, and calling for repentance. Even his lifestyle was disturbing, a wild-eyed figure carrying the simple lifestyle to excess.

It is difficult to be different. I recall my embarrassment travelling into Glasgow on a Saturday morning with a coffin on the seat beside me. I was going to a demonstration, but all the time wishing with all my heart that I could just be a normal Saturday morning shopper.

John's message was a clarion call to justice, reflecting the vision of the prophets of a world where crookedness, inequality and injustice were made straight – 'the axe laid to the root of the trees' – and the way prepared for the coming of God's Kingdom in Jesus. John never lived to see the completion of his revolutionary dreams.

Twenty years ago I took part in a Bible study led by a member of the Iona Community on the Jubilee message of Leviticus. He spoke of the cancellation of debt and linked it to the crushing 'debt' of the poor countries of the world. The idea had never occurred to us – we thought it impossible that governments would ever listen. Twenty years on, the movement to drop the debt is one of the fastest growing campaigns in the country.

People flocked out into the desert to hear John the Baptist. The message of justice is still urgently compelling. The world's poorest people are still on tiptoe with expectation.

Christian Aid

101. Struggling with temptation
Jesus was led by the Spirit into the desert, for forty days being put to the test by the devil.
(Luke 4:1–2)

In April 2000 South Africans were stunned by allegations that Hansie Cronje, captain of the national cricket team, had taken bribes for 'fixing' matches. The very idea that this national hero and role model would even contemplate doing something that was dishonest and corrupt was incomprehensible. When some of the allegations were confirmed there was a feeling of national mourning throughout the country. Public opinion was that if someone like Hansie Cronje could give in to such temptation, then anybody could.

Cronje blamed the devil for making him accept the bribes to fix results. The public's reaction to this was interesting. The declaration was treated with scorn and disbelief and seen as an attempt by Cronje to shirk responsibility for his actions. In a country that has a high proportion of Christian believers there was a widespread reluctance to see Satan as a reality at work in the world.

We have all, on occasion, been faced with temptation. Many of us have succumbed to temptation, to a greater or lesser degree. I don't think that any of us could imagine the magnitude and intensity of Jesus' confrontation with Satan in the desert. Yet these are the same kind of temptations that many people, especially those in positions of power, authority and leadership, are faced with on a daily basis. In the Church, in government, in business, in schools and in family situations, people are tempted to lord it over others, to get ahead by devious and ruthless means, to enrich themselves at the expense of the poor and needy.

Jesus was physically weak and vulnerable at the time of his testing, but he was also empowered by the Holy Spirit. The Spirit had led Jesus into the desert and, as long as he stayed rooted in his belief in God's plan for him, he would be protected and strengthened by the same Spirit. The same applies for our times of testing. We can resist temptation only by the power of the Spirit working in us.

Imelda Davidson
South Africa

102. True greatness

'*Whoever will be great among you must be your servant.*'

(Matthew 20:26)

There are many folk tales in Africa that teach us not to expect that good will always be repaid with good. A lion will attempt to devour the hunter who frees it from a trap. And while tradition expects us to be hospitable to all, including perfect strangers, there is sometimes a lack of appreciation which can be very irksome. There are times when our suffering results from the rejection we experience when we tell the bitter truth. But the grace of God sustains us even when we are neither attentive nor grateful. This fact should keep us gracious towards those along our path who treat us otherwise than we expect.

Today we confess that in our haughtiness we ignore how God deals with us, and act callously towards our neighbours. We act as if – and even sometimes say that – nothing can move us, forgetting to add that it is God who shields our lives. We seek lofty offices as if by right, for-getting that it is God who puts us in places of honour to be servants to the causes that God espouses. Sometimes we act as if we expect our authority among human beings to put us above the demands of God. With this mindset we proceed to put ourselves beyond the reach of those we ought to help. But Jesus points out that 'the greatest must be the servant'.

Serving others does not come easily and helping others to build themselves up is quite taxing. But that is what we are called to do as our witness to the love of God. Our deeds should become the Good News of the reign of God and thus lead others to walk with God.

If we want to follow the example of Jesus, especially in this Lenten season, then we should bear in mind that Jesus lived the will of God even when it involved dying. His life was one of praising God. What he did strengthened the faith of many. It released people from their fears and anxieties and turned their guilt to trust and generosity.

Mercy Amba Oduyoye
Ghana

103. Seeds of Hope

'Just as you did it to one of the least of these who are members of my family, you did it to me.'
(Matthew 25:40)

The real issue that faces us today is: 'What does it mean to be a nation in a world that is able to destroy itself at any moment?' If ever, it is today that politicians are called to be wise people, that is, women and men who can raise the issue of national identity and offer a vision of how to be a nation living in harmony among nations, freely using its power to serve rather than dominate. I sense that many personal sacrifices in the political arena will be necessary to reach the point of national discussion aiming at national conversion. Many who possess political power today will need to risk their own political futures and will have to be willing to let go of oppressive power in order to empower other nations and thus further justice and peace in the world. Without such sacrifices there will no longer be a true dialogue in the world of politics, but only a tyrannical monologue leading to the absurd silence not only of politicians but of all human beings. Then we will have created our own day of judgement and will have become our own judges.

This is precisely what the last judgement is all about. The Lord who becomes one of us in humility does not really judge us but reveals to us what we have become to one another. The day of judgement is in fact the day of recognition, the day on which we see for ourselves what we have done to our brothers and sisters, and how we have treated the divine body of which we are part.

Thus the question 'What have you done for the least of mine?' is not only the question of injustice and the question of peace, it also is the question by which we judge ourselves. The answer to that question will determine the existence or non-existence of our human family.

Henri Nouwen

Prayers

104. Author of Life, we come to you in repentance for the sins and abuses of the past, and beg your forgiveness for the destruction of communities and cultures and environments. Enable us to reach through our inertia and fear to feed your people wherever they are. Give us courage in the face of political pressure. Grant us the wisdom to use our resources to your will and to your glory. Give us the spirit of Jesus.
Amen.

Njongonkulu Ndungane,
Archbishop of Cape Town

105. A hymn for trade justice

God, whose people cry with yearning
for the lifting of debt's strain,
give to us the will for turning
from our ruthless search for gain.
Keep us struggling,
keep us faithful,
in the fight to heal earth's pain.

God, who made the earth for sharing,
help us work for fairer trade.
In our affluent lack of caring

help us see the price we've paid.
Grant repentance,
grant forgiveness,
for the unjust world we've made.

God, whose holy anger fires us,
make your cry for justice heard.
Light the vision that inspires us,
challenge with prophetic word.
Make us restless,
make us angry,
for the changing of your world.

God, embracing all creation,
bringing life and hope to birth,
give to every human nation
a true sense of what life's worth.
Give us freedom,
give us wisdom,
for the saving of the earth.
Amen.

(Tune: Rhuddlan)
Jan Berry

106. Asking forgiveness

For the times we have worshipped power and have succumbed to the
temptation of money over justice
we ask your forgiveness, good Lord.
For the times we have divorced ourselves from the reality of death
through believing in 'friendly fire' and 'collateral damage'
we ask your forgiveness, good Lord.
For the times we have given up something for Lent and remained inert
in the face of injustice and war
we ask your forgiveness, good Lord.
For the times we have pushed ourselves forward at the expense of
others and have forgotten your maxim 'the first will be last and the
last first'
we ask your forgiveness, good Lord.
For the times we have been too arrogant to admit to wrongdoing and
too proud to seek the path of repentance

we ask your forgiveness, good Lord.
For the times we have glibly talked about the need for forgiveness and
reconciliation without entering into the pain of injustice
we ask your forgiveness, good Lord.
Amen.

Annabel Shilson-Thomas

107. Choosing the narrow path

God, our companion along the road,
enter with us into the wilderness of uncertainty and the loneliness of
desolation, that through our wanderings and reflections we too may
choose the path of uncertainty and travel with those who have left
behind home and security.
Hear us in your mercy
and strengthen us to do your will.

God, our resistance,
strengthen our resolve to seek bread which nourishes and sustains,
that through our resistance of instant satisfaction we may learn to
value what we take for granted and seek solidarity with those who
have nothing.
Hear us in your mercy
and strengthen us to do your will.

God, our judge,
guard us against all arrogance, hypocrisy and self-righteousness, that
through choosing the fast that undoes the fetters of injustice we may
share our bread with the hungry and bring the homeless poor into our
house.
Hear us in your mercy
and strengthen us to do your will.

God, our beginning and our end,
remind us that we are but dust and to dust we shall return, that
through acknowledging our frailty and owning our mortality we may
draw closer to those who live in constant fear of death.
Hear us in your mercy
and strengthen us to do your will.

God, our cross bearer,

challenge us to take up our cross and to choose the narrow path, that
on our journey we may learn the cost of discipleship and identify with
those who give up home and livelihood for the sake of principle.
Hear us in your mercy
and strengthen us to do your will.

God, our challenger,
stir up our lives and shatter our complacency, that through the people
we meet and the life stories we share we may be challenged to change
and moved to action.
Hear us in your mercy,
strengthen us to do your will
and let our lives reflect your purpose.
Amen.

                                                    Annabel Shilson-Thomas

108. Almighty God, may my mouth speak for justice,
may my feet walk for justice,
may my hands work for justice,
but more than any of those,
may my heart and soul long for justice,
until your will is done on earth as it is in heaven.
Amen.

                                                        Peter Graystone

109. VOICE 1:   In a world of plenty,
VOICE 2:   our choices have condemned millions
                          to poverty and death.
VOICES 1 AND 2: Holy God,
ALL: **forgive our sins.**

VOICE 1:   In a world of great need,
VOICE 2:   we have chosen to keep what we have.
VOICES 1 AND 2: Holy God,
ALL: **forgive our sins.**

VOICE 1:   In a world where so much is fragile,
VOICE 2:   we have trusted in our own strength.
VOICES 1 AND 2: Holy God,
ALL: **forgive our sins.**

VOICE 1:	In a world crying out for peace,
VOICE 2:	we have made war.
VOICES 1 AND 2:	Holy God,
ALL:	**forgive our sins.**

VOICE 1:	In a world that needs to hear your word,
VOICE 2:	we have kept silent.
VOICES 1 AND 2:	Holy God,
ALL:	**forgive our sins.**

LEADER:	May God our rock,
	who leads us into life,
	grant us his healing and forgiveness,
	now and for ever.
	Amen.

Maggie Hindley

110. A prayer of commitment

Creator God, we believe that you have created all the nations of the world to live together in peace, sharing their riches, enjoying their diverse languages, cultures and colours, and caring for one another's need. Grant us the wisdom and the courage to break down all the walls that we ourselves built to separate us one from another. Empower us to rid ourselves of selfishness, indifference, intolerance and hate. Fill us with your glorious vision that springs from our common beginning as human beings created in your image and points to our common goal as your renewed creation.
Amen.

Christian Conference of Asia

111. The lighting of candles

LEADER:	We live in much darkness. We are often uncertain. We are sometimes afraid.
ALL:	**In the darkness, we light a candle of hope.**
	(The first candle is lit.)
LEADER:	We all have sorrows. We have known pain. Each of us carries special regrets. In our palm we light a candle of forgiveness.
	(The second candle is lit.)

LEADER: We are sometimes lonely, and the world seems cold and
           hard. In our loneliness, we light a candle of love.
           (*The third candle is lit.*)

LEADER: We have known awe, wonder, mystery and glimmerings of
           perfection in our imperfect world. In our wonder, we light
           a candle of praise.
           (*The fourth candle is lit.*)

LEADER: May our separate lights become one flame, that together we
           may be nourished by its glow.

ALL: **Amen.**

Christian Conference of Asia

112. Prayer to make poverty history

Christ our Lord,
your light shines into the shadows,
and shows us
where the obstacles to change lie.
We know that often
they are in our own hearts,
in the way we live,
and in our daily choices and actions.
We pray that we may accept
the light of your love
as a challenge to change
ourselves and our world.
We pray that, each day,
we make the choices and
take the actions
that will bring an end to poverty and hunger,
and lead us all
towards a fairer world.
Be with us, Lord,
as we face your challenge
and learn how to live
our lives in love.
Amen.

Linda Jones

113. We bring you, O Lord, the troubles and perils of people and nations:
      the sighing of prisoners and captives,
      the sorrows of the bereaved,
      the necessities of strangers,
      the helplessness of the weak,
      the despondency of the weary,
      the failing powers of the aged.
O Lord, draw near to each,
for the sake of Jesus Christ our Lord.
Amen.

                            St Anselm (1033–1109)

114. God of the big visions and the expanding horizons,
     you teach us to think of all the world and all of its people.
     Your aeons of engagement with creation urge us to look to the long-
       term.
     Your Son's cross draws all humanity to you
     and opens a bigger salvation than we can grasp.
     Your Kingdom defies our frontiers of place or time or thought.
     With you it is good to think big.

But now we need to think small.
We pray for a small room
and a handful of people with an agenda that may not be big enough.
We offer to you the meeting of the G8 (*or as appropriate*)
and the leaders of the world's richest and most powerful nations.

We pray that this may be
      a moment not just for the powerful, but also for the powerless;
      a moment not just for the rich, but also for the poor;
      a moment not just for the full, but also for the empty;
      a moment not justfor the secure, but also for the dispossessed;
      a moment not just for the few, but even for generations unborn.

And give to us who watch and wait outside the door renewed energy
and commitment to hold our leaders accountable, as we must hold
ourselves accountable, for the world's future and your Kingdom's
presence. Amen.

Holy Spirit, yours are the words we want to hear;
yours are the deeds we want to do;

yours is the way we want to go;
help us to hear; to seek and to follow,
Amen.

Neil Thorogood

115. Prayers of intercession

God of justice, God of love,
we keep praying for peace,
while harbouring resentment in our hearts.
> Have mercy upon us.
> **Help us live what we pray.**

We keep praying for an end to the world's hunger,
while enjoying the comfort of more than we need.
> Have mercy upon us.
> **Help us live what we pray.**

We keep praying for suffering people,
forgetting that we could be sharing their load.
> Have mercy upon us.
> **Help us live what we pray.**

And teach us again to keep praying,
not only with words,
but in all that we say and all that we do,
that your love and your justice
may be known on the earth
in each generation.
Amen.

Timothy Woods

116. Litany for *Make Poverty History*

On those bowed down by poverty
Lord, have mercy.

On those who struggle to survive
Lord, have mercy.

On parents who have lost children to disease
Lord, have mercy.

On children who miss school because of unpayable debt
Lord, have mercy.

On young people growing up with no hope for the future
Lord, have mercy.
On adults who work and cannot make a living
Lord, have mercy.

On farmers who cannot sell what they produce
Lord, have mercy.

On people working to rebuild their lives after disaster has hit them
Lord, have mercy.

For campaigners fighting for justice
Make their voices heard.

For citizens standing up for their rights
Make their voices heard.

For postcard-signers, email-senders and white-band-wearers
Make their voices heard.

For politicians and decision-makers
Give them wisdom, Lord.

For the G8 leaders as they prepare to meet
Give them wisdom, Lord.

For the leaders of Africa
Give them wisdom, Lord.

For ourselves, as we struggle with these issues
Make us the means of change.

For your world
Help us to make poverty history.
Amen.

Mary Bradford

117. People are calling for a voice

Give us, O Lord, churches that will be more courageous than cautious;

that will not merely 'comfort the afflicted' but 'afflict the comfortable';
that will not only love the world but also demand justice;
that will not remain silent when people are calling for a voice;
that will not pass by on the other side when wounded humanity is
     waiting to be healed;
that will not only call us to worship but also send us out to witness;
that will follow Christ even when the way points to a Cross.
To this end we offer ourselves in the name of him who loved us and
     gave himself for us.
Amen.

                                                    Christian Conference of Asia

118. Prayer

God of the struggling people
hallowed be your name.
Let the promise of abundant life be realised
and our longing for justice and peace be fulfilled.

Forgive our comfortable life
if we become unresponsive to the cries of the people.
Forgive our daily prayers
if we close our eyes and hearts to the needs of the many.
Forgive our act of charity
if it has thwarted us to work for justice.
Forgive our silence and solitude
if we departed from serving the oppressed wholeheartedly.

Look upon us.
Unjust trade is legalised.
Institutions and powers-that-be
make rules.
The mighty and the wealthy
continue to plunder the wealth of the earth
but the vast majority live in poverty and misery.

Listen to our cries.
Corruption and violence govern us.
The rich few exploit the many poor.
The workers are deprived of just wages.
Peasants and indigenous peoples are driven away from the land.

Heavy taxes and unabated price increases burden the vast majority.
Health, education and social services are not accessible.
Those who shout for justice and human rights are silenced.
Those who work for genuine peace are killed.

Continue to challenge our faith and love;
nurture the hope within us.
Strengthen our passion to serve and journey with the people.
Accompany us on our way.
Give us the strength of an eagle, the humility of a dove, the wisdom
of a serpent
as we join the people in the quest for a lasting peace based on justice.
Amen.

Norma P. Dollaga
The Philippines

119. Confessions

Forgive O Lord, our indifference to the needs of others. Our thoughtlessness and self-interest. How easy it is to forget, when we are loading our trolleys in the supermarket, that others toil to bring us our daily food.

Forgive O Lord, our voracious appetites for something new, regardless of where it comes from, and who produces it. The unrealistic prices we pay, and the subsidies we expect.

Forgive O Lord, that we do not equate the results of our own self-interest with the plight of so many producers who live in poverty.

Forgive O Lord, when we turn our heads and pretend we do not see.
Amen.

Irene Sayer

120. May the anger of Christ be mine,
when the world grows hard and greedy;
when the rich have no care for the poor,
when the powerful take from the needy.
In a world of restless change,
standing for love and faith and justice;

in a dark confusing time,
bearing the light, the shining light of Christ.

May the pity of Christ be mine,
when the outstretched hand's not taken,
when the needy stand in line,
when the lonely live forsaken ...
May the love of Christ be mine,
for the anguished, for the ailing,
for the frail disabled life,
for the fallen, for the failing ...

May the actions of Christ be mine,
bringing hope, bringing new direction,
bringing peace in a warring time,
offering welcome, not rejection ...

Colin Gibson
New Zealand

121. For a healed future

Blessed God, these are some of the things that belong
to our vision of a healed future:

A world that uses resources only as fast as they can be replaced,
so that the wealth of today does not destroy hope for tomorrow.

Leaders who are honest, respectful,
and more interested in doing their jobs than in keeping their jobs.

Material sufficiency and security for all, and therefore, by choice,
low death rates, low birth rates, and stable populations.

Work that dignifies people.

Incentives for people to give of their best to society, and to be rewarded
    for it.
And at the same time ways of providing sufficiently for people under
    any circumstances.

An economy that is a means, not an end,

one that serves the welfare of the community and the environment,
rather than demanding that the community and the environment
    serve *it*.

The kind of agriculture that builds soils,
uses natural mechanisms to restore nutrients and control pests,
and produces abundant, uncontaminated food.

Print and broadcast media that reflect the world's diversity
and, at the same time, bind together the cultures of the world
with relevant, accurate, timely, unbiased, and intelligent information.

Reasons for living and thinking well of oneself
that do not require the accumulation of material things.

Help each one of us, God, and all of us together
to believe in the possibility of such a future,
and by loving and by hoping and by working,
according to what each of us has to contribute, to help it to come
    true.
Amen.

Evan Lewis, after Donella Meadows
New Zealand

122. Prayer for change and transformation

O God, you love justice and you establish peace on earth.
We bring before you the disunity of today's world:
the absurd violence, militarism, exploitation and
oppression threatening life on the planet.
Human greed and injustice, which breed hatred and strife.
For change in our world we pray,
God, in your grace, transform the world.

O God, send your Spirit and renew the face of the earth:
teach us to be compassionate toward the whole human family;
lead all nations into the path of peace.
For the peace that only you can give we pray,
God, in your grace, transform the world.

Teach us how to trade with justice and love.

Remind us of avoiding greed and enable all of us to exalt people in
    poverty.
Remind us that all of us and the whole creation
belong to you and we are only stewards.
Forgive us for not abiding to your will of thy Kingdom on earth.
Give us strength and courage to work for justice and peace.
Amen.

World Council of Churches

123. Blessing

O Lord Christ, who became poor that we might be rich,
deliver us from a comfortable conscience if we believe or intend
that others should be poor that we might be rich;
for in God's economy,
no one is expendable.
Grant us instead the riches of love.
Amen.

World Alliance of Reformed Churches

124.   Christ, let me see you in others.
Christ, let others see you in me.
Christ, let me see:

You are the caller
you are the poor
you are the stranger at my door.

You are the wanderer
the unfed
you are the homeless
with no bed.

You are the man
driven insane
you are the child
crying in pain.

You are the other who comes to me
open my eyes that I may see.

David Adam

125. Make us worthy, Lord, to serve our fellow humans beings through-
     out the world who live and die in poverty and hunger. Give them
     through our hands this day their daily bread, and, by our under-
     standing love, give peace and joy.

     Mother Teresa of Calcutta (adapted)

126. Lord, make us to walk in your way;
     where there is love and wisdom, there is neither fear nor ignorance;
     where there is patience and humility, there is neither anger nor
        annoyance;
     where there is poverty and joy, there is neither greed nor ambition;
     where there is peace and true prayer, there is neither care nor
        restlessness;
     where there is the fear of God to guard the heart, there no enemy can
        enter;
     where there is mercy and prudence, there is neither excess nor
        harshness;
     this we know through the example of him who laid down his life for
        us,
     your Son, Jesus Christ our Lord.
     Amen.

     St Francis

127. Thou loving and tender Father in heaven, I confess before thee, in
     deep sorrow, how hard and unsympathising is my heart; how often I
     have sinned against my neighbour by want of compassion and tender-
     ness; how often I have felt no true pity for his trials and sorrows, and
     have neglected to comfort, help and visit him. O Father, forgive this
     heavy sin, and lay it not to my charge. Give me grace ever to allevi-
     ate the crosses and difficulties of those around me, and never to add
     to them; teach me to be a consoler in sorrow, to take thought for the
     stranger, the widow and the orphan; let my charity show itself not in
     word only but in deed and truth. Teach me to judge, as thou dost,
     with forbearance, with much pity and indulgence; and help me to
     avoid all unloving judgement of others.
     Amen.

     Johann Arndt (1555–1621)

Holy
Week

The testing of Jesus in the desert by the devil showed that a properly human approach to power requires neither domination nor submission. God shares his power with us so that we may stand upright, in all our human dignity.

Holy Week finally reveals the nature of the power of God as manifested in Jesus. As the Last Supper draws near, we see the gathering of the powers that will assassinate Jesus. The political and religious authorities are getting ready to take him by force, humiliate and kill him. These are dumb and brutal powers that are about to kill the one who is God's love for us in person. What they are about to do is absurd and nonsensical. When Jesus meets Judas he asks, 'Friend, why are you here?' And there is no possible answer, except to ask Jesus in turn, 'Friend, why are *you* here?' The absurdity of evil has only one answer which is the larger mystery of good.

Over against these powers of the world, Jesus embodies another sort of power. He makes signs. On that night, according to John, he enacted the sign of the washing of the feet. In Mark, Matthew and Luke, we find the sign of the bread and the wine shared, the new covenant. But the gospels show that throughout his ministry Jesus has been performing signs, turning water into wine, giving sight to the blind, multiplying the loaves and fish. It would be tempting to think that these are magical acts, as if Jesus were a first-century Gandalf, with Peter as Frodo. That would be to miss the point, which is not that Jesus was such a good magician that he could pull off amazing tricks.

These signs are momentous because of what they say. They speak of the Kingdom, of the end of oppression and humiliation. They are signs that all that we long for and more is beginning to happen among us. The signs of Jesus speak to us. They proclaim that the absurdity of suffering will not ultimately triumph, and that the history of humanity will one day bear fruit in justice.

So these two days, Maundy Thursday and Good Friday, are the breaking out of the conflict between these two forms of power. There is the brutal and dumb power of the military and the religious authorities, and there is the power of the man of signs, which is the power of meaning. The confrontation comes to a climax in the meeting of Pilate and Jesus on Good Friday. Pilate says to Jesus, 'Do you not know that I have power to release you, and power to crucify you?' (John 19:10). Jesus says to Pilate, 'For this I was born, and for this I have come into the world, to bear witness to the truth. Everyone who is of the truth hears my voice.' Pilate replies 'What is truth?' and notoriously does not wait for an answer. He does not need to since he has the soldiers behind him.

Those who have visited the so-called developing world will know that the conflict still appears to be going on. The capitalist economic system has brought wealth to some countries and raised the standards of living of many. But the great powers of this world want it above all to benefit us who live in the West, and so many more countries are being plunged into deeper debt. The gap between the rich and poor countries is increasing, and many countries, especially in Africa, appear to be staggering on towards ruin. Many people who work in development – though no one that I have met in CAFOD or Christian Aid! – are discouraged. Is there any point? Can all this self-sacrificing commitment make any difference? All this time and energy is spent in raising money, but far more money pours back out again to the rich countries. Trade barriers and subsidies seem doomed to make it almost impossible for many countries to become truly independent.

Faced with the powers of his time, Jesus made signs that spoke of the ultimate triumph of meaning. Often what we are able to do may look like little more than signs, but they speak of the coming of the Kingdom, and help to bring it about. Small signs are the signature of God. Jesus says that whatever we do to the least of his brothers and sisters we do to him. No sign is too small. Every small act for justice is a little window for God's grace, with consequences that exceed all that we can imagine or may ever know.

Jesus washes the feet of his disciples. It is a tender act, performed in the face of the brutality that he will endure. I was once bowled over by such a tender act in Phnom Penh, Cambodia. I visited an AIDS hospice set up by the Church. It is run by a priest called Jim. He and his helpers collect people who are dying of AIDS and bring them back to this simple wooden construction. There they are fed and cared for. Some are able to go back to their homes for a while but most of them come to die. One young man had just been brought in. He was emaciated and did not look as if he had long to live. They were washing and cutting his hair. His face was blissfully peaceful. You may ask, 'What is the point? He will be dead before long.' But this was an act of tender care that speaks of the Kingdom and brings it that little bit closer.

And Jesus shares bread and wine. At the moment that the little community of the disciples is falling to pieces, Jesus shares with them the bread, saying 'This is my body, given for you.' Just when it all seems hopeless, he performs our sacrament of hope. This is re-enacted not just in all our Eucharists, but all over the world when we gather people to share what we have, when we sink wells to raise water, when we do small things that speak of human dignity and hope. I think of another AIDS clinic, this time in Kigali in Rwanda, with sisters working in the poorest conditions. They had come to serve the people and they had come to stay. They were filled with joy, because they believed that goodness has the last word.

The next day is Good Friday. There is not much to say then. Jesus is mostly silent. The nonsense of evil appears to have triumphed and the powers of this world to have won. But on Easter Sunday the tomb was empty because the Word of life had risen from the grave. Absurdity and brutality cannot keep him in the tomb.

Reflections

128. A reflection for four voices
As he rode along, people kept spreading their cloaks on the road.
                                                            (Luke 19:36)

VOICE 1: Who is this coming into our city? From the noise of the crowd you'd think it was some general, parading his triumph and his wealth. But where is his chariot? Where are his armies, their spears and their swords?

VOICE 2: Who is this passing through our streets? A man on a donkey! A Galilean! A country-bumpkin prophet!

VOICE 3: Who is this riding into our midst? Doesn't look like anybody important. Just some poor man from the country. Probably hasn't got a job. Could even be foreign. How did he get here? Why doesn't he go back to where he came from?

VOICE 4: What's going on? Something's happening. I hope it's not a protest. These people are always out for more wages, or objecting to some injustice. But it can bring out the police or the army. That could mean trouble for all of us.

VOICE 2: This crowd's coming right into our holy place! And they're such a rough lot. Some are even women. The sort of women that look worn out. Maybe from carrying water or working dry soil. Or from bringing up children on their own. Or burying them.

VOICE 1: A lot of young people in the crowd too. Children that look old before their time. Child soldiers and street fighters. Dirty children that look as if they haven't got parents. Kids looking after other kids and working to put food on the table.

VOICE 3: What sort of a man gets a following like this?

VOICE 4: I'm trying to see his face. Such a ragged crowd. But he's smiling at them. There's something in how he looks at them. As if they are the important ones, not him.

VOICE 1: He looks as if he really knows them – what they've been through, what they are living. The sick ones and those looking after the sick. The dying and those grieving the dead. Even the ones who are mentally ill and the prostitutes. The ones who'd give him up to the authorities and the ones who haven't a clue why they are here.

VOICE 2: He looks so ordinary. He could be you or me. But doesn't he know what happens to people like him? Doesn't he understand politics, rigged trials? Doesn't he know about torture – the place where he'll have nothing to say, the hours when there are no companions, the way these things end – alone on some hillside, nailed up to be laughed at?

VOICE 3: I wonder if he does know. His eyes look knowing. But he keeps on coming. Yes, he keeps on coming – into our city ...

VOICE 4: our country ...

VOICE 2: into our church ...

VOICE 1: our lives.

VOICE 3: My brother,

VOICE 2: my sister,

VOICE 1: my child,

VOICE 4: myself.

Sandra Winton OP
New Zealand

129. Palm Sunday: the story of peace and justice

I do not rebel nor turn away. I give my back to the whip,
and my cheeks to those who pull out the beard,
I do not hide out from shame – they spit in my face.

(Isaiah 50:5–6)

This prophecy regarding the suffering servant made by the prophet Isaiah was fulfilled in Jesus Christ. Jesus was going to Jerusalem to offer his life for the salvation of the world. He knew that the Jews were out to kill him. He entered Jerusalem in humility but was welcomed as a king. The story of his triumphant entry into Jerusalem is the story of Palm Sunday. A huge crowd of people greeted him with palm branches in their hands. They spread their cloaks alongside the road as a sign of respect. They were shouting 'Hosanna' which in Hebrew means 'Please save' or 'Save now'.

'*God bless the king who comes in the name of the Lord! Peace in heaven and glory to God!*'
                              (Luke 19:38)

Jesus came with no sword in his hand or crown on his head. He was riding a colt (a young donkey) – a sign of humility and peace.

The story of Palm Sunday is the story of Jesus Christ's challenge to the existing exploitative and oppressive system. There was a nexus between merchants, Temple authorities and civil authorities. Devotees came to Jerusalem from all over the world and offered money in the temple to keep the commandment. Money-changers sitting in the temple premises were changing foreign currency into Jewish shekels at a very low rate. Money could not be changed outside. They were selling animals for sacrifice at much higher prices than the market rates. These could not be bought from outside. Jesus could not tolerate this injustice. He knew that no peace could be established without justice. He entered the Temple and drove out the money-changers. He turned their tables and quoted from the prophets! 'My house shall be called a house of prayer for all people' (Isaiah 56:7) and 'But you have made it a den of robbers' (Jeremiah 7:11).

The story of Palm Sunday demands the same kind of action today. St Paul exhorts us to have the mind of Christ in ourselves. This act of cleansing the Temple was a symbolic beginning of a movement against unjust and oppressive forces. Jesus challenged the corrupt system. He challenged the temple and civil authorities. We need to challenge the same kind of systems today. The menace of globalisation and liberalisation has badly affected the lives of the poor. Because of a market-oriented economy, poor people are losing their jobs, their land, their livelihood, their resources and their identity. In short, poor people are denied their right to live.

This is not that we in India have no resources. Nobel Laureate Amartya Sen has explained, 'The problem of poverty in India is not the lack of resources but the unavailability of resources.'

As we celebrate Palm Sunday, we must ask ourselves whether we are ready to challenge the forces which are responsible for such a situation. We need to make the people aware of their rights and initiate a strong movement against such forces. We have to work hard to build communities of resistance and hope to make life better for the poorest.

                                                        Daniel B. Das
                                                              India

130. Maundy Thursday: servants and masters

'Now that I, your Lord and Teacher, have washed your feet, you also
should wash one another's feet. I have set you an example that you
should do as I have done for you.'

(John 13:14–15)

Jesus washed the feet of his disciples, an act of hospitality and cour-
tesy. In hot and dusty Palestine, one could not be properly at ease
with sweaty, dirty feet. But to Peter, it was an offence that his master
should perform so menial a task. To wear a slave's garment, to get
down on the floor and clean off the dirt, offended every notion of
what should be offered up to holiness.

Every society has its people who it delegates to deal with its bodily
dirt and they always come at the bottom of the social scale – low
paid, dishonoured, sometimes destined through generations to be the
ones whose very name contains our fear of mortality: the 'untouchables'. And here was Jesus doing this work. But his disciples could not
deter him. This was something they had to learn: that there is no
untouchable area for God. Not the sweat of human bodies, not the
stink of the rubbish dump on which he died, not even the stench of
decay from the grave of Lazarus. No smell bad enough to keep God
away. No recoiling from corruptible human flesh.

Not even our own. Hard as it is for our society to value the servant
role properly, when every transaction is an economic one, it is even
more difficult for us to allow ourselves to be served, especially when
the service is a bodily one. It makes us vulnerable, exposes all our
weaknesses. No wonder we work to render invisible those who serve
us! In our heart of hearts, we know there is something lacking in the
terms by which we negotiate the meeting of our most intimate needs.
The dishonour, disgust and profound inequality we project onto
others are a measure of how hard it is for us to accept our own
deepest humanity, how hard it is to affirm intimacy. But Jesus
modelled a different kind of giving and receiving of service, one rooted firmly on mutual acceptance, respect and love for one another in
all our frailty. This embodied act of grace, more clearly than any
other in Scripture, awakens, confronts, embraces and transforms our
fear of loving and being loved.

Kathy Galloway

131. The difficulty of having power

Jesus, by washing the disciples' feet,
is saying something about the distinction so common in humanity
and throughout the history of humanity
between master and slave,
between those in power and the powerless,
between superiors and inferiors.
In many cultures, slaves did all the really difficult, strenuous, hard
      manual labour,
and were forced to work horribly long hours.
They were the ones who built the pyramids
and the palaces of the emperors.
They were the ones on whose shoulders
industrial societies depended,
as they worked in inhuman conditions and for a pittance.
Then, as now, immigrants in Europe did the work that others refused,
just as factory workers in the South
provide designer-label products for consumers in the North.

Jesus came to make things new.
For Jesus, each person is precious,
each one is loved by God,
each is called to become the 'home' of God;
each has a gift to bring to others,
each one should be deeply respected.

Jean Vanier
L'Arche community, France

132. A Gethsemane moment

*Then Jesus went with his disciples to a place called Gethsemane, and
he said to them, 'Sit here while I go over there and pray.' He took
Peter and the two sons of Zebedee along with him, and he began to
be sorrowful and troubled. Then he said to them, 'My soul is overwhelmed with sorrow to the point of death. Stay here and keep watch
with me.'*
      (Matthew 26:36–38)

I suspect that for many of us the facts and figures of the HIV and
AIDS epidemic are daunting. Perhaps like Jesus in Gethsemane we
will find our souls overwhelmed with sorrow.

How very much we would rather live in a world that HIV and AIDS had never entered. And from heaven I hear God's compassion echoing that. How very much I long for that world too. We may groan like Jesus, 'Must we drink this cup?' But we must. That is the world in which we find ourselves. This is the Gethsemane the world must pass through.

Many are simply asleep, like the disciples a stone's throw from Jesus, simply unaware or unconcerned about the relentless threat in parts of the world far from them. And in streets very close to them.

Others come armed, as soldiers were preparing to come to Jesus. Armed with hatred; armed with prejudice; armed with selfish desire to distance themselves; armed with the potential to make money from the difficulty in which people find themselves.

And there are others who come as angels, as Luke tells us happened in Gethsemane, bringing strength to the one who had become weighed down with human frailty.

But even with ministers from God to strengthen and to comfort, this is a crisis which the world must endure. It is a cup we must drink. And just as crucifixion lay ahead for Jesus before he was raised to life, so there is a journey that the world must go – through death – before this epidemic is at an end.

Christians have a genuine role to play in being God's ministers in this Gethsemane. The lesson of Gethsemane is that God does not expect us to do what is impossible, but he does call us to be faithful in what we can do.

Peter Graystone

133. *'The Son of Man came not to be served but to serve, and to give his life as a ransom for many.'*
(Matthew 20:28)

Recently more and more people have been expressing concern over what they see as the growing influence of religion in the public debate, and I can understand why. We've only to recall the bloody battles over beliefs that marred European life in the sixteenth and seventeenth centuries to appreciate that religion needs to be handled with care. I fully subscribe to the argument that a secular state is the best way to guarantee the civil rights and liberties of all its citizens, and yet I still believe that one's faith should influence one's political decisions as faith is not a private affair.

The events of Good Friday are a sober reminder of this. Jesus was executed because his loyalty to God took precedence over all other allegiances. The cross, therefore, is a symbol of the inextricable link between faith and life, the sacred and the secular. The grim reality of Jesus' public death means that no human experience or concern should be seen to be beyond the embrace of God; no human person as unworthy of our attention and respect. It isn't possible for us to accept Jesus' invitation to follow in his footsteps and at the same time to ignore what's happening in the world around us. War, poverty, hunger, oppression, injustice, unemployment, homelessness, health-care and education are as much to do with faith as with politics. These underscore the value that we give to human life and as such overlap with the core concern of the Gospel.

In recognising this, the Second Vatican Council called on Christians to let go of their own individual self-interest and to take an active part in promoting the common good by fostering justice and kindness at every level. Our sole ambition in this should be to serve humanity and not to seek political power and influence as a means to promoting our own beliefs to the exclusion of others. The events of Good Friday provide the spiritual vision that should keep us on track: 'The Son of Man came not to be served but to serve, and to give his life as a ransom for many' (Matthew 20:28). Wherever people are rejected and mocked the crucifixion becomes a present day reality.

Oliver McTernan

134. The Way of the Cross

… and carrying the cross by himself, he went out to what is called The Place of the Skull …
(John 19:17)

It was a hot day outside – even hotter inside the rackety old bus, stuffed with people heading home for Holy Week. We made a stop on the side of the highway to pick up a few more passengers – and more dust – which swirled around the inside of the bus until it found sweaty brows upon which to settle.

I was pressed against the window, my backpack at my feet, sharing the two-passenger seat with a mother and son. We were intimately stuck together by sweat. All I wanted was for the bus to get rolling so that I could breathe again.

I glanced outside the window and noticed a woman walking alongside the highway, balancing a large load of firewood on her shoulders and head. She was bent over, her face staring down at the hot pavement, walking to a place that seemed very far away.

For a split second the woman glanced toward the bus, just as it jerked forward and began to move again. Ah! Air to breathe. I went back to reflecting on the week's gospel texts and liturgical celebrations ... imagining the faces of the people with whom I would have the privilege of sharing another Holy Week in the mountain villages of Honduras.

Suddenly I sat up in my seat, and turned to look out the window. Where did she go? Where is the woman with the firewood?

It was as though I had just glimpsed the entire passion, death and resurrection of Jesus for the first time – embodied in the woman on the side of the road. Yes, of course! Jesus! The wood of the cross on her shoulders, the sweat dripping down her face like blood, walking – faithfully – to a place very far away. I could see her face – *his* face.

Like every mother in rural Honduras, she was collecting firewood for cooking, to make the corn tortillas for her family to eat. For her every supper is a last supper: Who knows if there will be wood and corn tomorrow? 'Take and eat. This is my body – broken for you. This is my blood – poured out in love. I have come that you might have life – life in abundance.'

There is only one *Via Crucis*, and Jesus walks it with us. Like a mother, he feeds us with his death, his resurrection, his bread, his love. 'Do not be afraid; I am with you always.'

Brian Pierce OP
Peru

135. *'Father, into your hands I commend my spirit.'*
(Luke 23:46)

The final cry of Christ from the cross, 'Into your hands I commend my spirit', is lost in the suffering of many in our world. In the face of daily hunger, crop failure, death at childbirth, from malaria, from TB, from AIDS, there is only pain and grief, then the silence of the tomb. For these there is no explanation for the torments they endure. Like Christ in the darkness of their own Calvary they can only cry 'My God, My God, why have you forsaken me?' Here there is no comfort of faith, no hope; there is no 'salvific purpose' in their suffering.

For others the death of Christ means nothing – a random and little understood fact, like so many other facts intruded into indigenous culture by foreigners. Their lives are like the voices of those at the foot of the cross taunting: 'Come down from the cross and then we will believe in you.' These are not just the drug dealers, the rich ranchers, the sexual exploiters, those who trade in human persons, but also the ordinary indifferent peasant. And yet it is for such as these, for such as us, that Christ was crucified, and is crucified again and again in his people, in their suffering and in their anguish.

The women of Jerusalem continue to weep in the Amerindian women beaten and bruised by their drunken husbands; Christ's abandonment is reflected in their desertion by good-time partners and loveless offspring.

The eyes of faith are blinded in those children whose parents forsake them to escape the Golgotha of poverty and boredom, exchanging the dark night of Guyana for the allure of the lights of Brazil. The faces of children fill with tears and misery as they weep not for Christ, nor for the womb that bore them, but for themselves and the generations yet to come. Is there any who will help to carry their cross?

In the absence of help there is illusion, the temporary relief of the gall and vinegar in the shape of rum, carrie and kasseri.* This offering is really only the Judas kiss of misery to all lips that touch it. They long for the heavenly Jerusalem and the false hope lasts but a night.

This Eden, the Rupununi, has its own tree of knowledge, making its own cross from which Christ hangs. The cross raised over the hillsides of this land, venerated but ignored, bringing life to all who will gaze upon it. But who is there to cradle the broken and bloodied body of Christ? The virgin mothers are the children of eleven and twelve made pregnant by intoxicated friends and family members. Their children are as unwanted and burdensome as they themselves were. Will they receive the Lord into their lap?

Christ: quo vadis? What have you done to your people? Come again not to judge us, but to save us.

Oliver Rafferty

(* Carrie and Kasseri are the local alcohol, made from the root crop cassava.)

Prayers

136. Jesus, Messiah and Prince of peace,
    make us instruments of your peace among warring families, communities and nations.

As you came riding into Jerusalem on a simple mule,
we pray that you would ride through our humble lives
and enable us to challenge, uproot, and destroy
strongholds that breed poverty, hunger, wars and death
as we work towards the realisation of your Kingdom here and now.
Your Kingdom come, O Lord.
Amen.

Joyce Karuri
Kenya

137. Jesus calls us to journey with him,
   to journey with him to a woman pouring perfume in a house at Bethany,
   to journey with him to a man pouring water, cleaning up after the devastation of war,
   to journey with him to a woman pouring lotion on the bruises of a husband's violence.

   Jesus calls us to speak out with him,
   to speak out for the beauty of a woman's extravagance,
   to speak out for the unveiling of rules that deny people's existence,
   to speak out for justice for the poorest of the poor.

   And Jesus calls us to celebrate in the dance of liberation.
   Jesus calls us to celebrate love wherever it is found.
   Jesus calls us to celebrate the many gifts offered by women and men.
   Jesus calls us to celebrate the dignity and worth of all people.

Clare McBeath

138. O loving Father, make me like Jesus:
   the Jesus who could spend nights in prayer,
   the Jesus who went about doing good,
   the Jesus who made time to talk to Nicodemus,
   the Jesus who could not bear to see the mother cry at Nain,
   the Jesus who took a towel and knelt and washed the feet of the men who were going to deny, betray and forsake him,
   the Jesus who could give a patient word when smitten on the face,
   the Jesus who could pray for the men who nailed him to the cross,
   the Jesus who was strong enough not to answer back when accused unjustly,
   the Jesus who could sleep peacefully in a gale and storm,

the Jesus who would not let the marriage at Cana be spoilt by lack of
    wine,
the Jesus who would not condemn the woman taken in an act of sin,
the Jesus who could shrink from the cup of suffering yet drink it to
    the last dregs.
O Loving Father, make me like the Jesus who came to the world to
show what you were like.

Personal prayer of Bishop Jacob,
Bishop of Travancore
South India

139. Servant Christ,
in setting your face towards Jerusalem,
in the struggle and the searching in Gethsemane,
and on the cross of Calvary,
you refused to choose a safe and expedient life.
May we resist the temptation to pursue our own interest,
to preserve the status quo,
and to participate in the conspiracy of silence
which protects the rich and harms the poor.
We make our prayer in your name.
Amen.

Caroline Ainger

140. *'Jerusalem, Jerusalem ... How often have I desired to gather your
children together ... '*
(Matthew 23:37)

As you weep over your broken world, Father, we acknowledge our
    share of responsibility for that brokenness.
Forgive our unwillingness to see.
Forgive our readiness to rationalise wickedness.
Forgive the ease with which we condemn others, while we are
    complicit ourselves.
Forgive our failure to act and to pray.
Grant us the grace of true repentance, that we may know your
    forgiveness and begin a new way with you. For Jesus' sake.
Amen.

Roy Jenkins

141. *Jesus answered: 'I tell you that if they keep quiet, the stones them-selves will start shouting.'*
(Luke 19:40)

The sound of a whistle blowing long and hard. The crowd's cheering turned to catcall and booing, and to one word shouted over and over again, 'Foul!' The referee, blowing his whistle, stopping the game, holding something red in his hand. A figure gesticulating and arguing; he turned, and shoulders slumped now, walked from the field.

The machine guns chattered in the village by the river as the troops stilled those who had spoken out against the government. But no referee blew his whistle.

The young girl, a runaway from her home for one or for a thou-sand reasons, was found by the man who led her into a life of drugs and prostitution. But no one called foul.

A nation starves, as the harvest fails, or as a cruel dictatorship burns the crops to bring them to heel. A red card may be held up, but no one leaves the field.

The ten thousand voices are dimmed for ten thousand different reasons. And the stones themselves shout to the sky as we are silent. The stones listen for the cries of others, but do so in vain.

We don't shout out, Lord. It's not our style. People don't listen when we shout. And anyway, we're not sure that shouting is the right thing to do. We can debate things, can't we, Lord? That's reasonable, isn't it? There must be two sides to every story. And the injustices continue. And they continue all the more when they know there is no one to hold up the red card, and that voices won't be raised to shout 'foul' at the tyranny of it all.

Perhaps we'll send some money, Lord, or give our old clothes to agencies who will help those who are displaced or starving, but we can't shout, Lord. What would the neighbours think? Forgive us, Lord, when we don't even whisper against the wrongs that we know are happening. Forgive us when we put our fingers in our ears if someone else blows the whistle and we don't want to hear.

The stones themselves cry out at our silence, Lord.
Amen.

Brian Hudson

142. Rainbow, cross and dove

As Jesus prayed,
so let us live

enfolded hand in hand,
encouraging and cherishing,
for peace is your command.

Chorus
Enrich us with each other's gift,
embolden by your love,
emblazon hope and unity
in rainbow, cross and dove.

As Jesus lived
so let us act
in anger but in love,
o'erturning bitter tables,
giving justice space to move.

As Jesus acted,
let us heal
the wounds within our touch,
and call the Spirit's power down
for pain that seems too much.

As Jesus healed, let us receive
a new life here and now
fulfilling every hope and dream,
release from hatred's vow.
> *(Originally written for the Week of Prayer for Christian Unity.*
> *May be sung to 'Auld Lang Syne'.)*
> David Coleman

143. Prayer of intercession

God of justice,
so many things in our world do not seem to be fair.
Just as the fig tree did not produce any fruit,
so we pray to you for those whose lives are barren,
or for whom life seems unfair,
for those who are killed,
or who lose their homes
as a result of natural disaster,
earthquakes, floods,
volcanic activity, especially …

(silence)

Caring God,
we pray for those whose lives are cut short early
by illness, or accident, or poverty, especially ...

(silence)

And we pray for those who mourn them.

All-seeing God,
we pray for those whose lives are made difficult
because of inequalities between the rich and poor:
the homeless,
those who do not have adequate healthcare,
or education,
or jobs;
for those who live in slums with inadequate basic facilities,
the hungry and starving especially ...

(silence)

Understanding God,
we pray for those who are disadvantaged by disability:
those who find it difficult to learn,
to walk,
to speak,
to hear,
to see, especially ...

(silence)

Embracing God,
we pray for those who are disadvantaged
or who face prejudice
because of their race,
or colour,
or gender,
or sexuality, especially ... .

(silence)

Loving God,
grant us the ability to begin to change unjust systems
and to repent when we have been responsible for anyone's difficulty.

We ask this in Christ's name.
Amen.

Lesley Husselbee

144. *Let us therefore approach the throne of grace with boldness, so that*
we may receive mercy and find grace to help in time of need.
(Hebrews 4:16)

When we refuse to share the resources of our wealth
when we are afraid to make sacrifices for justice
when the weariness of struggle stifles our longing for peace:
in the denial of dreams,
Lamb of God,
bearing the sin of the world
have mercy on us.

When unfair conditions add to the burden of the poor
when nations break promises and refuse responsibility
when violence is seen as a way of bringing freedom:
in the betrayal of trust,
Lamb of God,
bearing the sin of the world
have mercy on us.

When the longing for a better world is crushed by cynicism
when the suffering of the innocent cries out in despair
when vision is abandoned in the face of death:
in the shattering of hope,
Lamb of God,
bearing the sin of the world
have mercy on us.

When dreams are denied
Christ have mercy.
When trust is betrayed
Christ have mercy.
When hope is shattered

Christ have mercy.
Amen.

> *(A sung 'kyrie eleison' could be used in place of the spoken*
> *responses in this prayer.)*
> Jan Berry

145. *Christ Jesus ... who emptied himself, taking on the form of a*
slave ...
    (Philippians 2:7)

Christ our Lord,
you refused the way of domination
and died the death of a slave.
May we also refuse to lord it
over those who are subject to us,
but share the weight of authority
so that all may be empowered
in your name.
Amen.

> Janet Morley

146. Holy Thursday

My living Lord, with what intensity the hour had come, as at last you gathered your closest friends for that supper. Had you, for over a year, been pondering what had been said to you after feeding all those crowds by the lake: how *can* this man give us his flesh to eat, his blood to drink? When many had walked with you no more, except this little gathering who, though bewildered, said: 'To whom else can we go?'

And had you now, knowing how your final 'hour' had come, secretly moved the day and chosen the place for this supper? No wonder you sighed: How I have longed to share this meal with you, with you who have stood by me.

Outside the powers were mustering, threatened by all that you had lived for. And if we are honest, most of us wanted you, as did your cousin John, to be a divine Saviour who would destroy the powers and bring in justice and truth on behalf of the dispossessed of our world. But you have chosen, are choosing, another way. The mysterious way of God's unilateral disarmament. At three o'clock tomorrow all will be fulfilled. But now, at this ominous hour, you go down on your knees, abasing yourself in washing our feet. And you disappear into bread and wine.

Living One, Risen Victim, it was only later, as the light of your risen presence filtered through into the hearts and minds of your friends, that they came to know what you had left them, and us, at your supper. It was only in resurrection faith, shining back on your final 'hour' that we could know your time of degradation as the hour of glory and new creation. Oh, you are a hidden God!

As now we celebrate your presence in our Eucharists, may we know that it is you who believe in us more than we who believe in you. May we give our Amen to your presence which always 'goes before us'. And may we truly become you whom we receive, God's embodiment in our world.
Amen.

Thomas Cullinan OSB

147. The angels of God

There are memories of breaking, curses and brutality
but I will let them go now.
Not these memories
but of those who were there with me
and sought to repair the damage done
to save and protect from harm all that is good.
These are your disciples, Lord.
They have pushed back the darkness,
for they have hovered like faithful angels over the invasion and
    lessened it.
No, Lord, more than that, they have transformed it by their costly
    loyalty.
It is as though they feel the hurt more deeply than if it were their own.
And now they sit down and stay without judgement or fear for
    themselves
and the broken house is full of the warmth of their goodness.
Lord, as I begin again, it is your angels I will remember
and I will be for ever thankful for the blessing which they brought.
Amen.

Richard Carter

148. Simon of Cyrene

As they led him away, they seized a man, Simon of Cyrene, who was coming from the country, and they laid the cross on him, and made him carry it behind Jesus.

(Luke 23:26)

I. Simon of Cyrene is an extraordinary character on the way of the cross – the person who carried Jesus's cross and actually walked the route with him. Despite his brief appearance, he is perhaps a deeply representative figure – an ordinary person swept up in the great suffering of politics and power.

Like so many people in today's wars and disasters Simon does not choose his cross. He was going about his life when, torn suddenly from the role of passer by, he has a cross thrust heavily upon him and is frighteningly caught up in events that are not of his making. So many people – like Simon – have a cross thrust upon them.

Although Christ calls us to take up our cross and follow him, most people in war and disaster experience the way of the cross, like Simon, by force and not by choice. Grabbed from the path of their ordinary lives, they are wounded, raped, made destitute or bereaved – forced to carry a cross they have not chosen and to find God in the depths of a suffering they neither wanted nor expected.

We pray that in such forced cross-bearing they find the comfort of a God who shares its weight and helps them to survive to newness of life.

II. Like so many of us who watch things from afar on television or the web, Simon shares temporarily in someone else's suffering but is spared full participation in that suffering. Wrenched into a drama of terrible scale and intensity, he joins it only for a moment and then is just as quickly left alone with the shock of being powerless and peripheral to an outrage, yet shaken by it.

We often encounter those who suffer on our screens. Like Simon, we find ourselves brought close to a stranger's face, their sweat, their tears and their agony, only to be pulled far away from them again. This is not our suffering but we have felt and known it for a while.

We pray that after such momentary cross-sharing we do not feel discarded or confused but moved to remember and support those we do not know but whose suffering we somehow shared.

III. Simon's direct experience of the way of the cross changed him for ever. From such a short and sudden sharing with the crucified Christ, he was moved to seek and know the risen Christ.

We pray that in any experience of cross-bearing all your people may know the risen Christ.
Amen.

Hugo Slim

149. O Tree of Calvary,
send your roots deep down into my heart.
Gather together the soil of my heart,
the sands of my fickleness,
the mud of my desires.
Bind them all together,
O Tree of Calvary,
interlace them with thy strong roots,
entwine them with the network
of thy love.

Prayer of an Indian Christian

150. The shouts are too loud
they so often deafen my ears.
War, famine, destruction, death –
the sufferings of the world glide past my soul.
I have heard too much to care.

But then you, O God,
you stand in the midst of the world's woe,
and the shapes of those who suffer are no longer faceless,
for you have bequeathed to them your own face,
their pain is etched with the lines of your passion.
And I shall proclaim:
I had heard, but now I see.

The people are too many,
they blur together in my imagination,
races, colours, faiths and languages –
their shifting kaleidoscope dazzles my vision.
I am made giddy by their infinite variety.

But then you, O God,
you are the still point round which all revolves,
in you both light and shadow find an equilibrium:
you paint into life our many-peopled world,
your love refracts us into a rainbow of hope.
And I shall proclaim:
I had heard but now I see.

Clare Amos

151. A prayer to see God's face in the face of the suffering

Dear God who gave us life and designed us to be free,
and who weeps at the pain of separation and division,
stir in us the will to look at your face
in the faces of those who suffer.

We acknowledge with shame our inertia and fear
when we view others in our world
divided from us by poverty, disease and famine.
Enliven us with your love. Bring hope to the hopeless.

May we listen to the cries of the poor, and find direction.
May we come alongside the sick and weary, and find inspiration.
May we run to the hungry with food and bring water to the thirsty,
and find fulfilment
through Jesus Christ who died to bring life and love to us all.
Amen.

Grace Sheppard

152. Lament

The weight of the tears of the world
is too heavy to bear:
for the cost, and the waste of
young lives playing out
old men's games,
knowing terror and fear
never tasted by soldiers of lead.

Forgive us, I fear
that we know very well
what we do.

Ann Lewin

153. Easter Eve

O God,
you have searched the depths we cannot know,
and touched what we cannot bear to name:
may we so wait,
enclosed in your darkness,
that we are ready to encounter
the terror of the dawn,
with Jesus Christ.
Amen.

Janet Morley

154. Lord Jesus, you put a face to love.

It is your face.
But it is my face too.
It is the face of my neighbour
and the face of the stranger ...
We give thanks for those who,
on our behalf,
care for those aspects of our human existence
we would rather forget.
We pray to be like you, and them,
in generosity and grace.
Amen.

Kathy Galloway

155. God of truth,

we pray for all whom you call
to the task of being prophets.

To those crying for justice
in a world controlled by material profit,
Holy God, bring strength and perseverence.

To those imprisoned
for having dared to challenge the powers,
Holy God, bring courage and hope.

To those vilified or misunderstood
for threatening closely held assumptions,
Holy God, bring wisdom and determination.

To those ridiculed or ignored
for speaking peace in the midst of violence,
Holy God, bring a sense of your Kingdom.

And to your church,
unsure how to speak and be heard,
but struggling to find a prophetic voice;
**Holy God, bring faith
and the confidence that comes from confessing Christ as Lord.
Amen.**

Mary Cotes

156. Oh my heart's heart, in love and anger I will turn to you,
for my soul cries out, 'Where is justice,
when will the balance be redressed
for the fearful dreams of children who sleep with knives,
for the beaten women, and the shamed and helpless men?'
Where is justice?
For the agony of hunger is not to be set
against the insatiable appetite of jaded palates.

In the villages and camps, the children lie bleeding,
and great wounds gape in their throats and sides.
In the city, there is no safety for them;
as the leaves blow through the night streets,
they are swept away, they disappear without trace
as if they had never been.

In the marketplace, weapons are bought and sold;
they change hands as easily as onions from a market woman,
and killing comes lightly everywhere.
The value of people is weighed out on crooked scales
and found wanting,

they are discarded like bruised apples
because they lack the appearance of perfection.

But you, my heart's heart, you are careful;
like a thrifty housewife, who sees no waste in anything,
you gather up that which has been cast aside,
knowing its sweetness,
and take it home with you.
And I will see you in the camps and villages,
working late into the night,
showing patience in the midst of confusion,
reweaving the web of life.
I will see you in the cities,
seated in a circle, making new plans,
drawing attention,
naming the forgotten names.

I will see you in the marketplace,
dressed in black,
with the carved face of an old woman saying 'no' to war,
and you will stand your ground,
and you will seem beautiful to me.
For you are my sanctuary and my light,
my firm ground when the earth cracks
under the weight of warring gods.
As a woman in mortal danger flees to her sisters
and finds refuge,
so you will comfort me, and dress my wounds with tenderness.
And when the flame of courage burns low in me,
your breath, as gentle as a sleeping child,
will stir the ashes of my heart.

Teach me to know your judgement as my friend,
that I may never be ashamed of justice,
or so proud that I flee from mercy.
For your love is never less than justice,
and your strength is tenderness.
You contain my soul's yearning,
and in your encompassing, I am free.

                                          Kathy Galloway

157. We have squandered the gift of life.
The good life of some is built on the pain of many;
the pleasure of a few on the agony of millions.
To you we lift our outspread hands.
We thirst for you in a thirsty land.
We worship death in our quest to possess ever more things;
we worship death in our hankering after our own security,
our own survival, our own peace,
as if life were divisible,
as if love were divisible,
as if Christ had not died for all of us.
To you we lift our outspread hands.

Prayer used at the sixth assembly of the
World Council of Churches

158. Lord, take my heart and break it:
break it not in the way I would like,
but in the way you know to be best.
And because it is you who break it,
I will not be afraid,
for in your hands all is safe,
and I am safe.

Lord, take my heart and fill it with your joy,
not always in ways I like,
but in the ways you know are best,
that your joys may be fulfilled in me.
So, Lord, I am ready to be your friend, your servant.
Amen.

Michael Ramsey

Easter

On the evening of that day, the first day of the week, the doors being shut where the disciples were, for fear of the Jews, Jesus came and stood among them and said to them, 'Peace be with you.' When he had said this, he showed them his hands and his side. The disciples were glad when they saw the Lord. Jesus said to them again, 'Peace be with you. As the Father has sent me, even so I send you.'

(John 20:19–21)

When Jesus appears to the disciples, 'he showed them his hands and his side'. In fact the whole of this account of the appearance of Jesus in John's gospel appears to focus more upon the wounds of Jesus than on his resurrection. When Thomas comes back and hears about the appearance of Jesus, all he wants to do is to touch the wounds. 'Unless I see in his hands the print of the nails and place my finger in his side, I will not believe.'

Why does a story about the risen Christ focus so much on his wounds? It is because he is wounded and raised. When we think about the resurrection, we may be tempted to think that it is a stage in Jesus' life. He died, and then he rose and put hurt and death behind him. One might think that being wounded and dead are things of the past after the resurrection, just episodes from an earlier moment in his story.

But in the resurrection the Father gives back to Jesus the whole of his life, all that he has lived. He is *now* the wounded and risen Christ. One might even say that he is now the *killed* and risen Christ. That might sound rather paradoxical but it is, in every sense of the word, vital. In the Latin of the Preface which Catholics use at this time of the year it says that he lives 'for ever slain', '*semper occisus*'.

This is vital because it means that the risen Lord is now in touch with wounded humanity. All over the world, human beings are being wounded and killed. Some 20,000 people die a day just because they are too poor to go on living. Millions of others are wounded by torturers, in the conflicts between gangs, by inhuman labour in sweatshops. Good Friday goes on all over the planet. If the resurrection was Jesus simply putting all that behind him, like a man who leaves hospital recovered from his wounds, then he would have nothing to do with us now. We may hope for the resurrection as future comfort, but now we would be stuck in the hurt and the pain, remote from God.

A friend of mine, an American Dominican, went to work for a few years in Peru. At first he was rather horrified by how the religion of the indigenous people in the Andes seemed to be dominated by images of the crucified Jesus, with hideous wounds. He asked himself whether they really believed in Easter. Did their faith stop on Good Friday? As he got to know them he realised how wrong he was. They were indeed expressing their faith in the risen Lord, but the one who still shared their pain so that they might now share his life.

The disciples are locked in the room for fear of the Jews. They dare not go outside, in case they get lynched. They have seen what happened to Jesus and they fear that it may happen to them too. But it is the wounded Lord who says to them, 'Peace be with you' and sends them on their way. They will get hurt. The tradition is that nearly all of them died as martyrs. They can embrace that risk with courage because they have seen the wounded Christ and he is raised.

We all have our secure upper rooms in which we hide from hurt. Every one of us has his or her fears, against which we lock the doors. This fear of getting hurt may mean that we do not even want to know too much about the injustice and suffering of this world. We dread that if we get to know about it, then we shall have to leave our protected environment and take the risk of getting hurt or even killed. The disciples saw the wounds of the risen Lord but we have not. Jesus says to Thomas, 'Have you believed because you have seen me? Blessed are those who have not seen and yet believe.' How can we learn courage?

One of my brethren, Henri Burin des Roziers, is a French lawyer. He too has a reflection in this book on Easter, but he does not, of course, talk about himself and so I shall! For the last few years he has been fighting slavery in the Brazilian Amazon. There are enormous estates, some of them the size of Wales. The landowners lure the poor to work for them, promising wages and work and security. But once they have arrived, they find that they have to pay back the costs of their transport, and so slowly they discover that they are trapped and can never escape. If they try to, then they are usually hunted down by dogs and shot. One landowner admitted that he boiled up the bodies and fed them to his pigs. He could afford to make the admission because the police are in his pay.

Henri tries to take these landowners to court. It is often futile since the judges too are corrupted by the landowners. But he is beginning to get results. He frequently receives death threats. A few weeks ago they did kill his friend and collaborator, Sister Dorothy, of the Notre Dame Sisters. Anyone who kills Henri has been promised $30,000, an unimaginable fortune in the Amazon. When I was in contact with him recently, he said, 'I'm not afraid of dying. I have lived a long life.' When I stayed with him he lent me his room for the night. He did not sleep because it suddenly occurred to him that if they tried to get him that night, then they would kill me instead, which would be embarrassing. Fortunately the same idea did not occur to me!

All over the world there are tens of thousands of Christians, sometimes working with people of other religions, who daily take the risk of getting hurt and even killed. They invite us who have not seen the wounded and risen Lord to take the risk of getting hurt. If we do not do so, but remain safe in our upper rooms, then we shall be but half alive ourselves. Charles Peguy, the French writer, told the story of a man who dies and goes to heaven. When he meets the recording angel he is asked, 'Show me your wounds.' And he replies, 'Wounds? I have not got any.' And the angel says, 'Did you never think that anything was worth fighting for?'

If we do venture out of our safe places into this dangerous world, and risk getting hurt, then we shall surely be afraid. Courage is not being without fear; it is refusing to be enslaved by it. The brave admit their fears. Once Oscar Romero, the Archbishop of San Salvador, was sitting on a beach with a friend, and he asked his friend whether he was afraid to die. The friend replied that he was not, and Romero said, 'But I am. I am afraid to die,' and yet he had the courage to take the risk and he was killed. The risen Lord was with him then and now. Christ has died; Christ is risen, Christ will come again. We can dare to open the doors of our secure places and go out into the dangerous world, not without fear, but not ruled by it.

Reflections

159. Resurrection love

'Look at my hands and my feet.'
                                        (Luke 24:39)

On Easter Sunday, Jesus offers us the gift of presence and the gift of peace.

We are to know him in the breaking of the bread. Jesus does not want to be insubstantial; he does not want to be a ghost. Instead he comes to us and invites us to touch him. He offers himself to us in ways that are intended to nourish and nurture us. He promises companionship.

So where are we to touch him in today's world? Where are we to walk with him? Where are we to find his hands and feet? Where are we to offer him a piece of broiled fish and eat and drink in his presence? Christianity is an embodied religion. It does not live between the pages of a book. Rather, it invites us to engage with our world. So we are to recognise the presence of Jesus whenever there are wounded hands and feet that turn to us for healing and wherever there is a road that we can walk down in his company.

The gift lies in recognising him even when he presents himself to us in hidden and unexpected ways. We need to believe that we can touch him in our everyday lives. We need to understand that we can walk with him. Our task is to seek out people who are needy and to turn our faces towards them rather than away from them. This is not difficult to do, for there are many wounded hands and feet that clamour for our attention. There are many hungry people who would love a bowl of fish, let alone a loaf of bread.

If Jesus is risen from the dead then we need proof, we need evidence. How can we secure this in today's world? The Gospel seems to suggest that the way forward is to open our hearts in love. No one is to be excluded, no situation is beyond the reach of grace. By believing this and by putting it into practice, we can become witnesses and carry the echo of his saving mission forwards into our world. Christian faith is not a personal possession. It is always for sharing.

So everything comes full circle. We can be his witnesses. We can provide the evidence that he is risen.

Lavinia Byrne

160. Easter! Resurrection, light and life!

For freedom Christ has set us free. Stand firm, therefore, and do not submit again to a yoke of slavery.

(Galatians 5:1)

Cosmo was blind. His eyes had been ruined by the chemicals and fertilisers that he used to put on the farmer's fields, and five years ago he totally lost his sight. The farmer let him live in a small shack away from the house. He was fed twice a day at the same time as the dogs. Apart from that no one bothered about him and Cosmo lost virtually all human contact. He was shut up in the dark of his own little world, with only his memories. And he thought about the poor village that he had left behind seven years earlier in the hope of earning a little money in the *fazendas* of Parà.

One day some seasonal agricultural workers, also from Piaui, who had been cutting down trees in the forest, came to the farmer's house. Their wages hadn't been paid for three months and they wanted food and medical care for their colleagues stricken by malaria. They found Cosmo, their compatriot, dirty and unshaven, and he told them his story. The farmer refused to meet the workers and a couple of them ran off to complain to the Pastoral Land Commission of Xinguara (CPT).

They also told them about Cosmo. As a result the Ministry of Labour mounted a rescue operation and 30 rural workers, who had been treated like slaves, were set free, taken away from the farm, paid, cared for and returned to the village of Piaui. But Cosmo didn't want to go. He was terrified at the prospect of leaving his own little world, which, although wretched, was at least familiar to him. He was afraid that back in the village he had left so long ago no one would remember him. So CPT at Xinguara got in touch with their team in Piaui and tracked down Cosmo's family. Then Cosmo agreed to go back and was duly welcomed. He did not regain his sight, but he did find a new life. With the compensation that the farmer was forced to pay him he has rebuilt his life. And he is speaking out! He asked to join the CPT teams from Piaui at meetings of fellow agricultural workers and landless peasants, and warns them not be seduced by the false promises of agents recruiting people to work on

the big Parà estates. He tells them to listen to the union and to CPT,
to hang on to their freedom, to work for dignity.

I am the Lord, I have called you in righteousness, I have taken you by
the hand and kept you; I have given you as a covenant to the people, a
light to the nations, to open the eyes that are blind, to bring out the
prisoners from the dungeon, from the prison those who sit in darkness.

(Isaiah 42:6–7)

Henri Burin des Roziers OP

Brazil

161. A ray of hope

This horrifying story of violence, hatred and cruelty ends with an
    immense ray of hope:
death does not have the last word!
Violence and hate have been transformed
into tenderness and forgiveness
through the power of God, the Word of God made flesh.
Waters of life begin to flow.
people will now be able to receive these waters
of love and communion
and find inner liberation.
As disciples they will become a source of peace for our divided,
    broken world.

But this gift of the Spirit is not given without pain.
The pain and death of Jesus, freely accepted,
are followed by the pain and death that his disciples willingly accept.
Just as life flowed from the pierced heart of Jesus,
life will flow from the pierced hearts
of those who will suffer in the name of Jesus.
Disciples of Jesus throughout the ages
suffer rejection, are mocked, laughed at, pushed aside,
sometimes tortured and killed for their faith, for truth and justice.
They become like Jesus.
Paul tells his disciples:

I rejoice in my sufferings for your sake
and in my flesh I complete what is lacking in Christ's affliction,
for the sake of his body, the Church.

(Colossians 1:24)

Disciples who suffer in the name of Jesus become a source of life for
the church and for the world.
In 1982, Oscar Romero was assassinated by the military in El
    Salvador
because he sided with the poor,
with those who had no land.
He denounced the oppression of those in power.
Shortly before he was killed, Romero said:
'Even if my blood is poured out,
it will give life to others in El Salvador.'
He is one of countless many who have given their lives
proclaiming the message of love of Jesus.

Jean Vanier
L'Arche community, France

162. Secondary poverty: living in fear

A few weeks ago I had an appointment with my doctor to discuss my
latest blood monitoring test results. On the very same day in the
morning I received a call from a very worried friend who wanted me
to visit her sister who was finding it very difficult to accept her HIV+
status. This was a difficult request because I was supposed to pretend
not to know her status. I very begrudgingly agreed to visit her the
following day. I phoned the lady and she was very reluctant to invite
me to her home but eventually agreed to meet with me.

The discussion with the doctor also included helping me to
understand the link between HIV and depression. I made a
conscious decision to fight depression; I just could not afford to
entertain it.

I visited the lady in question the following day. I found her home
with the greatest of ease. She had a beautiful garden, which she later
told me, she tends herself. As she welcomed me into her home I was
struck by a heavy negative aura that filled her lovely house. It was
clear that she was not poor, yet I felt she was very poor because of the
heavy aura of anger, depression and fear. I was personally challenged
to the core by all this negativity within a context that was supposed
to be happy and healthy.

As I reflected on this experience, I was reminded of the woman in
Mark 5:24–34, the woman who had suffered from haemorrhages for
twelve years. She had spent all she had on doctors who could not help

her (v. 26). In a Jewish context her condition made her impure or unclean. After hearing about Jesus, she said to herself that if she could only touch the hem of his garment she would be healed. 'Her action violated the social code for proper female behaviour and religious law.' This to me sounds like a very bold step; it does not sound like something that could be done by someone who lived in fear. It is likely that this condition had isolated her from others who feared being infected. But she went ahead and touched Jesus' garment.

After her healing, Jesus wanted to know who had touched him. Judging from their response, his disciples thought his question did not make sense. But obviously Jesus knew something they did not know. It is only when the crowd knew her secret, that of touching Jesus, that she was filled with fear and trembling. The most important issue though is that she was healed.

Exactly what made her fearful and trembling? Was it the crowd or her confession? Jesus calls her daughter to show his unconditional acceptance. He also acknowledges the fact that it is her faith that had healed her.

Coming back to the woman I visited, how can a professional woman with all the resources and skills she needs live in fear of it being found out that she is HIV+, of being rejected, despised, undermined, discriminated (the list continues)? She has suffered greatly because of this fear and has even attempted suicide. I shared my story with her because I did not know what else to say. I also, of course, represented the very community that had forced her to live in fear. I was relieved when she decided to share her story with me. It was only then that we could discuss the available resources and possibilities for living positively for a long time.

What is our role as activists, communities and churches, in the creation of this cloud of fear, discriminatory myths and judgemental assertions that force those of us who are different or infected to live in fear? How much have we done to destigmatise HIV and AIDS and eliminate discrimination? Have we deprived people of opportunities to liberate, empower and inspire others or have we created an environment of love and acceptance? Without addressing the issue of fear in the lives of those living with HIV and AIDS, we still have a long way to go.

This prevents people from asking for relevant help or support.

This decreases the chances of people accessing the available resources.

This promotes a culture of dishonesty between partners.

Let us break the spirit of fear by encouraging people to be themselves, giving them the freedom to choose whether to disclose their status or not.

(Psalm 55:12–14; Psalm 56:1–4)

Phumzile Zondi-Mabizela
South Africa

Prayers

163. In the rising of the Easter dawn,
Christ is risen.
In the laughter of children at play during a ceasefire,
Christ is risen.
Where the hungry celebrate with feasting,
Christ is risen.
Where people find their voices and sing their songs,
Christ is risen.
When enemies give up violence and become friends,
Christ is risen.
When love is allowed to flourish and grow into community,
Christ is risen.
We welcome you our crucified and risen Christ,
Christ is risen, Alleluia.

Clare McBeath

164. A prayer of praise

Humble God,
born into the shabbiness
and dullness
of a dimly lit stable,
we glimpsed your glory then,
amid the dirt and din
of domesticated animals,
amid the blood and toil
of human birth.

Humble God,
living amidst the poverty
and ordinariness
of simple, down-to-earth folk,
we glimpsed your glory then,
in meeting and touching
the outcasts and untouchables,
in sharing bread, wine and stories
with tax collectors and sinners.

Humble God,
dying in the pain
and despair
of a torturer's cross,
we glimpsed your glory then,
in speaking kind words
with common criminals,
in concern and forgiveness
for those who had put you to death.

Humble God,
rising in the quiet
and beauty
of a garden tomb,
we glimpsed your glory then,
in the emptiness of the tomb.
'He is not here! He is risen!'
in the astonishment and disbelief
as women ran to tell the story.

Humble God,
risen with us now
in the fragile miracles
of human life,
we glimpse your glory now,
in the love, laughter and beauty
we share with one another,
in the depths of humanity,
as we respond to the needs and suffering of our world.
Amen.

Clare McBeath

165. Litany of resurrection

What if ... the women keeping vigil at the foot of the cross
witnessed not the cruel, senseless death of a revolutionary
but the torture and crucifixion of many people's lives?

What if ... the women crying outside a garden tomb
mourned not the emptiness and loss of a teacher
but the silencing and annihilation of many people's lives?

What if ... the women shocked into talking with angels
spoke not of the disappearance of a body
but proclaimed the presence of the risen Christ?

He is here, his presence is with us.

What if ... heaven and hell are not beyond-the-grave dreams
but here-and-now realities?

What if ... death is not revenge at the hands of an angry god
but the embracing of suffering by Christ's outstretched
arms?

What if ... crucifixion is not the passive acceptance of a
father's will but our struggle to overcome violence and
injustice?

He is here, his presence is with us.

What if ... women flinging insults and abuse across the
Holy Cross divide can form a friendship based on trust
and the beginnings of understanding?

What if ... instead of smiling with veiled eyes across a clinic
waiting room we could share the joys and frustrations of
shaping a new life?

What if ... instead of merely nodding to my asylum-seeking
neighbour our children could become friends?

He is here, his presence is with us.

What if ... the work of caring and nurturing was valued
more than juggling figures on a page?

What if ... the peace keepers put down their guns
            and became peace and justice makers?

What if ... we didn't just share bread around a piece of church
            furniture but had the courage to share bread across the
            world?

Not 'what ifs ... ?' We have rolled back the stone.
He is here, his presence is in us and among us.
The peace of the risen Christ be with you.
And also with you.

Clare McBeath

166. Arise

Lord Jesus Christ,
why have we forsaken you?
We see the goodness of your world lost and divided.
We hear you cry out.
We witness your hunger and your thirst.
We see you powerless and broken.
For we have tortured and wounded you.
Again and again we see you crucified
not once on Calvary
but here and now
in the Name of God.

Why are we persecuting you?

Arise Lord, arise.
You are the Prince of Peace.
You are the giver of life.
Yes, arise Lord, arise in us:
give us the courage of your Spirit
to forgive with your forgiveness
to heal with your healing
to speak out with your truth
to transform with your power
and to dare to love with a love that can never be defeated
now and for ever.
Amen.

Richard Carter

167. freedom

the elusive one;
once caught always lost
once lost always found
where is she to be searched for?
when does she discover you?

they look for her in their books
and search for her in their stratagems;
by policy papers and wordy manifestos
they fail to imprison her laughter.

they seek her in empty corridors
echoing with the sounds of powerless dictators
dined to bloating on their own importance
fed to obesity by a diet of propaganda.

they seek her in the warmth of missiles
and search for her among a bed of nuclear pillows
pulling back the blanket of macho security
to reveal the nakedness of fear.

they seek her in the words of hatred
where prejudice becomes the scapegoat's friend
and bullying the national sport
of nations too ashamed of difference.

they seek her in your heart
where she lies dormant
emptied of enthusiasm
lazy through lack of exercise
exhausted by inactivity.

freedom

the elusive one;
when will they learn
she is not a place but a sound
not a word but a whisper
not a weapon but a heart
not a prize but a gift?

when will they learn?

when freedom imprisons hate
and freezes out fear.

                                              Donald Macaskill

168. Broken bread

An Easter prayer, that our experience of the Eucharist may lead us to take action on behalf of the poor, especially those who live with hunger.

God, whom we meet in bread and wine,
in body broken and blood outpoured,
fill us with your compassion,
that we may hear the cries of the hungry
and reach out to those in need.
Engender in us a thirst for justice,
that the hungry will be satisfied
and the rich sent empty away.
Roll away our apathy
that, with arms outstretched,
we may offer life in place of death
and hope in the face of despair.
Amen.

                                         Annabel Shilson-Thomas

169. Overcoming the cross of hunger

An Easter prayer calling on us to move from apathy to action, from death to resurrection.

Risen Lord,
shed your light on those who live in the shadow of death
and warm the hearts of those who have lost hope,
that they who daily bear the cross of hunger
may find your Promised Land,
and move from slavery to freedom.
As we proclaim your Easter song
help us to die to greed and rise to justice,
to abandon apathy and take up action,

that rich and poor together may travel the road to freedom,
and be restored to your resurrection life. Amen.

Annabel Shilson-Thomas

170. Resurrection light

*Easter intercessions, asking that the light of Christ's resurrection may
lead us from despair and fear to hope and action.*

Risen Christ,
when darkness overwhelms us
may your dawn beckon.
When fear paralyses us
may your touch release us.
When grief torments us
may your peace enfold us.
When memories haunt us
may your presence heal us.
When justice fails us
may your anger ignite us.
When apathy stagnates us
may your challenge renew us.
When courage leaves us
may your Spirit inspire us.
When despair grips us
may your hope restore us.
And when death threatens us
may your resurrection light lead us. Amen.

Annabel Shilson-Thomas

171. An Easter prayer
(John 20:1–18)

ALL: **Good news!**
Glad tidings!
Christ is risen!

ONE: Gracious Lord,
like Mary we celebrate your resurrection.
As you were made known to her that first day of the week long
ago,

make yourself known to us today.

We rejoice as you call us by name, O Lord,
and we follow you.

ALL: **Good news!**
Glad tidings!
Christ is risen!

ONE: Loving Lord,
we tell the Easter story again and again,
from the shouts of Hosanna on Palm Sunday,
into the shadows of Maundy Thursday.
Who will keep watch with you?
Who will stand with you?
Your disciples disappear into the darkness.
Their resolve dissolves.
Denial.

Detained.
Assaulted.
Battered.
Like a detainee of today shuttled from pillar to post.
From Pilate to Herod, from court to court.

Crucified.
Yet, even from the cross you plead for us,
'Forgive them for they know not what they do.'

We rejoice as you call us by name, O Lord,
and we follow you.

ALL: **Good news!**
Glad tidings!
Christ is risen!

ONE: Lord of life,
we rejoice this Easter because death has loosed its grip on you.
The tomb cannot hold you.
The stone is rolled away.
The burial cloths testify to your triumph over death.
We sing our hymns of rejoicing to you,

because even as you are freed from death so are we.

We rejoice as you call us by name, O Lord,
and we follow you.

ALL: **Good news!**
Glad tidings!
Christ is risen!

ONE: Lord of justice,
even as we rejoice, we pause.
For we know all is not right in the world.
All is not as you desire.
You are crucified again and again, laid in a grave, a stone
sealing your tomb.
You weep with children who are left behind as they hunger and
thirst for the basics of life.
In them you are crucified anew.
You weep with the elderly who are neglected, forgotten, alone.
In them you are crucified anew.
You weep with the workers whose jobs are sent abroad in the
name of globalisation.
In them you are crucified anew.
You weep with the victims of violence.
In them you are crucified anew.

Yet, we rejoice as you call us by name, O Lord,
and we follow you.

ALL: **Good news!**
Glad tidings!
Christ is risen!

ONE: Risen Lord, you have conquered death.
In our baptisms we die to an old way of life and are born into
new life in you.
We are not afraid.
Not afraid to face up to the powers and principalities that
confront us,
Not afraid to work for justice,
Not afraid to say, 'This evil shall not stand.'
Not afraid to say, 'No longer shall the powerful go away sated

and satisfied and the weak go away hungry and hopeless.'
You are risen today and we proclaim you Lord of all.

We rejoice as you call us by name, O Lord.
Swell our hearts that they might be full of your love.
Open our eyes that we might recognise you in our world.
Unplug our ears that we might hear your cries.
Strengthen our hands that we might reach out to you.
Fortify us that we might have the courage to face the task.
Empower us to truly follow you.

ALL: **Good news!**
Glad tidings!
Christ is risen!
Christ is risen indeed!
Alleluia!
Amen.

Ana and Tod Gobledale

172. A prayer litany for Easter morning at the tomb

1ST VOICE: Woman, why are you weeping?
1ST WOMAN: We mourn these dark days of death and denial.
Abandoned, betrayed, forsaken.
Left alone. Jesus gone.
Where have they laid him?

1ST VOICE: Woman, why are you weeping?
2ND WOMAN: We are afraid for our Lord.
Humiliated in both life and death.
Robbed from the grave.
O where have they laid him?

2ND VOICE: Mary, do not hold onto me.

1ST VOICE: Women, why are you weeping?
WOMEN: We weep for Jesus, missing.
We weep for Columbian kin, missing.
We weep for children entangled in bitter domestic
disputes, missing.

1ST VOICE:	Men, why are you weeping?
MEN:	We weep for Jesus, humiliated and tortured.
	We weep for all political prisoners, suffering at the hands of oppressors.
	We weep for Muslims vilified by world powers and the media.
	We weep for peaceful protestors violently opposed.
1ST VOICE:	Women, why are you weeping?
WOMEN:	We weep for Jesus, abandoned and alone.
	We weep for the elderly, separated from family and community.
	We weep for children, orphaned by AIDS.
	We weep for our young, devastated by war.
2ND VOICE:	Do not hold on to me as I was.
	For I am with you, now, in the least of these.
	As you weep for them, you weep for me.
	As you serve them, you serve me.
ALL:	**Alleluia! Christ is risen!**
	Christ lives in the gardener,
	in the immigrant who mows our lawns and trims our shrubs.
	Christ lives in the teacher,
	the day care worker who minds our children.
	Christ lives in the tortured,
	the prisoners of 'the war on terrorism'.
	Christ lives in those for whom we weep.
	Alleluia!
	Christ is risen!
	Christ is risen indeed!

Ana Gobledale

173. Life goes on

On our TV screens,
if nowhere else,
we have heard and seen
the horrors of death and destruction.

What to be done?
Have we an option
beyond that of wringing our hands?

Remember we not
the Calvary Hill and
where Mary stood?

Remember his chosen friends.
How they ran from him
and were yet forgiven?

Did he not come to bring life?
and life goes on.

And the part for us,
involved no more
than at second hand,
is to believe.
To live the promise
he gave his life to bring:
to live on in the hope of his Word.

                                         Frances Makower RSCJ

174. Risen Christ, conqueror of death,
       bringer of new life, source of all love,
       we pray for justice.

       We pray for old people,
       for comfort, for healing, for hope,
       for your good news to the poor.
       Risen Christ,
       hear our prayer.

       We pray for the people of middle years,
       for strength, for vision, for hope,
       for freedom, for the prisoners.
       Risen Christ,
       hear our prayer.

We pray for young parents,
for resources, for food and clean water,
for recovery of sight to the blind.
Risen Christ,
hear our prayer.

We pray for children and babies,
for peace, for health, for far opportunities,
for release for the oppressed.
Risen Christ,
hear our prayer.

Mighty Jesus, your death and resurrection
changed the world for ever.
May the effects of that event
spread to all places of oppression and injustice.
May we know the year of the Lord's favour.
Amen.

Pam Macnaughton

175. God gives us power

God has given us the power

to create beauty
to make another smile
to be a healing presence in someone's sorrow
to bring justice to the oppressed
to console those in difficulty
to bring peace and joy to others
to help those in need
to laugh and enjoy life
to do good and turn from evil
to forgive those who have hurt us
and, most of all, to love.

Let us pray that God will continue to grace us with his love and mercy
and to spread that love to others during our journey.

Iris Perez
USA

176. Christ who was homeless, bless the wanderers.
          Christ who was hungry, bless the needy.
          Christ who was crucified, bless the fearful.
          Christ who was raised to life on Easter Day,
          Grant freedom and hope to suffering mankind.

                                              Christine Odell

Pentecost and Trinity Sunday

When the disciples were filled with the Holy Spirit and began to speak in other tongues, there were dwelling in Jerusalem Jews and devout people from every nation under heaven. And at this sound the multitude came together and they were bewildered, because each one heard them speaking in their own language. And they were amazed and wondered, saying 'Are not all these who are speaking Galileans? And how is it that we hear, each of us in our own language?'

(Acts 2:4–8)

Pentecost is the birthday of the Church. As with other newborn babies, there is lots of noise and wind. The Holy Spirit has been poured upon this tiny Jewish community. And yet there are signs of what is to come. These Galileans are understood by people from all over the Roman Empire as speaking in their own languages. This is a sign that this newborn baby has a global future. It is destined to be stretched open to all human cultures. What does this mean for us who seek a more just world?

We are endlessly told that we live in the global village. Humanity has been trying to cover the entire planet ever since some of us left Africa a few hundred thousand years ago. It seems to be part of being human. Now for the first time there is almost instant communication around the globe. It is true that many people, especially in Africa, are excluded from active participation in this communication. It is sometimes estimated that as many as 65 per cent of all human beings have never used a phone. And yet there is a degree of interconnectedness that we could never have dreamed of even twenty years ago. Is this what the Kingdom will look like? Is this a sort of realisation of Pentecost?

In some ways globalisation is wonderful. Never before have we been so much in contact with people from other cultures. Potentially it may bring tremendous wealth and richness to humanity. It would be stupid to simply reject it. On the other hand, it is a sort of Babel, and Pentecost was seen as the reversal of Babel. Babel is a symbol of all the efforts of human beings to impose unity on humanity, a unity which suffocates. 'Let us make a name for ourselves, lest we be scattered abroad.' It is a unity which is destructive.

Our global village is surely both a blessing and a curse. It is a blessing because human beings now have unprecedented contact with other cultures and traditions. We are beginning to recognise that we are truly each other's brothers and sisters. But the global village is also a curse because it is held together by trade which not only enriches but also impoverishes.

It is also knit together by violence. There are the bonds of the drug trade, the sale of arms, of money laundering, the criminal mafias, prostitution, the diamond trade and the sale of body parts. No one escapes those networks. Africa may be largely excluded from the networks of investment and legitimate trade, but civil wars in places like the Congo and Angola tie the continent in with the sale of arms, diamonds and minerals. Colombia may be marginal to many forms of legitimate economic trade, and yet, like Afghanistan, it is a centre of the drug trade. The feature film *Maria Full of Grace*, a joint production between the United States and Colombia, is the story of a young woman who becomes a mule, smuggling drugs from Colombia to the States. She has to swallow condoms filled with cocaine. If they burst in her stomach, then she dies. If she is caught, she will be imprisoned. If she fails to deliver her cargo, then she will be killed. One of her companions becomes sick, and so the drug barons in New York rip open her stomach to retrieve the drugs which are worth more than her life. But for Maria this is the only way to freedom and security for herself and her unborn child.

In the global village, hundreds of languages are spoken, and yet there is one dominant language, which is that of money. Everything can be converted into money and money into everything. Money is becoming ever more intangible, like a hideous parody of the Holy Spirit. It is just digits that twinkle on a screen. Money rules. Governments have to submit to the demands of money, especially if they are poor. If nations try to protect their fragile economies from the flow of money, then they will be threatened with the withdrawal of aid. If workers make problems or demand higher wages, then money moves and the workers cannot follow it. We cannot accept the rule of money, which demands that we bend our knees in idolatry before the false god of wealth. We cannot accept the unity which money imposes, seeing everything in terms of wealth. Money is good but only if it is our servant and not our master.

The Galileans were understood at Pentecost as speaking in all the languages of the then known world. We celebrate it not by imposing any language or culture or mentality, but by cherishing the voices that speak in the thousands of languages and traditions of our world. We prepare for the coming of the Holy Spirit among us by helping those who have no voice to be heard.

Agencies like CAFOD and Christian Aid support small radio stations all over the world so that those who are normally silent can be heard. This is what this meant to one Andean peasant woman:

> Yes, that was her voice coming out of the magical apparatus! The magic machine where only President Balaguer spoke, where Johnny Ventura and Fernandino Villalona sang and where Bishop Rivas gave his blessing ... All her life everyone had told her to shut up: her dad, her teacher, her husband, the priests, even her children. As they say around here, women should be seen but not heard. For years they had convinced her that she was only good for working, in the kitchen and in bed. But always in silence, obedient. Now her voice was coming out over the radio and her friend Hipólita, her neighbours and all her family were listening.[1]

The Holy Spirit does not give us a divine Esperanto so that we can all speak the same language. It works within us in a more beautiful and subtle way, making us attentive to other accents, other human stories. In the era of the national state, the Church's role was often to be witnesses to the transnational, the global. Today, faced with

1. *Making Waves: a thematic review of CAFOD supported community radio projects in Latin America*, p. 19.

globalisation, perhaps we must cherish the local voices and the small stories. Doing so will stretch open our hearts and our minds to strangers, so that slowly human beings learn to speak with the spaciousness of the Word of God. Then we shall gradually begin to glimpse what it might mean to be children of the Kingdom.

Reflections

177. Pentecost

Her image is permanently imprinted on my mind, as if she had been, spiritually, a branding iron. In the morning we had walked the slums of an Indian mega-city, where our colleagues worked among the people. Oh, I already *knew* about such things. In the cool, clean, comfort of my first-world country, we had tried to inform ourselves about the precarious existence of these 'others' – so that we might *know* our own complicity, *do* something about it, *live* with a new gratitude.

Around noon we came upon a vacant lot. It served as a rubbish tip. There sat the woman at the edge of the tip, under the blazing sun, hair matted with sweat and dust, intent upon her squalid task, salvaging, piece by filthy piece, bits of plastic from the foul-smelling heap. The stench of refuse-filled open drains hung in the hot air. This was the place of the woman's 'employment', where she worked for her daily rice. We passed close by and I saw her face. What was she thinking? Appalled, I thought, 'She is somebody's family, she could be my own sister!' Suddenly it hit me: 'she *is* my sister!'

This happened a few days after Pentecost when, as often before, I had reflected on the first Pentecost – what had actually happened inside those people, how does the Pentecost experience happen in us?

Later it dawned on me. Wasn't that encounter with the woman an occasion of the Holy Spirit acting in me? Wasn't that confronting insight a small ray of the Pentecost experience? *Veni, lumen cordium*! Come, light of our hearts. For Pentecost is surely about seeing differently, with Christ's Spirit, bringing not so much new ideas as new enlightenment of the heart, impelling action. The Holy Spirit, Love Itself, *is* the very Spirit of solidarity, bridging every divide, transcending language and every other barrier. The One who teaches us to experience not 'others' but sisters and brothers is indeed the selfsame Spirit who cries 'Abba' in our hearts. Could I, even now, learn a new sensitivity to the presence of this Spirit, who alone can guide our work aright? *Come, Holy Spirit – come today!*

Gabrielle Kelly OP

178. Pentecost

On Pentecost 1977, Archbishop Oscar Romero of El Salvador observed that faithfulness to the Gospel brings with it persecution: 'Always when one preaches the truth against injustices, abuses and the trampling down of others, the truth has to hurt,' he said.

Romero practised what he preached in a land plagued by poverty and oppression. He spoke out against human rights violations. He admonished the powerful. He took the side of the common people, the poor and all those who were persecuted and tortured. And his voice cried out to the highest heavens for justice.

He once observed: 'At this moment, I know that I am being an instrument of the Spirit of God in his church to guide the people, and I can say like Christ: "The Spirit of the Lord is upon me; he has sent me to bring good news to the poor."'

On 24 March 1980, he paid the ultimate price for his faithfulness to the Spirit's command. While he was saying Mass, he was shot in the chest and tumbled to the floor by the altar. But his legacy, his spirit lives on in the Salvadoran people, as he had foretold.

Faithfulness to the Spirit's direction impels us to proclaim the reign of God with courage no matter what the price. For this we need inspiration, to be set on fire by the Spirit.

The Spirit descends where it wills, in tongues of fire or in the whispers of the wind. As the Infant Jesus Sisters prayed during their General Chapter in France in 2001: 'Your spirit is blowing within each of our hearts ... sometimes like a gust of wind and sometimes like a gentle breeze. And we ask: "Lord, in what direction is the breath of your Spirit leading us?"'

In the sequence for the feast of Pentecost, the Church prays to the Holy Spirit: 'Without your strength, nothing is in humanity, nothing without blame. Wash what is dirty, bathe what is dry, heal what is bleeding. Bend what is rigid, heat what is cold, straighten what is bent.'

May we always be faithful to the Spirit of Pentecost by our actions for justice and the risks we take for peace, by our courage to proclaim the Spirit, who heals the broken-hearted and sets the captives free, who opens prison doors and makes the blind to see.

Anil Netto

179. Pentecost: an experience of love?

While I was talking to a colleague about Pentecost, he remarked that it is an experience of love. This phrase struck me because I have always understood Pentecost as a feast of harvest for the Jews (at the completion of the grain harvest), and also as the anniversary of the sealing of the law at Mount Sinai, fifty days after the exodus. In the New Testament Pentecost is the day when the Holy Spirit descended on the disciples giving them new life and power to continue the work that Jesus had began. So I began thinking about it and continued the conversation. Can this event be understood as an experience of love?

Surely for Christians the experience of Pentecost empowers them to show love to all, irrespective of colour, language or gender. This experience, transcending the language barrier, embraced not only the disciples, but also hundreds of strangers who heard them. Not only were the disciples able to hear one another, but others were able to hear the disciples. This was the true gift of Pentecost – bringing people together. The following stories show something of this experience being put into practice.

In solidarity with those working on flower farms

Flowers are a great thing to have in our homes and our churches. They colour our occasions or ceremonies. Yet we often fail to understand the difficulties of those who work in the flower farms. Their problems include starvation wages, arbitrary dismissal, often no health, maternity or other benefits, sexual harassment of women workers and inability to form unions which could speak on their behalf. These workers are also exposed to chemicals, which cause infertility, lung damage, skin reactions, fainting, stomach problems, miscarriage and reduced vision.

Anita has worked in a flower farm for a number of years. A year ago while she was harvesting flowers in the greenhouse, her colleague sprayed the flowers with chemicals. This affected her eyes and she began losing her eyesight. The company sent her for medical attention. The diagnosis recorded that she had severe allergic conjunctivitis around the left eye with secondary bacterial infection. The doctor explained that she was reacting to the chemicals she was exposed to in the course of duty. She was either to be moved to another job or given goggles to protect her eyes. The management refused to do anything about it and she lost her eyesight. The company then terminated her contract to work.

However, her fellow workers have stood with her and have continued to agitate for the rights of the workers. Some flower farms are now taking precautionary measures.

Stigma on those affected by and infected with HIV and AIDS

Ngendo had AIDS and no one in her church would visit her. As a committed member of her churchwomen's group, she was deeply hurt when rumours started to spread through the group that she had AIDS because she had sinned. Others refused to visit, fearing that they might get AIDS from being close to her. She continued to attend the church services even when people did not want to spend time with her.

One day a visiting preacher talked about the Holy Spirit and the power to live a new life. Ngendo's pain and isolation turned to productivity. She refused to give in to the false rumours about her. She devoted all her days to educating community groups about AIDS, concentrating on church groups. She believed the church should be in the forefront of the struggle to prevent AIDS and to care compassionately for all those affected by AIDS. Through this action, Ngendo has helped her church to start dealing with the issues of stigma towards people who are infected and affected with HIV and AIDS.

Rescue centre for girls escaping early marriages

The practice of early marriage in some African communities is common. Some girls are betrothed when they are young; others are married when they reach puberty or when they are finishing their primary school education. Marriage at this age destroys their chances of having a good education and being able to join the decision-makers in society to make a difference. They end up joining the circle of illiterate and poverty-stricken groups. For most of them their future is ruined. Both the church and the government speak about the evils of early marriages but only a few groups or individuals take up the case of rescuing the girls from early marriages.

Mary's story

Mary had just finished her primary school and was preparing for secondary school. One day her father came home with an old man who was to marry her. Mary refused this old man but she was taken by force because this man had paid a dowry. When members of the local church heard that Mary had been taken away, they began looking for her. They found out where she was, rescued her and took her to the church centre for girls who are forced to marry young. Mary has now finished her schooling and joined a group that is campaigning against early marriages for girls.

In our broken world, how else shall we understand the Pentecost
if not as God's gift of unifying and reconciling the world to God's self
through Christ, through that fire of love, which burns away all disunity and preserves that ultimate unity which characterises God's very
being.

Esther Mombo
Kenya

180. *'Have you anything here to eat?' They gave him a piece of grilled fish
and he took it and ate it in their presence.*
(Luke 24:41–43)

We need to look at what *our* resurrection means
in the light of the resurrection of Jesus.

We are truly men and women of resurrection
because that which we yearn for has already happened.
This new life, new birth, is given at baptism
when we are reborn in the Holy Spirit.
Yet it also remains so hidden and unassuming:
like a tiny seed
that grows and develops in the vulnerable earth of our being.

We are a wounded, broken people,
our reactions springing from fear and anguish.
Our vulnerable hearts are so frightened of pain and rejection
that we put up barriers.
But if we allow the Holy Spirit to enter into our hearts,
they will be changed and transformed, little by little,
through her presence.

Jean Vanier
L'Arche Community, France

Prayers

181. Pentecost

Spirit of truth
whom the world can never grasp,

touch our hearts
with the shock of your coming;
fill us with desire
for your disturbing peace;
and fire us with longing
to speak your uncontainable word
through Jesus Christ.
Amen.

Janet Morley

182. Chosen by God

'I chose you and appointed you.'
(John 15:16)

Galvanised
by your Spirit, O Lord,
we torch the fire
with passion.
Energised
courageous
determined
bold.
Touched
by the flame of
compassion, O Lord,
let our quest be
freedom
justice
truth
hearts burnishing with
your love.

Margaret McNulty

183. A morning prayer

Mysterious and Loving God,
open my mind and my heart this day
that I might lose myself in wonder and awe
at the glory and grandeur of your creation.
May I grow each day in awareness
of my unique place in your loving universe.

All-caring God,
allow your energy and compassion to flow through me
towards all who are in pain,
all who are alone and frightened,
all who feel lost and confused,
and above all towards those who endure cruelty and injustice.

Mysterious Divine Healer,
in everything I think and say and do this day,
make me a finger of your healing hand.
Make me sensitive to the wounds and brokenness
of all my brothers and sisters,
the good, the bad and the indifferent.
May they heal me as we all stretch out our hands to one another.

For we are all one in you and your Holy Spirit, through your Son,
Jesus Christ.
Amen.

Albert Nolan OP
South Africa

184. Spirit of Pentecost

Spirit of God,
enlighten our hearts and minds that we may see the faces of our sisters and brothers whose labour provides us with the food we eat, the clothes we wear and the computers, phones and washing machines we use.
Spirit of God come to us.

Spirit of God,
embolden us to speak out on behalf of those who suffer injustice, so that they may enjoy the fruits of their labour and have enough to feed, clothe, nurse and educate their families.
Spirit of God come to us.

Spirit of God,
consume us with a passion to change our way of life. May we put the needs of others before our desire for more possessions at bargain prices.
Spirit of God come to us.

Spirit of God,
through the witness of our lives,
standing in solidarity with all peoples,
may we spread
the warmth of your love,
the light of your wisdom,
and the fire of your justice,
so that all may live in peace and security.
Amen.

Sue Cooper

185. Spirit of Pentecost, Life-giving Spirit

In a world of so much poverty, where hunger and exclusion lurk in the corners of our cities and villages and consume the lives of millions of the poor.

In a world where governmental and international policies do not come to the aid of those most in need of succour.

In a world where small acts of charity may only create more dependency.

Wild bird of Pentecost, Spirit of gentleness, give us the strength to work for transformation. Reawaken in us the power of dreaming and acting with conviction for justice and peace.

Spirit of Pentecost, Life-giving Spirit, you are our hope.

In a world where wealth, avarice and the desire to possess lurk in the corners of our hearts and consume the lives of some, in all our contexts.

In a world where a never-ending quest for personal satisfaction threatens to destroy the fabric of our lives.

In a world where the acquisition of material goods burns into our lives.

Wild bird of Pentecost, Spirit of gentleness, give us the strength to work for transformation. Reawaken in us the power of dreaming and acting with conviction for justice and peace.

Spirit of Pentecost, Life-giving Spirit, you are our hope.

In a world where divisions among us lurk in every corner of our societies – a world where fear of the other, prejudice and intolerance threaten to break unity.

In a world where expression of racial or caste-based violence raises its ugly head once in a way. In a world where sexism and discrimination ensure that some half the population of our societies do not have access to the gifts of freedom and justice.

In a world where a small minority of people have the power to keep the majority in a position of powerlessness.

Wild bird of Pentecost, Spirit of gentleness, give us the strength to work for transformation. Reawaken in us the power of dreaming and acting with conviction for justice and peace.

Spirit of Pentecost, Life-giving Spirit, you are our hope.

In a world where greed and the desire to dominate and control the earth lurks in the corners of our hearts.

In a world where the earth and the things of the earth have been used and overused for human consumption.

In a world where the gifts of the earth, common goods such as fresh water, are now exploited, packaged and sold to those who have the means to pay for it.

In a world where science and technology move rapidly into new and extractive ways to make life even more comfortable for human beings (for some, not for the whole) at the cost of the environment.

Wild bird of Pentecost, Spirit of gentleness, give us the strength to work for transformation. Reawaken in us the power of dreaming and acting with conviction for justice and peace.

Spirit of Pentecost, Life-giving Spirit, you are our hope. In you lies our power. Amen.

Aruna Gnanadasan
World Council of Churches

186. Gentle God,
who, in Jesus Christ,
showed us humility and compassion,
we thank You for your gracious love.
Forgive our sin of pride and apathy,
empower us to struggle for justice.
For the sake of the most oppressed
and totally broken in body and spirit.

Compassionate Jesus,
teach us to be true disciples
in our times
in all places today.
Enable us to change attitudes and structures

that enslave.
Give us eyes to see and hearts to be.

Divine Wisdom, Holy Spirit,
in your grace, transform the world
in us, through us.
Cleanse our hearts and renew our spirits.
With serving hands and liberating actions,
we humbly pray for courage and inspiration
to do your will beginning today.

In Jesus' name, we hope and pray,
Amen.

Elizabeth S. Tapia
The Philippines

187. Creating and re-creating God
our hope is in you.
Hear our cries and laments.
Bless our vision for
transformed relations
sustainable communities
a pacific, peace-loving world.

Holy God, creative Power
our strength is in you.
We long for you.
Guide us, inspire us
as we join in the dance of life.

In your grace, and in the mission of our Lord
Jesus Christ,
abundant life is offered and is possible.
In your transforming grace and power
we become a people of joy.

In the name of the Triune God, we pray.
Amen.

Elizabeth S. Tapia
The Philippines

188. Proclaiming global justice at Pentecost

Holy Spirit,
give us
tongues of fire and inspire us
to speak of justice without fear or prejudice.
Change us
so that the language of liberation may spread from our lips
as we challenge the economics of oppression.
Teach us
to understand the sufferings of workers who are forced to labour in
   sweatshops round the world.
Guide us
to recognise the temptations of consumer choice and to dedicate
   ourselves to universal human rights.
Make us
raise our voices by shouting out loud the good news and proclaim
   global justice for all.

Tony Singleton

189.

We shall go out with gratitude within us
for signposts, guides and waymarks in our lives,
and friendships formed in laughter and in sadness;
for when we sense support, our hearts revive.

May we in strength fulfil the needs of others,
not let our fear destroy the truth within.
May we seek justice for a whole creation
and stay in tune with one who is our origin.

We praise this source of all that is created,
the model of our creativity.
May we be one with all that is life-giving,
not lose our way in negativity.

For we would walk in happiness and sorrow,
yet keep in touch with wellsprings deep inside.
So shall we come to know abundant living,
and share in God a love that is both deep and wide.

(Tune: Londonderry Air/O Danny Boy)
June Boyce-Tillman

190. Liberator Lord

To those whose lives are bitter, the poor and dispossessed,
your word is one of justice, of balance redressed,
the riches of creation, a commonwealth possessed.
May your Spirit be upon us, our Liberator Lord.

To those who live in bondage of body and of mind,
who are prisoners of ignorance or the hatred of their kind,
your word is one of liberty, the captive to unbind.
May your Spirit be upon us, our Liberator Lord.

To those whose eyes are blinded, who will or dare not see,
your word is calling softly – come face reality
and in it the dear truth, your lives will precious be.
May your Spirit be upon us, Liberator Lord.

To those who know the anguish of love that cannot flower,
whose race or class or gender define another's power,
your work is one of freedom to grow and not to cower.
May your Spirit be upon us, our Liberator Lord.

You have spoken through the prophets and saints of history,
through the sobbing of the voiceless and the groans of the unfree,
and your voice is still proclaiming, 'Now you must speak for me.'
May your Spirit be upon us, Liberator Lord.

Kathy Galloway

191. A responsorial prayer

God of healing and hope,
we bring before you now all who live with HIV and AIDS,
families and communities broken and struggling to survive.
Give them the strength and courage of your peace.

In the power of the Spirit,
bless all who offer loving care and who work to sustain and rebuild
    communities.
God of healing, God of hope,
Save us and help us.

God of knowledge and understanding,

we bring before you now all those deceived by ignorance and rumour;
all those possessed by prejudice and fear;
all who act harshly and oppressively.
Give them the freedom of your redeeming truth.

In the power of the Spirit,
bless all who work in AIDS prevention and education,
and who seek to raise awareness;
all who are searching for new forms of treatment.
God of knowledge, God of understanding,
Save us and help us.

God of love and faith,
we bring before you now all who are shunned and condemned by
their neighbours;
all who find themselves isolated and alone;
all who fear for their children's future without them;
all who are denied treatment;
all who are abused.
Give them the assurance of your unfailing love.

In the power of the Spirit,
bless all who welcome, support, befriend,
all who respect and value the dignity of fellow human beings,
all who take action on their behalf.
God of love, God of faith,
Save us and help us.
Amen.

Diakonia Council of Churches
South Africa

192. Bring about change

Creator God,
as we journey through this world
give us the grace to allow your Holy Spirit to work through us.
Help us to speak, think and work
with honesty, and compassion,
to celebrate all that is life-giving,
to restore hope where it has been lost,
and to bring about change where it is needed.

We ask this in the name of Jesus Christ, our companion.
Amen.

Ann Smith

193. May the spirit of the Lord rest upon us,
      may the call of God sustain us,
      as we seek to be God's people,
      transformed by the Gospel,
      announcing good news to the poor,
      proclaiming freedom for those in prisons
      of wealth, poverty, disease and disorder,
      committed to making a difference
      to the world's kingdoms
      for the sake of Christ's Kingdom.

May we deploy our resources as the Spirit guides,
not shirk difficult decisions about the priority of mission,
pledge ourselves anew to work with all our fellow Christians
and use the gifts of all God's people
so that all may be filled
with the Spirit of healing, justice and peace.
Amen.

URC Assembly prayer

194. *He was not the light, but came to bear witness to the light.*

(John 1:8)

We praise you, God, for all those who are 'not the light' and yet in
their words and actions bear witness to the light. Thank you for those
you call throughout history to proclaim the values of your Kingdom.
Thank you for calling us to be part of your mission.
We, too, are 'sent from God'.

We find it hard to live up to our calling. We rely too much on our own
strength, instead of opening ourselves to your Holy Spirit. We leave
mission to others.
We, too, are 'sent from God'.

We pray for people throughout the world in whom your image is
darkened: people traumatised by conflict, people without food,

people living with illness. Help us to play our part in working for
your better world.
We, too, are 'sent from God'.

May we be loving and brave in standing for justice and for all that
leads to light and truth. Give us a passion for your Gospel and a
vision of your Kingdom in which we are all included.
We, too, are 'sent from God'.

Gray Featherstone

195. A prayer for others

Move us to action, loving God,
so that we do not avoid the pain of the world by escapism,
but engage in work for justice and peace.

Move us to action, compassionate God,
so that we do not care only for ourselves or our own,
but care for all those in need, friends and stranger alike.

Move us to action, healing God,
so that we do not aim simply for our own health,
but share our resources with all who are dis-eased.

Move us to action, friendly God,
so that we do not exclude those different from us,
but welcome with generous hospitality those in need.

Move us to action, wonderful God,
so that we do not lie lukewarm in apathy,
but give ourselves in courage and daring for your cause.

In the power and grace of the Spirit of Christ,
we offer ourselves and our prayer,
for you to make us your wonder.
Amen.

Terry Oakley

196. Why are you waiting, people of the living God?
We are waiting for forgiveness.

Our brother dies of cholera upon our television screens.
Our sister screams her hatred in our city streets.
Our father turned to vapour in our bright atomic sun.
Our mother sleeps in doorways, dies, forgotten in a corner.
Our children choke on ozone, and will farm a ruined earth.

We seek forgiveness.
We did not wish for these things to happen,
but did not prevent them.

We dwell in quiet luxury through unjust terms of trade.
We seek the quiet life in face of prejudice and lies.
Our taxes gird us round with weapons and with armies,
but we do not care for Christ-like folk,
the poor, the damaged.
We drive our cars, we waste our food,
we pour filth on the waters.
We are involved in these sins, by our silence, by our weakness.

Do you turn from these things?
We do, God help us.
As he has promised, the Creator makes us new.
As he has promised, the Son sets us free.
As he has promised, the Spirit leads us into life.

Come, we shall sin no more, but live for God and justice.
Amen, Thanks be to God.

Extract from a prayer by Vince Gilbert

197. Affirming our faith

It is not true that this world and its inhabitants are doomed to die and
be lost;
This is true: for God so loved the world that he gave his only Son so
that everyone who believes in him shall not die, but have everlasting
life.

It is not true that we must accept inhumanity and discrimination,
hunger and poverty, death and destruction;
This is true: I have come that they may have life, and have it abun-
dantly.

It is not true that violence and hatred shall have the last word and that war and destruction have come to stay for ever;
This is true: for to us a child is born, to us a son is given, in whom authority will rest, and whose name will be prince of peace.

It is not true that we are simply victims of the powers of evil that seek to rule the world;
This is true: to me is given authority in heaven and earth, and lo, I am with you always, to the end of the world.

It is not true that we have to wait for those who are specially gifted, who are prophets of the church, before we can do anything;
This is true: I will pour out my Spirit on all people, and your sons and daughters shall prophesy, your young people shall see visions and your old folk shall dream dreams.

It is not true that our dreams of liberation of humankind, our dreams of justice, of human dignity and peace, are not meant for this earth and its history;
This is true: the hour comes, and it is now, that true worshippers shall worship God in spirit and in truth.

Adapted extract from presentation by Allan A. Boesak
South Africa

198. Prayer for the Holy Spirit

Lord God, we are waiting.
Send your Holy Spirit on us today – we are ready.
Open our ears to listen,
our mouths to speak,
and our hearts to be filled with love for you.
Blow us inside out with your wind.
Make us blaze with your power.
Change us. Transform your world. We are ready.
Amen.

Maggie Hindley

199. A prayer of supplication

Oh God, by your Spirit root out prejudice and selective love from our hearts, actions and speech. Make us friends towards people who are poor, disadvantaged, troubled or sick. Make your church a welcoming community, accepting of human diversity, made up of people who forgive the failings of others and who refuse to harbour grudges.

We pray for people trapped in a spiral of debt, under the pressure of mortgage payments, council tax, credit cards, rent or repayment of student loans. May they have access to sound advice and firm support and find ways to manage their money well.

We pray for people who are trying to build a new life for themselves after a prison sentence. May they find others who will trust and respect them.

We pray for the rich and powerful nations of the world, and powerful elites in poorer countries. May resources be moved from armaments and grandiose expenditure to the relief of poverty. May the crippling burden of Third World debt be eased by the debt's cancellation.

Amen.

Barry Vendy

200. Prayers of petition

When we are rejected and yearn to belong,
when we are isolated and long for company,
when we are lonely and miss our family,
Spirit of love, breathe on us.

When we are abused as children,
when we are despised as outsiders,
when we are exhausted by shame and guilt,
Spirit of healing, breathe on us.

When we are underpaid workers,
when we are tortured victims,
when we are hungry refugees,
Spirit of justice, breathe on us.

When we speak peace but act with violence,
when we preach love but practise hate,
when we shout liberation but live oppression,
Spirit of forgiveness, breathe on us.
Amen.

Beverley Humphries

201. The healing of your people

Loving Creator, you have made us in your image
and we yearn for the healing of all your people.
fill our hearts with the fire of your love
and our minds with a thirst for justice.
Embolden us to cry out against oppression,
empower us to work for the coming of your Kingdom,
and enrich us with your life-giving Spirit
so that all creation may feel your touch and be healed.
We ask this in the name of our crucified, risen Lord,
our liberator and redeemer, Jesus Christ.
Amen.

Annabel Shilson-Thomas

202. May the God who dances in creation,
who embraces us with human love,
who shares our lives like thunder,
bless us and drive us out with power
to fill the world with her justice.
Amen.

Janet Morley

203. Look upon us, O Lord,
and let all the darkness of our souls
vanish before the beams of thy brightness.
Fill us with holy love,
and open to us the treasures of thy wisdom.
All our desire is known unto thee,
therefore perfect what thou hast begun,
and what thy Spirit has awakened us to ask in prayer.
We seek thy face,
turn thy face unto us and show us thy glory.
Then shall our longing be satisfied,
and our peace shall be perfect.
Amen.

St Augustine (354–430)

204. Holy Spirit, giver of life and new beginnings, help us to faithfully respond to God's call to be ministers of reconciliation.
Come, Holy Spirit, renew us all.

Help us to find ways of encouraging people to open their hearts and confess their part in the past injustices and find ways to build a just and secure future for our children. Give us wisdom and courage in this difficult task. When the pressures of the situation make us despair, come with your Holy Spirit and renew our strength and hope.
Come, Holy Spirit, renew us all.

Sustain with your power those, who in the midst of all difficulties, are building quietly the culture of reconciliation, justice and peace. They may not be many right now, but we remember that the work for God's Kingdom among us started with only a handful of faithful and committed people.
Come, Holy Spirit, renew us all.

Come, Healing Spirit, and change us and open ways for us to change others. Remove all injustice and fill our land with a just peace. Remove all hatred and fill us all with true love.
Come, Holy Spirit, renew us all.

Remove all insecurity and bring in real security. Remove all occupation and bring in freedom for all.
Come, Holy Spirit, renew us all.
Merciful God, accept our prayer and yearning. You are the only strength we have. No one can take the power of prayer away from us. In the name of Jesus – our Liberator and Redeemer – we pray.
Amen.

Bishop Munib Younan
Evangelical Lutheran Church of Jordan and Palestine

205. O Lord,
you love justice and you establish peace on earth.
We bring before you the disunity of today's world;
the absurd violence, and the many wars,
which are breaking the courage of the peoples of the world;
human greed and injustice,
which breed hatred and strife.
Send your Spirit and renew the face of the earth;

teach us to be compassionate towards the whole human family;
strengthen the will of all those
who fight for justice and for peace,
and give us that peace which the world cannot give.
Amen.

From Monday morning worship in the Ecumenical Centre,
World Council of Churches

206. God,
We are created in your image.

The only way to show your peace and justice
is through us.

We are responsible for your world and
for each other.

Transform us through your Holy Spirit.

Open our eyes!

World Council of Churches

207. Lord Christ, you see us
sometimes like strangers on the earth,
taken aback by the violence,
by the harshness of oppositions.

And you come to send out a gentle breeze
on the dry ground of our doubts,
and so prepare us to be bearers
of peace and reconciliation.

Brother Roger of Taizé

208. Give us courage, O Lord, to stand up and be counted,
to be counted for those who cannot stand up for themselves,
to stand up for ourselves when it is needful for us to do so.
Let us fear nothing more than we fear you.
Let us love nothing more than we love you,

for then we shall fear nothing also.
Let us have no other god before you,
whether nation or party or state or church.
Let us seek no other peace but the peace which is yours,
and makes us its instruments,
opening our eyes and our ears and our hearts,
so that we should know always what work of peace
we may do for you.

Alan Paton

209. Lord Jesus,
when our lives have gone wrong
and we don't know how to put them right,
show us your love.
Teach us what we should do.

When our thinking is confused
and we don't know how to sort it out,
show us your love.
Teach us what we should do.

When our intentions are good
but we don't know how to put them into practice,
show us your love.
Teach us what we should do.
Lord Jesus,
you separate the wheat from the chaff,
the sheep from the goats;
help us to prepare for your coming.
Show us your love.
Teach us what we should do,
that we may be baptised with the Holy Spirit and with fire.
Amen.

Mary Cotes

210. Gracious and Holy Father,
give us wisdom to perceive you,
diligence to seek you,
patience to wait for you,
eyes to behold you,

a heart to meditate on you,
and a life to proclaim you;
through the power of the Spirit
of your Son, Jesus Christ our Lord.
Amen.

St Benedict

211. Give us, Lord, the determination, which no unworthy affection can
sap;
give us the strength, which no affliction can undermine;
give us the integrity, which nothing unworthy of you can destroy.
Pour upon us your Holy Spirit so that we may receive
understanding to know you,
persistence to seek you,
wisdom to find you,
faithfulness in the end to embrace you;
through your Son, Jesus Christ our Lord.
Amen.

St Thomas Aquinas

212. Almighty and everlasting God, thou lover of peace and concord, who
hast called us in Christ to love and unity: we pray thee so rule our
hearts by thy Holy Spirit, that we, being delivered by the true fear of
God from all fear of man, may evermore serve thee in righteousness,
mercy, humility and gentleness toward each other, through thy dear
Son Jesus Christ our Lord.
Amen.

Bunsen's Collection

Jesus Continues His Ministry

Ordinary Time 2

The day after Pentecost, we go back, in the liturgy, to ordinary time. Ordinary time sounds boring but, as I explained before (see page 79), it is not. It is about being ordered beyond ourselves. When we looked at the first block of 'ordinary time' we saw how Jesus summons us to belong to each other: 'I am because we are.' In this second period, the emphasis shifts towards how we are ordered towards God's Kingdom.

The colour of the vestments of ordinary time is green, the colour of life and fertility. Ordinary time is the time that is necessary for anything to grow. Jesus said, 'The kingdom of God is as if a man should scatter seed upon the ground, and should sleep and rise night and day, and the seed should sprout and grow, he knows not how. The earth produces of itself first the blade, then the ear, then the full grain in the ear. But when the grain is ripe, at once he puts in the sickle, because the harvest has come' (Mark 4:26–29).

Advent teaches us the excited patience of waiting for a birth. The time is limited and we can see the moment approaching as the mother's womb swells. Ordinary time teaches us the quieter patience needed when nothing appears to be happening at all. One of my brethren was out jogging and got hit by a bus. The accident took a few seconds. The knitting together of the bones takes months. So much time just sitting there, wasting time, getting bored, but meanwhile the body is quietly and invisibly repairing itself. So it is with the life of Jesus. After the drama of birth there were the quiet years of growing up, of which we know nothing, slowly maturing until he appears suddenly for baptism by John. There are then those years, perhaps three, of mission, of preaching, before the drama of death and resurrection.

Sometimes CAFOD and Christian Aid face dramas which grab the headlines, like the tsunami of 2004. Then everyone is motivated to acts of tremendous generosity; thousands of nurses and doctors fly out to the scenes of disaster, the churches are filled with people praying for the afflicted. But much of our commitment is in 'ordinary time'. This is the daily and patient collaboration with those in need, in small and undramatic projects which, we pray, quietly heal the body of humanity. This requires of us fidelity and patience, being in for the long haul. They will produce no headlines and will be largely unnoticed and yet they are fundamental for the greening of humanity as we make our imperceptible way towards the Kingdom.

Thomas Aquinas, a thirteenth-century Dominican friar, taught that the essence of courage is endurance. Courage is not at its core the macho virtue of the aggressive but the quiet strength of those who carry on. G. K. Chesterton reminds us that we all owe our existence to the courage of our mothers who endured nine months of pregnancy. Then there are the long years of courage, as our parents raise us. There is daily courage in getting out of bed to face another day. It may be another day of working in an AIDS clinic, when levels of infection go on rising; another day of meetings in which we try to see how we can best work in partnership with groups from a different culture, day after day after day; another day addressing envelopes. Often it may look as if nothing at all is being achieved, and yet the seed is slowly germinating in the soil.

The temptation is to despair of achieving anything. Is it all a waste of time? This is Macbeth's sense of futility, of 'to-morrow, and to-morrow, and to-morrow, creeps in this petty pace from day to day'. This is the temptation to think that life 'is a tale told by an idiot, full of sound and fury, signifying nothing'. But ordinary time is ordered time. It expresses the faith that human beings are destined to flourish. The green of ordinary time is the statement of our conviction that God intends human beings to arrive at the fullness of being, and that we shall do. If nothing much appears to be happening, then it is because the deepest changes are often invisible. We talk of watching the grass grow. One cannot see it happening and yet it does! 'For as the rain and the snow come down from heaven, and return not thither but water the earth, making it bring forth and sprout, giving seed to the sower and bread to the eater, so shall my word be that goes forth from my mouth; it shall not return to me empty, but it shall accomplish that which I purpose, and prosper in the thing for which I sent it' (Isaiah 55:10–11).

The Christian is one who waits for the Lord. But we do not wait passively. All the labouring for a more just world order, the advocacy of the poor, the development of partnerships that cross the barriers of our world, all this is an active reaching out for the Kingdom. It bears fruit now, but also stretches forward towards humanity's flourishing in God. The Latin word for 'to wait' – *adtendere* – means to reach towards. The Second Letter of Peter talks of us as living good lives now, 'waiting for and hastening the coming of the day of God' (3:12). This 'ordinary time', spent doing small acts that seek justice, is a hastening of the coming of the Kingdom.

In this time of the hatching of the Kingdom, Jesus sometimes performs dramatic miracles. Miracles are not magic. They are moments in which we are reminded that God is at work all the time, bringing about the Kingdom. We must find our own signs that speak our hope.

When I was in Burundi during a time of civil war between two ethnic groups, the Hutus and the Tutsis, I spent a few days driving around the country with two of my brethren, trying to make contact with the scattered members of the Order and their families. One of the brethren with me was Hutu and one was Tutsi. Every night we would celebrate the Eucharist together. Often we had had a hard day, visiting this country filled with violence and hatred. But in the evening we shared the sign that Jesus performed in the face of his own suffering and death, which looked to the Kingdom in which all hatred and pain will be finished, and all human beings will flourish together. Often we did not know what to say to each other but we had something to do, which was a sign of a hope for which we had no adequate words. We do not know when or how this hope may come to pass, but God's Kingdom will come. All work for justice and peace is our small Amen to the Lord's Prayer in which we pray for the coming of the Kingdom, an expression of hope.

Reflections

213. Ordinary time and Matthew 20:1–16
'For the kingdom of heaven is like a landowner ... '

I enjoy mocking the phrase 'Ordinary Time', as if the bulk of the Church's year is notable only for coming before or after something else. Whereas it is the ordinary, not the special or the spectacular, that mainly determines the quality of our own lives. A character in Pasternak's novel, *Doctor Zhivago*, claims that the most distinctive feature of the teaching of Jesus is not any specific commandment but the fact that Jesus teaches through parables from ordinary life, that profound truths are explained in terms of everyday reality: therefore, that everyday reality carries a deep and eternal significance. And there's nothing more everyday than work – work in the home or professional work – even if the fashionable expression 'work–life balance' strangely suggests that work is somehow apart from what–ever we imagine our 'life' to be.

In Matthew's parable about work, it's natural to feel sympathy for those labourers who complain that the master's 'generosity' is unjust. It's true that they have worked through the day's scorching heat. It's also true that the landowner's procedure, paying the latecomers first, misleadingly inflated their expectations: perhaps this detail of the story is artificially included to anticipate the decisive saying, 'the last will be first and the first last'.

However, I began to understand this parable when I lived in Liverpool and learned that the casual labour system in the docks there survived till the 1960s. Workers signed on morning and afternoon Monday to Saturday, so twelve times per week. A strong young man could make decent money. But dockers in their fifties, maybe after a couple of industrial injuries, were typically hired only at peak periods, though their families' needs were surely not less. So every docker, after decades of arduous labour, ended working life poor.

That surely is the burden of Matthew's parable. Those hired at the eleventh hour may have been 'idle', in the sense of 'unhired'; but they are not 'lazy'. Far more likely, they have been desperately searching for work since morning. The landlord's payment of a full day's wages recognises that human need and dignity come before certain models of efficiency or even of 'fairness'. In this parable, the 'option for the poor' is not impartial and seems to penalise the guiltless – who themselves may well fall into poverty later in life. But favouring 'the last' is an option for respect of the weak, and against dehumanisation.

Frank Turner SJ

214. Labourers in the vineyard

I was reminded of this parable recently when listening to the first words of Pope Benedict when he said that the Lord had called him, a humble worker, into the vineyard of the Lord. I thought it a beautiful phrase.

But I have to admit that, throughout my life, I have often struggled to find the wisdom and lesson in this parable. Why did the vineyard owner pay those who worked for the whole day the same as those who had worked for only part of the day? Was that just? Was the vineyard owner naïve or just a fool?

I suspect Christ may have two messages for us in this parable. The first is the recurrent Gospel theme that 'the last shall be first, and first last'. He pays those who came last – first. The second message is about the reward. The vineyard owner has come at different stages of the day and he has found people still searching for work. Throughout the day, as he encountered them, he has made a contract of work with them. At the end of the day he honoured each contract without differentiation.

That lack of differentiation, it seems to me as a human rights lawyer, may be the profound lesson in this parable. Christ reminds us that we have the invitation simply on the basis of our humanity. The parable's lack of differentiation is a rich example in the Gospels of the universal nature and message at the heart of Christianity. It speaks powerfully of a full embrace of human rights where each of us is valued for our intrinsic worth, not for our status or achievements. This is a world where social and economic rights are not relegated to the second division, but are central and simply given on the basis of our shared humanity.

What of today's world and this parable? Some would say it is an irrelevance, an irrational response or a utopian dream. And I doubt whether many of us would want to see such a system where hard work or talent are ignored. But just imagine for a moment a world based more on this model of economic justice. It would likely be a world with less hunger, disease, unemployment, deprivation and

poverty. A world more concerned with human security in its full
sense. A world based on respect for each human being. In all likeli-
hood it would be a more equitable and therefore perhaps a more
stable world. So perhaps the vineyard owner was not such a fool after
all.

Cherie Booth QC

215. Mind the gap
A meditation based on Luke 16:19–31

He doesn't think about me seeing him
(and pretends he doesn't see me).
Natty dresser. Overfed, jowled,
careful not to let even the hem of his cashmere coat
touch the running sores that cover every inch of my body.

For years I worked at his factory, stitching footballs,
barely making enough to feed my family.

It was the work of my hands that has made him fat and rich.
Across the ocean, people pay what is several months' wages to me
to see leather, stuffed and sewn by me,
kicked about by young men with more money still.

No one sees me.
No one sees that, without me, there is no game.

The preacher tells me my day will come … on the other side.
But the cries of hungry children stop up my ears.
I cannot believe that God blesses this state of affairs.

He doesn't think about me seeing him
(and pretends not to see me).
Averts his eyes, sweeps his coat to the side.
But I know he knows.
I know he knows my name and he knows my need.
Knows it well enough to know that I will do what he asks,
if it will give me daily bread and milk for the baby.
He'll know it even on the other side,
where he will dare to ask for cool comfort from my fingertips,
where he would will me to life for a word of warning to his brothers.

Always a toll, a thing, to be used,
that is what I am to him.
This is the great chasm,
fixed by his refusal
to see and to know
I am who I am.

I see him, better than he sees himself.

God sees all.

Carla Grosch-Miller

216. The transfiguration of all

Here is a mountain-top experience, in a rarified atmosphere, and yet we are called to share in it. We are all given the opportunity to be alone with Jesus and to see him for what he truly is. And in seeing him and his glory we will be changed.

Robert Browning says of the moment when he first saw his loved one: 'And suddenly life awoke.'

It was the same for the disciples. The transfiguration was not only a vision of the glory of Jesus, but an awakening to what all of life is about. Vision, if it is true, always demands change within us and about us. Vision awakens us to new potential, to new ways of seeing and doing what is asked of us.

Only those who keep their eyes open are truly able to see. Many of us go through life unable to see what is about us. Jesus had purposely taken Peter, James and John with him to the mountain top. By setting them apart for a while he gave them an opportunity to see him more clearly. There is a suggestion that it was only possible for them to see Jesus and his glory if they were fully awake. They were called to be sensitive to him and all that he came to do.

Here is not only a glimpse of glory but of the one who fulfils all that the law and the prophets looked forward to. Here is a vision of humankind as it could be, how through fulfilling the law and the prophets each of us can reveal and share in the glory of God.

The glory of our Lord still waits to be revealed in much of our world. God is revealed when the laws of justice and right relationships are fulfilled. We are given a glimpse of the glory of God when freedom and righteous dealings are achieved. When slums are transfigured, when communities and peoples are redeemed from hurt and harm, when warring factions find peace, then the Kingdom comes nearer to us and we reflect God's glory.

David Adam

217. Keeping on keeping the faith
Based on Luke 18:1–8 (Parable of the widow and the unjust judge)

Talking of liberation

'I sat and waited. I'm sick of the waiting. I have sat quietly but it got me nowhere. Now I have shouted. I have almost lost my voice shouting at the window. I've been here for hours and I am sick of this waiting. I know he's in there and I know that he can hear me. He's trying to pretend that I'm not here. I know his game, but it's not going to work.'

Black people have struggled against seemingly unequal forces for centuries. Forced removal, captivity, negative propaganda, frustrated external control and desperate material poverty; we have waited and continue to wait for our liberation. When will the waiting end? When will our cries for justice be heard?

'I began to throw stones at the window … Small stones at first, then bigger ones and eventually, almost boulder size. The man inside had to acknowledge me now. Now he heard me. Now he wanted to talk. Began to call me a vandal. An uncouth thug and worse. But all I want is justice. How come I get labelled when all I want is to get what is owed to me? To get what I deserve. Is that too much to ask?'

Such is the inequitable system in which black people have existed for several hundred years, that we now find ourselves on the receiving end of the negative barbs and assertions of others. We are the victims and yet our cries for justice remain unheard and we get the blame for the condition in which others have placed us.

'The police came by, asking me to move on. I was creating a disturbance. Now that's rich, I thought to myself. I'm fighting for justice and the man whose job it is to see that I get it is ignoring me; but yet I'm still the one at fault. How can that work? But I refuse to be moved. If they think that I'm going quietly then they simply don't know anything about me. I've been here too long, seen too much, faced too much heartache and pain to give in and give up now. I am

*going to get him inside to deal with me. He will deal with me. He will.
He will.'*

The struggle for liberation has taken on many forms and phases.
Slavery gave way to colonialism, which in turn moved into economic
colonialism and dependence; and now there is AIDS. We are still
shouting at the people who can give us justice. Our prayers continue
and we are still waiting ...

Anthony G. Reddie

218. The Samaritan woman at the well
(John 4:5–30)

The woman comes to the well alone in the midday heat. A man is
there. Flaunting convention, he speaks to her. 'Give me a drink.'
Every man this woman meets wants something from her. She is
vulnerable and alone but she challenges him, feisty and flirtatious,
masking her fear. He offers her water that will quench her thirst for
ever, and she longs for this abundance that would liberate her from a
life defined in terms of survival and thirst. But there is a catch. 'Go,
call your husband.' 'I have no husband,' she says defiantly. Then he
astonishes her, for he seems to know all there is to know about her.
He knows about the struggle, the poverty, the weariness of her life.
He knows about the hungry, thirsty children, and the men who
abandon her. But he also knows about her deeper thirst, her yearning
for love, her sense that there must be more to life than this. She feels
something stirring within her, coming alive. It is more fragile than
faith. It is the first trickle of hope. 'He cannot be the Messiah,
can he?'

As a woman and a Samaritan, this woman is doubly marginalised,
and no self-respecting Jewish man would speak to her. The theology
and social priorities of our churches give the impression that Jesus is
most visible among those whose lifestyles conform to the status quo,
but this story tells us that Jesus reveals himself to those who lack the
disguises of affluence and respectability. He comes to us as the thirsty
stranger who offers life without end. It is when we respond to the
needs of others that he shows us the truth about ourselves and offers
to share his life with us.

There is always a risk that we either spiritualise Christ's message
so that we fail to take seriously real physical hunger and thirst, or that
we politicise it so that we become immune to the spiritual needs

around us. Many poor communities are home to the most vibrant forms of faith, while our affluent Western cultures have become spiritual wastelands. Only if we hold together these two dimensions of the Gospel message – the thirst for water and the thirst for life – can we experience the promise of Christ.

Tina Beattie

219. Some random reflections and comments

The Canaanite woman
(Matthew 15:21–28, Mark 7:24–30)

This is the first time that Jesus goes out beyond the boundaries of the Holy Land into unholy, polluted and pagan territory, to people who will not enjoy God's Jubilee. (By this time Israel had forgotten the more universalistic thrust of the prophet in Isaiah 66, and of Ruth and Jonah.)

The attitude of Jesus is puzzling and gives rise to speculation on his interior struggles. It does seem that the mission was in trouble, the thousands had gone away and he was left with only a remnant of faithful if oscillating companions. She shouts out to him repeatedly and at last is prevailed upon by his disciples to attend to her. His first words define his position with regard to her: he is sent only to Israel and its lost sheep. To preach to the Gentiles would be to throw the children's bread to the dogs. (Is this the same man who said 'Come all you who labour and are burdened ... '?) He sounds narrowly nationalistic, chauvinistic and sectarian. But the woman has grit and answers wittily that even the pups can eat the crumbs. A great humility born out of desperation: she'll take any little bit he can give. Jesus is surprised by her faith, her trust, her confidence in him. How is it that faith in God can be found outside of Israel? He did not bring faith to her, the Spirit of God was already there, waiting to be evoked.

If Jesus had been a Columban lay missionary we would have expelled him from the programme. That was no way to do mission. The one sent on mission is to be alert for the signs of God's presence already there. Let there be no self-deception that somehow the missioner brings God. How many of us, having gone to evangelise, were ourselves evangelised?

The woman bent over
(Luke 13:10–17)

By the time we get to this episode we see that Jesus is very much in conflict with the religious authorities. This time over a woman!

The scene is very familiar. Jesus is in the synagogue to fulfil the Sabbath regulation, and he sees a woman who has suffered for years bent over without ever having lifted her head. A woman of her time perhaps – head always bowed in a world she could not call hers, in a synagogue which was not hers either.

Jesus sees the woman, calls her over and cures her. This provokes the ire of the president of the assembly and he criticises the action of Jesus. And Jesus responds and situates himself as on the side of those for whom the Sabbath is an opportunity to do good (not necessarily to do 'proper').

The surprising thing here is that Jesus calls the woman a daughter of Abraham. Shocking because there was no such thing as a daughter of Abraham, only a son of Abraham.

This is the first time in the history of extant Jewish literature that the phrase 'daughter of Abraham' is used of a Jewish woman. This is a radical break with Jewish religious patriarchy, a shaking of the theological and anthropological foundations of Jewish identity. Never before had the phrase been heard.

How many Christian women may be waiting to hear similar words from their Church, their leadership, their institution?

Who will be the Christian leader to stand up and say to women: 'You are daughters just as we are sons, sharing in the same baptism, the same vocation, the same destiny'?

Is it any wonder that Luke is called the feminists' gospel?

Frank Regan SSC

220. The greatest in the Kingdom
'Unless you change and become like little children, you will never enter the kingdom of heaven.'
(Matthew 18:3; Mark 10:15; Luke 18:17)

What could possibly make a child greater than an adult? In worldly terms, probably very little, and in Jesus' time even less. Children had no status, their opinions were not sought, and they could not legally own property. In fact, historians tell us that children were no better than slaves.

We read very little in the Bible about children. Apart from his escapade at the Temple when he was twelve, we know virtually nothing about Jesus as a child. Children were not deemed people in their own right until they reached adulthood, so this makes it all the more remarkable that Jesus took a child as his example of greatness.

But Jesus reverses all the human ideas of greatness. The child in her dependent state – dependent on nurture and care from others – is the one to be emulated, not the people who can stand on their own, dependent neither on God nor on others. And not only were the disciples themselves to become humble, like children, but they had actively to welcome these children. The weakest among them were to be given respect. The rules of social conduct were to be changed and based on humility and service rather than on power and authority.

Imagine how radically our communities would be altered if the ground rules about power were changed so dramatically. What would it be like if we were all so dependent on each other in the way that children are dependent? What would it be like if children were given a voice and their opinions mattered? What would the life of our churches be like if worship and service focused on the needs of children?

And children can be great instruments of change. In South India, groups of children have been taught puppetry, drama and song and have been the messengers going round villages teaching about sanitation, domestic violence and bonded labour. Conventional wisdom would say that this is the realm of adult action, but the children have been remarkably effective. They were the ones who convinced their elders that new ideas were not all bad – after all, what harm can a toilet do to you!

Eildon Dyer

221. I am the bread of life

'You are looking for me, not because you saw miraculous signs but because you ate the loaves and had your fill. Do not work for food that spoils, but for food that endures to eternal life.'

(John 6:26–27)

We might expect Jesus to be frustrated that his words and actions continue to be misunderstood, and people fail to distinguish between 'food that spoils' and 'food that endures to eternal life'. However, the discussion here shows his deep patience and an attitude of forgiveness of people's failures. Having eaten with them, Jesus continues to nourish them.

Jesus connects with people through eating with them. Communing thus with him is also to feed on him. It is to be forgiven; to be fed and sustained by Jesus. In giving of himself in this way, Jesus gives life. In John, Jesus' followers, who failed, misunderstood and betrayed him again and again, find sustenance in the memory of the meals Jesus shared with them. And participating in Holy Communion sustains us in the context of daily life and struggles.

One of the most memorable meals I have had was given to me by Maria, who lives on the slopes of a volcano in El Salvador. Maria gathers coffee beans left or dropped by coffee pickers. She sells them, keeping some back for herself. When I visited her, without prior arrangement, I was treated like an honoured guest. She went out and collected wood, lit it, and placed a pan of water on it. Then she went out again and came back with a parcel. It was locally collected honey.

The water came to the boil. In went two large pinches of her own coffee. She gave me coffee and she gave me a small bowl of honey. She gave me what she could. When I left she gave me a little bag of coffee. About four tablespoons full. She bid farewell and said, 'Remember me.' I still have the coffee. I cannot bring myself to use it. It is too precious. It reminds me of her. I remember Maria whenever I have coffee or honey.

Bit by bit, poverty has consumed Maria's body. The honey and coffee she gave me was a sacramental meal. Its memory, kept alive by the coffee she gave me to bring home, continues to inspire and feed me.

Inderjit Bhogal

222. Feeding the crowds

Jesus replied, 'You give them something to eat' ... Taking the five loaves and the two fish ... he gave thanks and broke them. Then he gave them to the disciples to set before the people. They all ate and were satisfied.
(Luke 9:13–17)

Too often the news of the day is filled with overt signs of violence and human cruelty. But to me there is no image more shocking and more violent than the sight of children scavenging for food in a dump, which, tragically, is a common scene in the developing world. Knowing that we all have a mandate from our Lord to 'feed the hungry and clothe the naked' should shape our commitment and inform our vocations. Often it is understood as no more than rhetoric.

I have dedicated myself to the principle that the developed world, out of the implicit relatedness of being human, has a moral responsibility to forgive the indebtedness of the developing world. Why, you might ask? Because much of this debt was organised under corrupt and deceitful regimes; much of this debt has long since been repaid, only the interest remains. And it is those interest payments that take the food from the mouths of our children.

But there is more. I have redoubled my efforts to work for economic systems which put people first and profits second, and for systems based on respect for the environment. And finally I am working for democratic accountability and transparency. All of this and more is what I am about in the new South Africa. But our Lord's command to 'feed them' remains.

We cannot turn the clock back to a pre-colonial period, so we must ask our families in the North, who have long enjoyed the benefits of our work and our resources, to support these transitions. You have the ability to think and act. You have the ability to influence authority and persuade those in power. You also command resources and investments. Think of us and think of Jesus, who said, 'Feed them.'

Njongonkulu Ndungane,
Archbishop of Cape Town

223. A sandwich for supper

'Go away from me, with my curse upon you … for I was hungry and you never gave me food; I was thirsty and you never gave me anything to drink; I was a stranger and you never made me welcome; naked and you never clothed me; sick and in prison and you never visited me.'
(Matthew 25:41–43)

A story tells of a man who went to the office every day in his expensive car, and made important decisions and signed big contracts. When this important man enjoyed business lunches he would try to distract the attention of his influential guests from the unsavoury spectacle of the beggars on the streets of his city.

One evening after a hard day making money he packed his briefcase to go home, where supper would be waiting for him. As he was locking his desk for the night he caught sight of a stale sandwich lying abandoned at the back of the drawer. Without much thought he crammed it in his coat pocket. No need for it to go mouldy and mess up his desk. On the way out to the car park he saw a beggar on the steps, huddled in an old blanket. 'Here, my friend,' he said to the beggar. 'Here is something for your supper.' And he gave him the stale sandwich.

That night the man dreamed that he was away on a business trip. After the day's meeting, he was taken with his fellow directors to the town's most luxurious restaurant. Everyone gave their orders, and settled down with their aperitifs to look forward to a convivial evening.

The orders arrived. *Pâté de fois gras*. Medallions of venison. Lamb cutlets with rosemary and garlic. The dishes being brought to the table brought gasps of delight from all the company. Then his own order appeared. A waitress set in front of him one small plate, on which was ... a stale sandwich!

'What kind of service is this?' the man demanded, enraged. 'This isn't what I ordered! I thought this was the best restaurant in town!'

'Oh sir,' the waitress told him, 'you've been misinformed. This isn't a restaurant at all. This is heaven. We are only able to serve you what you have sent on ahead while you were alive. I'm very sorry, sir, but when we looked under your name, the best we could find to serve you was this little sandwich.'

(adapted from a Jewish folk tale)
Margaret Silf

224. The homeless stranger

The weather had turned and although the sun was still bright, the thin, high clouds were racing across the pale blue sky, mirroring the strong wind that was cutting through his thin coat.

He had no money and owned nothing but the dusty threadbare clothes he wore and the sandals on his feet. The wind threw grit into his eyes and caused him to turn his head slightly down and to one side as he trudged on.

The last town he had been in had not been friendly to him. Some people were just simply frightened when they saw him trudging into their safe little prosperous communities. Was it his presence that made them feel so threatened? How could such an obviously poor and powerless man make them react that way? He smiled to himself, thinking about how his life had panned out.

This state of homelessness was not new to him. He had been born homeless and had spent his earliest years as a stateless refugee. His good and loving parents had struggled to make a home and settled down and, yes, things had gone well for a good few years. As a young man, he had even gained a trade and helped to run the family business. But that was all behind him now.

The strap on one of his sandals was coming loose again and as he stopped to adjust it for the umpteenth time that day, he felt his stomach rumble. It would be good to stop somewhere and, perhaps, get something to eat and drink. In the last few years he had always been like this – always dependent on the goodwill of others for shelter, food and clothing. He smiled as he reflected on the wonderful generosity most people showed him.

Looking up from his sandal, he realised that he was not far from where he was aiming to spend the night, and as he passed over the brow of the hill, he could see the small village in the bottom of the valley. Even from here he could recognise some of the people gathering in the small clearing by the well. Friends he had grown to know during his years on the road were there along with others who looked familiar.

The loose sandal was causing him to limp a little as he took the steep path down the side of the hill, and the wind that had been troubling him began to buffet him with renewed force. Despite these and the ache in his belly, he smiled. A little boy from the village saw him and trotted up the hill to take a look at this travel-worn, hobbling tramp.

In the village one of the elders looked at him as he approached this small gathering and stood up as if to tell him to move on. His scowl turned to surprise as a man in the crowd stood up and called to the tramp.

'Jesus, Master. Please, we have a seat for you here, out of the wind. The people are eager to hear you speak.' Then, as he gestured to the seat, another brought a drink and Jesus sat within the circle, ready to share his good news with these people.

Ian Smith

225. Peter's declaration
(Matthew 16:13–20; Mark 8:27–30; Luke 9:18–20)

The sanctuary of the Church of the Immaculate Conception is draped for Lent, a purple cloth looped over the life-sized wooden corpus that hangs on the cross above the altar. In my week-long peregrination around Los Angeles, that multiethnic microcosm of the global Church, I have been in many such hued spaces. It is a late Tuesday morning and my travels have taken me through *barrios*, ghettos, industrial landscapes, suburban developments and neighbourhoods of elegant gated estates. The area in which the church is situated has gentrified its shopping district so that sophisticated bistros and trendy boutiques line its streets. In the church, however, it is not the well-heeled matrons or the handsome young professionals sipping their lattes who are found but two of that vast army of Mexican immigrant workers who daily travel into neighbourhoods like this to wash the restaurant dishes, change the hotel sheets, and collect the accumu-lated trash of an affluent, acquisitive society. The man kneels in the darkened church, his eyes upturned and back erect, a profound attentiveness claiming him as he waits before his Lord. Further back a middle-aged woman also turns her gaze to the wooden crucifix but she is choked with tears, hunched over in what can only be a grief so raw it cannot express itself in any other posture. His almost military alertness and her ragged sobs are offered up wordlessly to the figure above the altar.

Each of the synoptic gospels records Jesus' urgent question put to Peter: 'Who do you say that I am?' In each, Peter gives voice to his intuition: 'You are the Messiah,' he replies and Jesus affirms this intuition. When he ventured this identification Peter was recalling the ancient hope for an anointed one, a king who would deliver his people. Whether or not Jesus was the type of king that Peter imagined, he had, according to the gospel of Luke, in fact pointed to the Kingdom he was sent to inaugurate when at the outset of his public ministry he read from the prophet Isaiah in the synagogue 'He has sent me to bring good news to the poor ... to proclaim liberty to the captives ... sight to the blind ... to set free the oppressed.'

In a graffiti-scrawled neighbourhood, inside the church called Our Lady of Victory, a woman softly sings a Spanish song of praise; at Epiphany Church a young mother tenderly lifts her toddler daughter to the base of the plaster statue of *Sagrado Corazon*; at the shrine of the Sorrowing Mother and her Crucified Son at *Nuestra Señora de Guadalupe* hundreds of dog-eared photographs – of children lost to jail or drugs or violence or exiled half across the world because their only hope of escape from poverty has been military enlistment – flutter in the breeze like prayer flags; outside Our Lady of Lourdes a mortuary hearse idles while inside two young gang members crouch in a back pew and pray with tight-gripped fists. All over the archdiocese of Los Angeles the poor and marginalised gather at the foot of the cross and gaze – with hope, with love, with anguish – upon the face of this Messiah, this anointed one who proclaims God's kingdom, the good news to the poor.

Wendy M. Wright
USA

226. The judgement of the nations
(Matthew 25:31–46)

How do we recognise Jesus? Matthew 25:31–46 gives a disconcerting answer to an apparently simple question. It starts in a rather conventional way. Jesus is portrayed as a king surrounded by angels, who renders a judgement. He separates the sinners from the true believers. We like to see Jesus as a powerful figure. It is probably because we would not mind sharing his power. Many Christians sincerely believe that they honour God by attracting honours on themselves and developing mighty networks of influence.

But the rest of the passage leads us in another direction. The ones who will enter the Kingdom are those who give food to the hungry, water to the thirsty, comfort to the sick and consolation to the criminal. Matthew does not say that Jesus supports those needy people. That would restrict the meaning of the text. Jesus is the one who suffers from hunger, thirst, sickness or isolation. When you see somebody in pain you see Jesus. For we who live in South Africa, for instance, Jesus is the young woman who dies of AIDS without having told her boyfriend because she is afraid of being beaten by him. Jesus is the street child who sniffs glue and snatches your bag when you visit the city centre. Jesus is the old man at the crossroad who begs for a job with a tear in his eye.

How can Jesus be all these people? Does it mean that he is anonymous? The answer is yes. He is invisible. Those who take care of him, the text says, do not know what they do. They do not know that the person they assist is Jesus himself. This entirely contradicts the popular image of Jesus as a king in majesty. Far from being a figure of power and authority, Jesus, our Saviour, identifies himself with the lowly. If Jesus was among us, his message would not be on the internet and nobody would act as his media officer. For Christians who struggle with the lack of visibility of the church in a secular world, this message should bring some comfort. Jesus, and God his Father for the same reason, does not need to be recognised to exist. He is present in his very absence. To save the world he does not need to rule it.

Does this mean that Jesus is insignificant? In no way. The scene described by Matthew shows exactly the opposite. This anonymous Jesus whom we struggle to recognise is indeed a king. The strength of the gospel lies in this paradox: unless we recognise our Saviour in the lowly and the needy, we won't enter the Kingdom of God. His power here means real power, not the fictitious power of politicians, corporate leaders and media tycoons. This power is of a totally different nature: it is not discernible to the eye. But it is real. It is the power to be with God and share his beatitude.

Philippe Denis OP
South Africa

227. *'The kingdom of heaven is like yeast that a woman took and mixed in with three measures of flour until it was all leavened.'*

(Matthew 13:33)

This parable is the only one of the 'Kingdom parables' that deals with a woman. In it the Kingdom of God is compared with a woman taking yeast and mixing it with flour until it was leavened. The parable is subtly subversive on at least two counts. The first is that Jesus is comparing the Kingdom of God to what may be considered a very ordinary, everyday activity for women in that historical situation. In a context where all religious matters belonged to the sphere of men, to compare the work and the activity of a woman to such a significant religious and spiritual phenomenon as that of the Kingdom of God, is certainly making a statement.

The second way in which this parable is significant can be found in the choice of yeast to make his point. Yeast, both in the Old Testament (Exodus 12—13) and New Testament (1 Corinthians 5:6–8) is considered morally impure. *Zyme* (leaven; yeast) is considered impure as opposed to *azymos* (unleavened). Yet Jesus chooses to use *zyme* (yeast) to make his point. In the historical context of the time, women, like yeast, were also considered 'unclean' in many respects. Yet Jesus uses women and yeast to make his point. What was Jesus trying to tell us about the Kingdom of God? As we reflect on this parable I would like to suggest at least three things:

1. The Kingdom of God welcomes all – including women. While making bread and other such 'domestic' matters are stereo-

typically assigned to a woman, Jesus takes this activity and transforms it into something as powerful and as significant as explaining the Kingdom of God.

2. The laws of purity and impurity do not govern the Kingdom of God. Rather it is that which promotes life. In this parable the yeast, when added to the flour by the woman, produces an end product, bread – the 'bread of life'. It is the bread that sustains us, not laws of purity and impurity.

3. Finally, the small act of putting yeast into the bread results in the feeding of many. In the same way, the Kingdom of God does not depend on the 'pure' and the 'religious' who perform big, outward acts of service that may in the end amount to nothing. It depends on the 'little' acts of people who others may consider 'impure'. It is these little acts consisting of life-giving measures, rather than discriminating ones that enhance the Kingdom of God.

Dr Sarojini Nadar
South Africa

228. Unconditional acceptance – the elder son

'My son, you are always with me, and everything I have is yours. But we had to celebrate and be glad because this brother of yours was dead and is alive again; he was lost and is found.'

(Luke 15:31–32)

Awareness-raising workshops on social issues have been difficult in some of our communities because of misunderstandings and lack of information. Many people believe that some problems only belong to certain classes, for example. Gambling is often seen as a problem of the rich, drugs a problem of the poor. HIV/AIDS tends to be seen as a disease of the poor and those who lead immoral lives. These myths have been challenged by inviting people from different social classes and races to come together to share their experiences. This is done with the hope that our communities will become more understanding and supportive.

Our churches are often the most judgemental institutions. Churches always struggle to embrace and accept those who are perceived as different. When they see a link between a person's condition and a presumed contravention of Christian ethics, it results in discrimination, rejection and mistrust.

The father in today's parable challenges his elder son who does not understand why his 'disobedient' younger brother should be given special treatment. The elder brother resents the fact that he has not been rewarded for his obedience.

As activists and as Christians, we should take our lead from the forgiveness and unconditional acceptance of the father in the story, supporting, empowering, crying and rejoicing with those who are suffering or are in 'unacceptable' situations.

Phumsile Zondi-Mabizela
South Africa

229. Christ is that tramp who comes in need of a night's lodging

What is the use of loading Christ's table with gold cups while he himself is starving? Feed the hungry and then if you have any money left over, spend it on the altar table. Will you make a cup of gold and withhold a cup of water? What use is it to adorn the altar with cloth of gold hangings and deny Christ a coat for his back? What would that profit you? Tell me: if you saw someone starving and refused to give him any food but instead spent your money on adorning the altar with gold, would he thank you? Would he not rather be outraged? Or if you saw someone in rags and stiff with cold and then did not give him clothing but set up golden columns in his honour, would he not say he was being made a fool of and insulted?

Consider that Christ is that tramp who comes in need of a night's lodging. You turn him away and then start laying rugs on the floor, draping the walls, hanging lamps on silver chains on the columns. Meanwhile the tramp is locked up in prison and you never give him a glance. Well, again I am not condemning munificence in these matters. Make your house beautiful by all means but also look after the poor, or rather look after the poor first. No one was ever condemned for not adorning his house, but those who neglect the poor were threatened with hellfire for all eternity and a life of torment with devils. Adorn your house if you will, but do not forget your brother in distress. He is a temple of infinitely greater value.

St John Chrysostom (*c.* 347–407)

Prayers

230. God of justice
(Persistent widow)

O God of justice,
you have called your prophets throughout the ages
to persist in proclamation
in the face of callousness,
and to be resilient in faith
confronting stupidity:
we pray for those
who have refused to be silent before injustice;
who have been repeatedly turned away but are not discouraged;
whose outrageous faith has caused the mighty to tremble;
whose stubborn humour gives their sisters* heart.

For the earth shall be full of the knowledge of God
as the waters cover the sea.

We pray for those
whose efforts in the cause of justice have left them damaged or bitter;
who are repudiated by those they struggled for;
who have lost all hope of remedy,
and whose voice is not heard.

For the earth shall be full of the knowledge of God
as the waters cover the sea.

We pray for those
who have the power to do good and will not;
who attend to no voice but their own;
who dismiss the causes of oppression,
and ignore the plight of the powerless.

For the earth shall be full of the knowledge of God
as the waters cover the sea.
Amen.

                                                  Janet Morley

(* Or 'allies' or 'brothers' as appropriate.)

231. Loving God, you could have walked this earth in splendour and might, but instead chose to come among us as a little child. Help us to learn that the world's view of greatness is not your way, and may we follow you in dependence and humility.
Amen.

Eildon Dyer

232. Holy God,
we have tried so many ways to find you.
Forgive us,
for our failure to see you beside us,
and communing with us.
We bless you
for staying with us,
forgiving us and feeding us
in Jesus the Bread of Life,
day by day.
Amen.

Inderjit Bhogal

233. Lord of the Transfiguration,
awaken us and we shall be changed.
Transfigure our churches, our relationships, our world;
transfigure our hopes, our dreams, our way of living.
Lord of the Transfiguration,
awaken us and we shall be changed.
Amen.

David Adam

234. A prayer of response

God of pain and fear,
do you feel the tears
falling as leaves to a barren earth,
decked in the splendour of autumn's richness,
beauty masking their imminent death?

You were there long ago –
when a precious jar was broken,
its fragrant contents poured out,

an unnamed woman foretelling death,
her touch evoking intimacy,
her actions inciting dispute.

You keep vigil with us, waiting
as the long night draws in,
trusting experience to the rhythms of life.
Anoint us with the touch of your intimacy,
knitting together wounds too deep for words.

God of intuitive wisdom,
grant us the maturity to offer extravagance
in the face of another's pain,
evoke in us the memory of her story
weaving through the patterns of time.

                                    Jill Thornton and Clare McBeath

235. *The Lord gave and the Lord has taken away, blessed be the name of the Lord.*

We live in a world which progressively blurs the distinction between necessity, comfort and luxury so that we are unable to tell the difference.
My soul is restless and it shall remain restless until it rests in you, O God.

Money offers everything – material possessions, influence, status, power and happiness. It is God's rival.
My soul is restless and it shall remain restless until it rests in you, O God.

We are constantly bombarded by the idea that who we are is measured by what we have.
My soul is restless and it shall remain restless until it rests in you, O God.

Grant us courage to learn poverty, that we may discover your riches;
to become foolish, so that we may speak with your wisdom;
to celebrate weakness, resting in your strength;
to rejoice in being nothing, because Christ has become all things.
Amen.

                                    Voices from the South

236. Loving God,
you show yourself in those who are vulnerable,
and make your home with the poor and weak of this world.
Warm our hearts with the fire of your Spirit,
and help us to accept the challenges of AIDS.

May we, your people, using all our energy and imagination,
and trusting in your steadfast love,
be united with one another in conquering disease and fear.
We make this prayer in the name of one who has borne all our
    wounds,
and whose Spirit strengthens and guides us,
now and for ever.
Amen.

Voices from the South

237. The rich fool
(Luke 12:13–21)

God of Life, Creator of the earth and all that is in it, we lift our
    prayers of thanks to you
for the beauty of the earth that surrounds us,
for spring flowers that dazzle us and summer's greenery that delights us,
for autumn's bounty that sustains us, and winter's hibernation which
    settles us.
**Thanks be to you, Lord of the heavens and the earth, to whom all
    things belong.**

God, we enjoy your abundance, yet are seduced by accumulation.
The mantra, 'More is better,' lulls us.
New inventions become seeming 'necessities'.
We fill our cupboards and closets, basements and barns to over-
    flowing.
Yet we despair, feeling our lives stand empty.
God, let us not be possessed by our possessions.

God, we claim to enjoy your peace, yet we persist in worry
    about things.
Even as Scripture reminds us that Solomon's finery cannot compare
to the flowers of the fields,
we worry about our house, our cars, our clothes, our shoes.

Yet we despair, sensing our coveted treasures bring no lasting
  meaning to life.
God, let us not be possessed by our possessions.

God, we sing of your 'blessed assurance,' yet crave promises from our
  banks and pensions.
We worry if our Individual Retirement Accounts will see us through.
We store up more and more riches for our earthly security.
Yet we despair, discovering we are not 'rich towards you'.
God, let us not be possessed by our possessions.

God, we commit ourselves to care for others,
yet we stock our pantries for tomorrow, while millions suffer empty
  bellies today.
We focus on our shoe collection while millions go bare-footed.
We lament our fashion follies while others lament that their children
  go naked and cold.
We deposit ever more into our bank accounts while millions live from
  day to day.
God, let us not be possessed by our possessions.

God, our life span is short, at any moment to be taken from us.
Free us from greed, and fill us with generosity.
Release us from insecurity and restore us to contentment with the
  treasures of your Kingdom.
Strip us of our fear and strengthen us to love one another as you have
  loved us.
In Jesus' name we lift our prayers to you.
**Thanks be to you, Lord of the heavens and the earth, to whom all
  things belong. Amen.**

                                        Tod and Ana Gobledale

238. On a donkey riding

On a donkey riding, bound for Jericho,
one lone weary trav'ller still has miles to go.
Suddenly some robbers spring out with a knife:
steal his precious money, almost take his life.

On the same rough highway to Jerusalem
holy people pass him – no concern to them.

Victim in the gutter with deep wounds that bleed:
who will prove a neighbour in the hour of need?

Comes at last a stranger with a rescue plan,
one whom none have time for, a Samaritan.
Rubs in healing ointment, takes him to an inn,
pays the bill, behaving just like next-of-kin.

Jesus told the story, tell it us today:
leaves us with a question that won't go away.
Ev'ry day's a challenge with some fresh surprise:
shall we each show mercy or just close our eyes?

David Mowbray

239. Friend to friend

Let us now as God's own people, give the sign of peace,
proclaiming our love for one another, binding friend to friend.

Refrain
Christ Jesus calls us to love one another, to be one in him,
friend to friend, in love to each other, we shall give our hands.

In our care for one another, by each kindly word,
by every loving deed, we make known the love of Jesus Christ.

We feed the hungry, clothe the naked, give drink to those who thirst,
for Jesus came in love as a servant, and we follow him.

Eduardo P. Hontiveros
The Philippines

240. Prayer to become a living example of a loving community

We pray for the Church throughout the world that she may be a living example of a loving community, and a voice for those who are hungry for justice.
Lord in your mercy,
hear our prayer.

We pray for the world's leaders, that they may work to overcome the barriers between peoples and foster a spirit of global community.

Lord in your mercy,
hear our prayer.

We pray for our own local community here in ...
We pray for those who feel excluded from our local community,
through poverty, disability or illness.
We pray for people affected by HIV and AIDS, and especially for
those excluded from our communities through discrimination and
prejudice.
Lord in your mercy,
hear our prayer.

Diakonia Council of Churches
South Africa

241. Restless God,
we know that children should have space to play and be educated and
not have to work to support their families; that mothers should not
have to see their babies die for lack of access to clean water; that
workers should get a fair wage and not have to work in dangerous
conditions; that elders should live in safety and comfort and not have
to scrabble around on rubbish tips to find food.
We know that things should be different in our world.

We know that people should have balanced lives and not have to
work long grinding hours whilst others can't find work; that prejudice and discrimination should have no place in society; that all
should be free from abuse and brutality.
We know that things should be different in our world.

Merciful God, we are sorry for our apathy, for our lack of action, for
our ignorance, for our indifference.

Forgiving God, help us to be free from the feeling of being overwhelmed, free to reflect, pray, focus and act in whatever way possible.
Help us not to deceive ourselves but always to grow towards truth
and action.

Loving God, help us in our journey with you to be growing, imaginative, generous, letting-go people.
Amen.

Ingrid Shelley

242. At the banquet

At the banquet we laugh and rejoice with each other
make a toast to friendship
give thanks to God.

Together we marvel at the feast laid before us
sit down in communion
our meal, a prayer.

Each guest brings an offering to share at the table
each plate is different
each gift the same.

God invites us to share our love and our differences
embracing our neighbours
praising his name.

At the banquet we laugh and rejoice with each other
God's gift is diversity
come take your fill.

Yashoda Sutton

243. A prayer of intercession

Loving God, in your Son, Jesus Christ, you call all people to yourself.
We pray for those who seek you in your Church and beyond, who
wait to hear your voice.
Good Shepherd, lead them,
and keep them safe in your hands.

In him you laid down your life for the world you made. We pray for
all people who suffer political oppression, economic exploitation, or
the ravages of war, and for all who listen for a message of peace.
Good Shepherd, guard them,
and keep them safe in your hands.

In him you shared the life of a human family and community. We
pray for those carrying the stigma of homelessness, unemployment or
addiction who are excluded from our community life, and who long
to hear words of acceptance.
Good Shepherd, embrace them,
and keep them safe in your hands.

Through him you fed the hungry, healed the sick and restored the
dead to life.
We pray for those who lack the basic securities of shelter, clothing,
food and clean water, and for the sick and dying who wait for words
of hope.
Good Shepherd, sustain them,
and keep them safe in your hands.
Amen.

Judy Bainbridge

244. A prayer for healing

Jesus, you ask, 'Do you want to be healed?'
Oh yes, Lord, we want to be healed.

From our self-preoccupation and self-pity, and our indifference to
    those in need,
from our greed for material things and our wasting of the gifts we
    have been given,
Oh yes, Lord, we want to be healed.

From our reluctance to let go of hurts, and our pursuit of petty
    revenge,
from our fear and anxiety, and our inability to trust you or our
    neighbour,
Oh yes, Lord, we want to be healed.

From our lethargy and cynicism in the face of the need to change and
    be changed,
from our narrow judgements, our unthinking prejudice and our easy
    acceptance of stereotypes,
Oh yes, Lord, we want to be healed.
Amen.

Judy Bainbridge

245. Look around you.
    Here are the children of God.
    See your neighbours,
    each different from each other
    and made in the image of God.

Think of our world
and its millions of people.
They are our neighbours,
each different from each other
and made in the image of God.

Open your hearts
to meet with the Creator of us all.
Offer your praise as we come together,
each different from each other
and made in the image of God.

Rachel Poolman

246. A prayer for justice

Gracious God,
in a world where the rich build ever bigger barns and banks
and millions live in shanty towns and slums,
let there be justice, let there be peace.

In a world where many eat and drink to excess
and millions more simply long for clean water,
let there be justice, let there be peace.

In a world where many make merry
and millions grieve,
let there be justice, let there be peace.

In a world where many join health clubs
and millions long for basic health care,
let there be justice, let there be peace.

In a world where many are stressed out with work
and millions feel their labour is in vain or unwanted,
let there be justice, let there be peace.

In a world where many are materially poor and yet spiritually rich,
and millions are materially rich and yet spiritually poor,
let there be justice, let there be peace.
Amen.

Andrew Roberts

247. Prayers of intercession

God, our rock,
bless your church,
that it may be built on the sure foundation of your word.
May your people be so deeply rooted in the promise of your love
that they may be good news for a broken world.
God of justice,
hear our prayer.

God, our rock,
bless your world with the gifts of justice and peace.
Hear the cry of the poor;
humble the rich and the powerful;
bind up the wounds of those whose lives are scarred
by famine, disease and war.
God of justice,
hear our prayer.

God, our rock,
bless this community, gathered in your name.
Help us to dig deep foundations for our life in you,
and be a blessing for those among whom we live.
Make us attentive to the ways you speak to us,
especially in the voices and the lives of unexpected people,
and help us to make better connections
between our worship and our lives.
God of justice,
hear our prayer.
Amen.

Maggie Hindley

248. Dalit woman,
beautiful, refined,
like mother, grandmother before,
you carry your burden of stone,
weighty, heavy on your head,
in this ancient place of pilgrimage,

Head held high, proud and upright,
keep it thus positioned
or the stone may drop!

You walk away to dump the rock,
far from all intrusive sight.

Colourful sari, elegant folds,
float around as you walk
barefoot in the dirty earth,
drops of sweat on clothes and brow.
Surely even custom makes this far from easy?

Young man, rock-breaking, what do you think?
Can you bear to see her burdened thus,
ceaselessly tiring, unendingly weary,
working all the daylight hours?
Yet your burden is enough for you alone.

Where caste and gender dictate place
to thousands upon thousands like her,
we pray it will not always be thus; your words
'Come to me and I will give you rest'
will be heard for all burden-carriers.

O God, move this woman into a different place,
where all your children are equally regarded.
Lift up the poor and give them rest;
remove the weary weight of history and culture
through human regard and life-giving action.

Bring all your creation into harmony with you
as we take your yoke and learn your way.
Give rest for souls, as we rest in you.
Lift up our spirits and may hearts rejoice
as we come to your new place of pilgrimage.
Amen.

(This meditation/prayer was inspired by a visit to the sixth-century shore temples at Mamallapuram, Tamil Nadu, South India in January 2005 during a visit of a Cambridgeshire Ecumenical Council group to their partner, Vellore Diocese in the Church of South India. This church is engaged in relief work after the tsunami and more generally amongst the Dalit people. Many former Dalits have become Christian as a result of the churches' commitment to outreach programmes which ensure the social 'uplift' of these people. This prayer could be

read accompanied beforehand or afterwards by some Indian music,
perhaps with Tamil Christian lyrics.)

Deborah McVey

249. Set us free

Pilgrim God,
journey with us as we seek you amongst the poor and dispossessed
and guide our feet that we may travel with those who long to find the
    way home.
Your Kingdom come
your will be done.
Wait with us as we listen to discern your voice amongst the cries for
    peace
and touch our hearts that we may join with those who long for
    justice.
Your Kingdom come
your will be done.
Search with us as we struggle to find your light amongst the shadows
    of oppression
and kindle our flame that we may be a beacon of hope to those who
    sit in darkness.
Your Kingdom come
your will be done.
Join with us as we prepare to face your truth amongst the challenge
    of repentance
and feed our desire for justice that we may reach out to those in need.
Your Kingdom come
your will be done.
Rejoice with us as we listen to your promise to set us free
and raise our voice of liberation that we may give courage to those
    who live in fear.
Your Kingdom come
your will be done
on earth as it is in heaven.
Amen.

Annabel Shilson-Thomas

250.
You were accused, Good Teacher.
You ate with sinners.
You touched the unclean.
You offended common decency.

We had thought you came to bless us,
but you keep going to those we do not understand,
those we do not trust,
those we fear.

We want you to confirm our prejudices,
but you shatter them.
Samaritans, children, lepers, women, tax collectors, a sick friend, a
    dead daughter,
all of these you blessed and healed.
Those we distance ourselves from, you actually touch.

We grumble at you,
not sure that we can follow you in this way,
not strong enough to overcome what we have always been taught,
not open enough to see the depth and breadth of your grace.

Forgive us, Jesus,
turn our grumbling into acts of courage.
Turn our codes of conduct into the conduct of compassion.
Turn our condemnation of the failures of others
into the awareness of our failure to love others with your grace and
    compassion.

Forgive us, Jesus, and make us new,
until we become one with the lost ones,
until we become lost in your love.
Amen.

                                   World AIDS Day ecumenical order of service

251. A prayer for peace for use with children

*Place a large bowl of water in the middle of the floor. Give a small
pebble to every child. Drop one pebble into the water and together
watch the ripples spread out. Say the words below:*

Imagine that this pebble is a droplet of love (*pause*).
God calls us to be like droplets of love in a world where there is
    hatred and war.
(*Drop another pebble into the water.*)
If we could let our love spread like ripples on a lake,
God's love would spread through all the world.

(*Drop another pebble into the water.*)
Real peace comes through love and understanding.
It starts with us and how we treat others – here – now – today
    tomorrow.
(*Invite all the children to come forward and to drop their pebbles in
the water one by one.*)
Lord Jesus, help us to love one another and make this world a place
    of peace.
Amen.

Roots

252. A prayer for all saints

For the people of God who are sent to support us,
for the people of God who are sent to disturb us,
for the people of God who are sent to inspire us,
for the people of God who are sent to trouble us,
for the people of God who are sent to enthuse us,
for the people of God who are sent to still us,
thanks be to God.
Amen.

Peter Privett

253. Lord, in all ways we are connected to people we will never meet,
dependent on people we will never know.
Lord, you love us all.

People who make our clothes and our games,
people who produce our food and our drinks.
Lord, you love us all.

Help us to be grateful for all these people,
help us to see that the riches of the world are for all to share.
Lord, you love us all.

As we stand for a moment in silence,
we think of the men, the women and the children
who work hard so that we can have so much.
Lord, you love us all.

We pray that you will help us to be responsible,
and fight for a fairer and more just world,

where we can all live in harmony and peace.
Lord, you love us all.

(*silence*)

Lord of all,
Amen.

Roots

254. A prayer for human rights

Dear Lord Jesus,
we know you must feel angry
> when anyone says bad words about black people,
> or about poor people, homeless people,
> old people, disabled people,
> and people with nasty illnesses like leprosy
> or any kind of disease.
Forgive this sin.
> These people are all in the Kingdom of God.

Help us to protect human rights for everybody in the world.
Help us to know about the principle of justice.

Jesus, you went on trial and forgave your enemies.
We want justice for people in courts and in prisons.

Help us Christians to be like you.
Help us to feel happy.
Help us to be free.
> We need to trust one another.

Soldiers fought for our country,
> for freedom for Britain.
We remember this.
We are happy to be free.

In other countries soldiers are killed in battle,
> villages are destroyed,
> children lose their homes,
> countries are in debt.
All that must make you sad.

We pray for all the world of countries.
We want human rights for everybody,
        because human rights mean freedom.

We know that justice, freedom, truth,
        and human rights all belong to you.
Through Jesus Christ our Lord,
Amen.

Richard Bowers
(a young man with Down's syndrome)

255. The kingdom of God made present

The cantors sing the 'Caribbean Lord's Prayer'. They continue humming the tune during the spoken responses.

LEADER: Where is wisdom that we may find her? And how may we learn to be prophets, able to do what God is asking of us? How can we fulfil our mission of helping to make real the vision that Christ spoke of as 'the Kingdom of God'? How can we work to bring it about now, in our time, in this place, where we are, on earth? We find guidance in the *Christian manifest* – 'on earth as it is in heaven' – embedded in the prayer Jesus gave us.

Let us stand to proclaim it in song and speech.

CANTORS: Our Father who art in heaven, hallowed be thy name.
ALL: **We value the sacredness of God's creation.**
We give respect to the call of each person's name.

CANTORS: Thy Kingdom come, thy will be done.
ALL: **We respond to God's invitation to be partners in the completion of the work of creation.**

CANTORS: On earth as it is in heaven.
ALL: **Our ultimate goal is to make the reality of God's Kingdom, where justice reigns, present now in our whole world.**

CANTORS: Give us this day our daily bread.

ALL: We must take only enough for our needs, ensuring all life's gifts are distributed fairly.

CANTORS: And forgive us all our trespasses.

ALL: We need to recognise where our neglect and deliberate offences cause harmful consequences. The exploitation of debt and the abusive denial of the means to good health must be put right. We must foster compassion one for another, tolerating damage to no one and oppression by no system.

CANTORS: As we forgive those who trespass against us.

ALL: When we can accept hurt done to us, then we can begin the process of forgiveness. We will work for a spirit of reconciliation with respect for right relationships, and the common good of all.

CANTORS: And lead us not into temptation.

ALL: We want a culture that resists indulgence and bigotry and is able to frolic in a community that encourages all respect for our common humanity and global interconnectedness.

CANTORS: But deliver us from evil.

ALL: Let us work for constancy in our ability to empathise, for in its absence evil lurks. We will work for appropriateness to the propriety of the culture of life, where all are empowered, enhanced and encouraged to live simply, act justly and love tenderly.

LEADER: Our Christian manifesto is a call to us all, especially those in positions of authority, to reject all power play, and rather to use the authority we may be given to serve in a spirit of love.

ALL: We are all called to live justly, compassionately and with integrity, particularly being mindful of our responsibilities to those with whom Christ identified – the poor and the powerless.

Amen, amen. It must be so, for hallowed is God's name. (*repeat*)

Lala Winkley

256. A prayer for suicide bombers

Dear Lord of life and love,
we look with pity on those who kill and maim their brothers and
    sisters with bombs, destroying themselves.
Frustrate their efforts to take innocent lives.
Fan into flames our love for one another,
that our fears may be transformed into love and their anger into hope,
so that together we may build a world where justice reigns
and your Kingdom of peace is established among us.

Through Jesus Christ our Lord,
Amen.

Grace Sheppard

257. A prayer for political leaders

O Lord of all the earth,
grant to our leaders integrity, courage and vision.
Give them the ability to make wise decisions which benefit the whole.
Enable them to handle power with humility.
Help them to make decisions in the light of your truth and intention
that all shall thrive and flourish, and love one another.

Through Jesus Christ our Lord,
Amen.

Grace Sheppard

258. God,
The image of your Son is deformed by our sin,
because we sin against you and our neighbours.

Forgive us when we ignore the suffering of your people
and violence and injustice near and far.

Give us the courage to confront our fears and
help us to act as agents of peace.

Restore to us the vision of one Church.

Open our eyes!

World Council of Churches

259. O God, graciously comfort and tend all who are imprisoned, hungry, thirsty, naked and miserable; also all widows, orphans, sick and sorrowing. In brief, give us our daily bread, so that Christ may abide in us and we in him for ever, and that with him we may worthily bear the name of 'Christian'.

Martin Luther (1483–1546)

260. God our Father,
who gives us the ability to produce wealth,
and who cautioned us through our Saviour Jesus,
that we should not lay our treasure on earth
where thieves break and moths destroy,
may your Holy Spirit
cut through our comfort and complacent lifestyles
and cause us to see the stretched out avenues of ministry
to your hungry, poor and dying children,
for whatever we do to any of these little ones,
we do it for Jesus.
In his precious name we pray.
Amen.

Joyce Karuri
Kenya

261. God and Father of all human beings,
in your love you have made all the nations of the world to be one family.
Help those of different races and religions to love and understand one another better.
Take away hatred, jealousy and prejudice,
so that loving you more deeply
we may work together for the coming of your kingdom of righteousness and peace.
We ask this through your Son, Jesus Christ our Lord.
Amen.

Evelyn Underhill

262. Almighty God, maker of heaven and earth, giver of light and life, so teach us those things which belong to the heavenly Kingdom, and those duties which are of the earth, that we, stirred by the light and

life of the peace of God, may be enabled faithfully to do the things committed to us, looking ever unto thee for light and life, that, being lifted above ourselves, the life of God in the soul of man may be ours, and the peace of God, which passeth all understanding, may then keep our hearts and minds, through Jesus Christ our Lord,
Amen.

George Dawson (1821–76)

263. Bless me, O God, with the love of thee, and of my neighbour. Give me peace of conscience, the command of my affections; and for the rest, thy will be done! O King of peace, keep us in love and charity.
Amen.

Thomas Wilson (1663–1755)

264. O God of love, who lovest the stranger, defend and nourish, we entreat thee, all sojourners in strange lands and poor helpless persons, that they may glorify thee out of grateful hearts; and to such men as are tyrannical and oppressive give searchings of spirit and amendments of ways, that thou mayest show mercy on them also.
Amen.

Christina C. Rossetti (1830–95)

Harvest

All creatures look to you in hope to give them their food when it is due. What you give them they gather up; they eat their fill of good things.
(Psalm 104:27–28)

Most cultures and religious traditions gather for an annual celebration to thank God or the gods for their harvest. This is a key moment in the rhythm of the year. If there was no harvest, then how could we survive? Our ancestors lived precariously from harvest to harvest. Those of us who live in the West, the wealthy of the global village, have no such moment in our year. Somewhere on the planet it is always harvest time. The fruit and the vegetables come to us all the time: we do not have to wait and have no special time to give thanks to God, and so easily forget that God exists.

It is good, though, to keep a time every year when we remember that all that we need to survive and flourish is ultimately a gift. It may be bought in a supermarket, but it is the fruit of the earth. Our ancestors were naturally religious because they lived close to the miracle of fertility, the astonishing fecundity of animals and soil. But we, who buy our food wrapped in plastic, may forget the miracle of new life upon which we depend, and forget God, 'the giver of all good things'.

If we forget that everything is gift, then we may fall into the terrible blindness of imagining that we may claim absolute ownership of the earth and its fruit. Beginning in Tudor England with the enclosures of the common land, we can plot the growing worship of a new idol, which is private property. Instead of thanking God who is the source of all that is, we worship the rights of private property and think of human beings as those whose dignity lies in ownership.

This has been called the 'commodification' of creation. Land, water and even human beings become commodities that can be owned absolutely, and so bought and sold, products on the market.

Harvest Festivals challenge this perception of the world and call us to remember that everything is gift, and is given by God so that humanity and all animals may flourish. We are merely stewards of the common good. Thomas Aquinas, that wise friar, accepted that private property was necessary, since we look after things that we own personally better, as anyone who lives in a religious community knows! But he, with the whole of the old Christian tradition, maintained that the rights of private property are not absolute. When there is a conflict between private property and the common good, then it is the common good that has priority.

When the poor have not got what they need for survival and their human dignity then they have the right to the excess wealth of the rich. Thomas quoted St Ambrose of Milan: 'The bread that you keep for yourself belongs to the hungry, the cloak that you store away belongs to the naked, the money that you salt away is the price of the poor person's freedom.'

We have all heard the statistics so often. One sixth of all human beings live in extreme poverty, on less than $1 a day. Eight million people die every year just because they are too poor to go on living. In this world, Christians must champion the common good of humanity and refuse the idolatry of private property. The wealth of the planet belongs to humanity. It is simply crazy that the four hundred richest Americans can have an annual income of $69 billion in comparison with the $59 billion which was the combined income of the 161 million inhabitants of Botswana, Nigeria, Senegal and Uganda.[1]

The commodification of the planet is continuing rapidly. The latest form of this is intellectual property rights. The poor of our planet depend upon the fertility of the land. They struggle to live from the annual miracle of planting and harvesting. The rich do not need to take ownership of their land. It is enough to own the fertility of the seeds as their intellectual property. About ten major companies are buying germ plasm. According to Jeremy Rifkin, President of the Foundation on Economic Trends in Washington, they 'then slightly modify the seeds or strip out individual genetic traits, or recombine new genes into the seeds and secure patent protection over their

---

1. Jeffrey Sachs, *The End of Poverty: How We Can Make It Happen in Our Lifetime* (Penguin, 2005) p. 305.

"inventions". The goal is to control, in the form of intellectual property, the entire seed stock of the planet.'[2] We become rightly indignant when President Mugabe of Zimbabwe robs white farmers of their land. It is even more unjust when the rich multinationals try to rob the poor of the God-given fertility of their seeds.

Intellectual property rights are also at the centre of the struggle to ensure that poor countries, especially in Sub-Saharan Africa, are able to buy retroviral drugs and combat AIDS. The pharmaceutical companies, with the support of the United States Government, have done everything possible to stop the production of these drugs at prices that would be affordable by countries whose very future is at stake. They put private profit before the common good, even though this would cost the lives of millions and even bring about the collapse of whole nations. This is truly idolatry, the sacrificing of human blood. Thanks be to God that some victories have been won.

At Harvest Festival we thank God for the good things that we have received. It is not just what I have received for my private benefit. We thank God for the whole miracle of fertility which is a gift to all that lives and breathes. Ultimately the private good of individuals and of nations and the common good of humanity are not in competition. No one can fully flourish if humanity does not. Humanity cannot flourish if the planet does not. At Harvest time, we remember the common good, which is the good of every person, bound up with each other as we are. We long for the Kingdom of God, the great harvest when God will gather in the whole of humanity and we shall delight in God and in each other. All that we are, with our joys and sorrows, our richness and our poverty, will be gathered in. Nothing will be wasted.

2. Jeremy Rifkin, *The Age of Access* (Penguin, 2000) p. 66.

Reflections

265. Harvest
Now, barbarous in beauty, the stooks arise
around; up above, what wind-walks! What lovely behaviour
of silk-sack clouds!

exclaimed the priest-poet, Gerard Manley Hopkins,[3] in a poem that easily connects harvest's exuberance with the Creator's love. Such connections seem remote today, especially in Western cultures long alienated from the earth's rhythms. Lacking our medieval ancestors' rootedness in the seasonal processes of sowing and reaping, and overwhelmed with the supermarket's willingness to produce every kind of fruit and vegetable from far-flung countries at all times of the year, does it make sense to celebrate harvest liturgically any longer?

In my personal life this was poignant, as, for a period my husband and I ran a pick-your-own strawberry farm. Not only did most of the public have little idea of when the correct time to harvest strawberries would be, but the notion of personally gathering in the fruits, an ancient and biblical idea, was deemed inferior to acquiring the neatly packaged supermarket product, readily available at all times. Who ploughs the fields and scatters in this day and age?

Do holiday experiences offer surrogate possibilities for experiencing harvest? I confess to revelling in other people's harvests when, for example, on holiday in Crete, enjoying local tomatoes, olives and melons. But mentioning olives brings us into contested terrain, to the fact that politics prevents harvest in many countries. In Palestine, the wall newly constructed by the Israelis has separated hundreds of Palestinian farmers from their olive groves: there will be no harvest for the Palestinians. In Iraq, not only is it difficult for farmers to harvest the land in war conditions, but newly arrived US corporations are insisting that they buy expensive varieties of seed from them.

Disastrous climatic conditions also prohibit harvest. In drought-stricken Rajasthan, where I have been involved for 17 years, the

3. Gerard Manley Hopkins, 'Hurrahing in Harvest', in *Poems* (Harmondsworth: Penguin,1953) ed. R. H. Gardiner, p. 31.

failure of monsoon rains frequently means that crops cannot survive. People can withstand one year's drought because they have stored grain from previous years. But in the second year of drought, the spectre of famine looms. Only through carefully conserving every drop of monsoon water when it comes is it possible to re-charge the wells, and enable crops to grow. This process we call water-harvesting. It is the ancient wisdom of the desert peoples. It is little short of a miracle to see the transformation of village communities who, through practising water-harvesting, are once more able to achieve solid crops to enable them to survive.

Solidarity with the global struggle is important, yet harvest can still be celebrated here. Apples are one of the glories of this country, and apple picking is a possibility for many. Once churches were surrounded by apple orchards – and there are echoes of this in popular carols, like 'Jesus Christ the Apple Tree'. Hedges are still bursting with blackberry bushes in September, although very few seem to be willing to stop and pluck. What is very clear is that the traditional character of Harvest Festival must change. The task is two-fold: our own responsibility to rediscover roots in the rhythms of sowing and reaping so as to celebrate the ingathering of the fruits is one aspect, but the political struggle to enable vast numbers of poor communities around the world to experience the reality of harvest just to survive is now an urgent Christian priority.

Mary Grey

266. Tap dancing

Ho, everyone who thirsts. Come to the waters …
(Isaiah 55:1)

Fresh sparkling water flows through the garden turning all to a lush,
    green pasture …
Precious water, life-giving water, free-to-all water …

A tap is turned.

The flow is stopped and the hand that turns holds the power,
reversing the garden to a barren desert.
Creation becomes uncreation,
water and food withdrawn at once.

The dancing children stall and turn,

their eyes of laughter sink into their cheeks,
fit to burst,
begging for life.

Water, flowing and pure, against water, stagnant and diseased.
So easily, at a turn of a tap.
Life and death, unhappy neighbours, sit side by side.
How is this justice?
... Those who have ...
... Those who have not ...
The spring of life is extinguished with the turn of a tap.

Tap, tap, tap.

And the political dance goes on.

The turn of a tap.

And life can flow again. Justice at last, essentials for all. So easy, so
    easy.

We are the brothers and sisters of our world,
sitting side by side,
children who may dance in the rainbow of water and light.
Hope for the world.

                                                        Martin Hazell

267. A story from Mozambique

*This is a traditional bedtime story told to the children of
Mozambique, but it has a simple moral that is entirely relevant to our
theme. It may be possible to turn it into a simple drama, with children
miming the parts of gazelles. Make horns from wire coat-hangers,
shaped into increasingly comic and elaborate shapes to sit on
children's heads.*

Once upon a time there was a family of gazelles. They wandered the
forest in Mozambique with their horns held high on their heads.
Their mother said to them: 'God has made your horns very beautiful.
They are just right for what you need. Make sure you keep them that
way.' Every day they would walk to the deep pool of water from

which they drank. They would look at their reflection in the water and admire their horns. They would say, 'Thank you, God, that we have just what we need.'

The gazelles took their mother's advice and were a contented family. All except the youngest one. One day he looked at his reflection in the water and said to himself, 'I have the most beautiful horns of all. Two little horns are not enough. The world would be a better place if I had more.' And as he said that, to his astonishment, an extra pair of horns, bigger than the first pair, grew.

The next day he went back to the water pool where everyone was drinking and showed off his new horns to his brothers and sisters. And when he looked at his reflection, he thought to himself, 'My, how these bigger horns suit me! The world would be a better place if I had even more.' And as he said it, to his amazement, another pair of horns, even bigger than the previous ones, grew.

His mother started to be worried. 'My dear son, don't do this!' she pleaded. 'It's not good for you to have more than you need.' But the gazelle did not listen to her. He kept growing more and more horns, and they kept getting bigger and bigger. And the more he had, the prouder he grew of what he had achieved.

But then one day, something terrible happened. A drought came to Mozambique. The pool where the gazelles came to drink became drier and drier. When the mother came to drink, she had to put her head deep down into the hole in order to reach the water. When the young gazelles came to drink, they too had to stretch deep, deep down to reach the water. But when the youngest gazelle tried to drink, he couldn't. He had so many horns, and they were so big, that he couldn't get his head into the hole. No matter how hard he tried, his horns got in the way. And because he couldn't reach the water he grew more and more thirsty. And without water to drink, he wasted away and died.

When parents in Mozambique tell this sad story to their children they explain the moral: The world has enough for everyone to have what they need. But there is not enough for everyone to have more than they need. Learn from the gazelle that we will not make a better world for ourselves by wanting more and more.

Christian Aid

Prayers

268. A prayer of confession
You show me the path of life ...
                              (Psalm 16:11)

Giver of Life. In the midst of a plundered world we groan with creation.
Lord, have mercy on us. Christ have mercy on us. Christ have mercy on us.

Giver of Life. In the midst of poisoned waters we groan with creation.
Lord, have mercy on us. Christ have mercy on us. Christ have mercy on us.

Giver of Life. In the midst of polluted air we groan with creation.
Lord, have mercy on us. Christ have mercy on us. Christ have mercy on us.

Giver of Life. In the midst of mountains of waste we groan with creation.
Lord, have mercy on us. Christ have mercy on us. Christ have mercy on us.

Giver of Life. In the midst of a world at war we groan with creation.
Lord, have mercy on us. Christ have mercy on us. Christ have mercy on us.

Giver of Life. We who are made in the image of God have gone astray, and creation groans with us.
Lord, have mercy on us. Christ have mercy on us. Christ have mercy on us.
Amen.

                              Christian Conference of Asia

269. Creator of the world we share
'When you pray say, "... Give us each day our daily bread ... "'
                              (Luke 11:2–3)

Generous, loving God we ask you
to give us today our daily bread.
Creator of the world we share
give us today our daily bread.
As we store the crops
and fill the barns
stack the shelves
pile high the tins
and wander the aisles
of supermarket choice
show us how to see the world
through the eyes of the hungry
teach us how to share with all
our daily bread.

Linda Jones

270. Community life

... where can I flee from your presence?
(Psalm 139:7)

O Lord Jesus Christ,
when we wake each day as the sun rises,
when we kneel in silence and speak to you in prayer,
when we come to the altar and receive your body in our hands,
when we study your Word and try to understand,
when we wash our clothes with our hands in a bucket of water,
when we stir up a fire and blow it into flames,
when we meet, laugh together and share our stories,
when we ride on the back of a truck with dust in our eyes,
when we are burnt by the sun as we walk the roads,
when we stand in the mud of our garden,
when we work in the plantation and the sweat runs down,
when we cook food in the smoke of the kitchen,
when we are hungry and share together the food you provide,
when we are tired and dirty and swim in the river,
when evening comes and the oil lamps are lit,
when we lie down to rest in the darkness of the night
O let us be filled in all these things with love for you,
let us never forget that you are always with us
and all our lives belong to you.
Amen.

Richard Carter

271. In times of need

... so that we may ... find grace in time of need.
(Hebrews 4:16)

Because the world is beautiful
and beauty is easily destroyed
and we are the stewards of creation:
we need you, Lord.
We need you.

Because we are weak and fail,
because we know so little but pretend so much,
because we are afraid:
we need you, Lord.
We need you.

Because we cannot live without you
we cannot walk in darkness:
we need you, Lord.
We need you.

Because you came among us
and sat beside us
and heard our stories
and healed our pain
and let us curse you, and even kill you
but loved us to the end
and won a victory over all our hatred:
we need you, Lord.
We need you.

Because we have your message to proclaim,
because we have your Kingdom to build,
because we have your children to save:
we need you, Lord.
We need you, now, and for ever.
Amen.

Richard Carter

272. Candles at harvest-time

... and what does the Lord require of you but to do justice, and to love kindness, and to walk humbly with your God?

(Micah 6:8)

As each candle is lit, the one lighting the candle will say:

I light this candle:
for those suffering hunger and injustice
as a result of natural disaster or the misuse of natural resources.
(*Mention any place that is known.*)

(pause)

I light this candle:
for those across the world
whose hands grew some of this food,
packed it and brought it to our land.
(*Mention any countries known as sources of the food.*)

(pause)

I light this candle:
for the gardeners, farmers and distributors in this country
who worked with weather and soil,
with road and with rail
to make the land productive
and to deliver its harvest
so we can eat food produced at home.
(*Mention any we know.*)

(pause)

I light this candle:
for the supermarket employees
who stack this food on the shelves
and take our money at the tills
with cheerful smiles.
(*Mention any we know.*)

(pause)

I light this candle:
for those who cooked and carried this food here
so that it can be shared by all of us who gather here
as a sign that we are friends
and share a common fellowship.
(*Mention any we know.*)

(pause)

I light this candle:
for ourselves, who belong to the earth
and are caught up with each other and the web of life.
May we learn to live justly together,
to honour the earth and walk humbly with our God.

                                                        Christian Meeting Point

273. A Harvest litany for the marginalised

VOICE 1:   Let us pray for the scavenging child.
    VOICE 2:   She goes about collecting tins
                  from richly furnished rubbish bins:
                  for those who dress in hope and rags
                  can find a use for plastic bags.
    RESPONSE: **Lord, you are there:**
                  accept our prayer.

    VOICE 1:   Let us pray for the homeless man.
    VOICE 2:   When sorrow cracked his crazy heart
                  flimsy achievement fell apart.
                  His home was bleak, his work was tough:
                  better to sleep alone and rough.
    RESPONSE: **Lord, you are there:**
                  accept our prayer.

    VOICE 1:   Let us pray for the woman who walks miles to fetch water.
    VOICE 2:   The village pump is far away.
                  She makes the journey twice a day.
                  Tied to her back – a little daughter.
                  But on her head – a weight of water.
    RESPONSE: **Lord, you are there:**
                  accept our prayer.

VOICE 1: Let us pray to the Lord who was despised and rejected.
VOICE 2: Dear Lord, who died beyond the pale,
your steadfast love can never fail.
Give us the grace we need to stand
with those who live in no man's land.
RESPONSE: **Lord, you are there:**
accept our prayer.

VOICE 1: Let us pray to the Lord who lives and loves for ever.
VOICE 2: Let every loner find a friend,
let sad recrimination end.
May all your people never cease
to grow in love and joy and peace.
RESPONSE: **Lord, you are there:**
accept our prayer.

John Coutts

274. Lord of the earth's resources

Lord of the earth's resources, of oil and wheat and trees;
Lord of all nature's forces and of the seven seas!
We contemplate with wonder, the skies, the everglade,
confessing that we plunder the good earth you have made.

We ransack God's creation, pollute the atmosphere;
then, in blank consternation, protest when faults appear.
Broad bowls of dust grow broader, strong chemicals defile;
the seasons, in disorder, withdraw their friendly smile.

Forgive, Lord, our wrongdoing, indifference and greed
and for the earth's renewing make stony hearts to bleed.
We'll dedicate our labours to make the desert flower
and with our global neighbours we'll work towards the hour.

Yet, Lord, so much in nature we cannot halt or change:
flood, hurricane and earthquake – destructive, sudden, strange.
Lord of the earth's resources we ask, bewildered, why?
Amid these mighty forces, teach us humility.

Praise, praise to God the Father: praise Jesus Christ the Son,
and praise the Holy Spirit while years eternal run!

God's love from the beginning looks far beyond the Fall
and, in the End, is winning a homeland for us all.

David Mowbray

275. We plough the fields and scatter

We plough the fields and scatter the good seed on our lands,
but nations who are deep in debt are left with empty hands.
The world is full of people who struggle to survive,
while we have food in plenty – O God, our care revive!
> Some good gifts around us have been acquired by stealth;
> forgive us, Lord, and move our hearts that we may share our
> wealth.

The fields of many countries are tilled to pay their debt,
while labourers go hungry, with basic needs unmet.
Their good, unfairly traded, make losses for our gain,
as most of all the profits in wealthy hands remain.

Your beautiful creation is fast becoming spoiled,
and deserts overrun the land where once the farmers toiled.
Forgive us this pollution of much that you have made,
and show us the solution for fair and equal trade.

Alison Blenkinsop

276. Summer joy?

'Summer suns are glowing' –
fine for Northern hymns:
not so good when blowing
sand clogs up our stream.

How shall those who're farming
grow what they must eat
when through global warming
harvests fail in heat?

'Everything rejoices' –
so it used to be:
but the bird's sweet voices
now fail silently.

Somewhere, planes and cars are
burning fuel fast:
this, they say, brings profit;
but folks starve at last.

In your mercy, Jesus,
our mistakes forgive.
Bring us to our senses!
Let the people live!

Daphne Fraser

277. Our Father
who is in us here on earth
holy is your name
in the hungry who share their bread and their song.
Your Kingdom come,
a generous land where confidence and truth reign.
Let us do your will.
Bring a cool breeze for those who sweat.
You are giving us our daily bread
when we manage to get back our lands
or to get a fairer wage.
Forgive us
for keeping silent in the face of injustice
and for burying our dreams.
Don't let us fall into the temptation
of taking up the same arms as the enemy,
but deliver us from evil which disunites us.
And we shall have believed in humanity and in life
and we shall have known your Kingdom
which is being built for ever and ever.

Christian Aid

278. **Prayer of Confession**

Creating God, you give light and life,
and express delight in your creation.
You gave the command to till and care for your garden,
but we have abused the beauty of creation and the keeping of your
  word.

We confess the plundering of finite resources.
We confess to stealing our descendants' birthright to life.
We confess the flagrant pollution of land, sea and air.
We confess the churches' lack of concern for the well-being of
    creation.
We confess the excesses within our own lifestyle.
Creating God, we have desecrated your creation and darkened your
    light.
In a moment of quiet we confess our profligate lifestyle and human
    greed.

Words of renewal

God of life and God of light, as we seek a new relationship with your
created order, may we sense the grace and peace of a new relationship
with you. Amen.

In the dawn of the day lead us to the garden of life that we might ...
prune the excess,
root out injustice,
water the wilting,
nourish the withered,
empty the potting shed of poison,
and at the eve of the day, rest, and wonder at God's garden.

www.ecocongregation.org

279. Loving God, source of all life and goodness,
    we are motionless and speechless before you.
    Enthralled and beguiled we praise you.
    Every fibre of our being quivers at the beauty and grandeur of your
        world,
    a world created by your hand, sustained by your laws and fashioned
        for our delight.

    Yet the world is fragile,
    created with such infinite balance,
    each plant and creature has its appointed life and worth,
    but is easily damaged by abuse, disregard and neglect of its resources.

    Forgive us that we have so often been careless, lacking respect for the
        earth and its peoples.
    We have taken for granted what you have created.

We have not walked gently on this earth but have trampled through life, aware only of our own needs and cares.

So often we have masked the beauty and integrity of your world and your world by petty rules and regulations, with little thought for your purposes.
With shame we acknowledge that we have so often spoilt what you have so generously gifted to us.

Yet still you call us to be co-creators and sustainers of life with you, to redeem that which has been damaged and to claim a new beginning.
Help us to live responsibly and with integrity so that all may enjoy your world and be nourished by it.
Amen.

Stella Bristow

280. You who turn storms into gentle winds,
and troubled seas into tranquil waters,
you who make yams grow
and bananas blossom,

wash our people with justice;
teach us with righteousness;
speak to us daily;
strengthen us to serve you.

Your Will Be Done
Christian Conference of Asia

282. O God, pour out on us the water of life that we may quench our thirst and draw strength from you. Help us to stand alongside those who struggle daily for clean water so that all may be refreshed and renewed by your love.

Christian Aid

283. Making the connection

Think of the difference fair trade brings,
the dignity of wages for work that is valued.

Pride in the history of learning to grow,
to carve, to stitch: that sense of purpose.

Think of the power of a coffee bean,
the taste of satisfaction. Crops grown,
enjoyed by others, appreciated,
giving the pleasure of making plans.

Think of the fingers that made that stitch,
weaving us together, thread to thread,
touch upon touch, smile meeting smile.
Imagine the dream and feel it taking shape.

Think of connecting hope with reality,
one world with another, lives and hearts
and voices in a joyful celebration.
Rejoice in the difference fair trade brings.

                                          Fiona Ritchie Walker

283. A prayer of intercession

Flow over your creation this day, O God.
offering to the world the living water of your life
so that the seeds of compassion may break forth,
in the greening of new possibilities for good
and the blossoming of justice.

Warm our cold hearts with the flame of your Spirit
so that we may feel again the passion of caring for others,
leaping up in the sharp colour of action for trade justice,
moving outwards in the fires of determination
that all the world may know a different day.

Take our hands, Jesus Christ,
leading us in courage to confront with courage
the forces which oppress and divide,
which exploit and tear from the people the fruits of their harvests.
Take our hearts, Jesus Christ,
and open them to the truth which will set others free to live.
Amen.

                                          Dorothy McRae-McMahon

284. A prayer for justice in trade

Tilt the scales,
      O God of the tiny seed:
      that the poor shall see justice.
Share the feast,
      O God of Eden's abundant garden:
      that each crop may fetch a fair price.
Upset the tables,
      O God of the upside-down kingdom:
      that the least can benefit from their trade.
Open our eyes,
      O God of life in all its fullness:
      that we may learn to walk the way of your Son
          tilting, sharing, upsetting this world
      not satisfied until the gifts of the harvest
      give a better deal, to all who hunger for one.
In the name of Jesus,
Amen.

                            Christian Aid

285.

Lord, thank you for all the tastes and colours we enjoy.
We remember those whose harvests are threatened.
Feed the hungry; change our priorities.
In this place and in all places
let your will be done.

Our systems and actions have
transformed your world of plenty;
the rich reap what belongs to the poor.
Forgive us; change our priorities.
In this place and in all places
let your will be done.

Sow in us your desire to see justice.
Grow in us some of your harvest generosity.
In all places, through us in this place,
let your will be done.
Amen.

                            Christian Aid

286. Pumpkins, peas, pears and rice,
potatoes, tomatoes, chillies and spice!
Lord, as we taste your harvest,
help us to remember
those who have grown it,
and where it has come from.
We lay down our selfish demands,
we accept our responsibility
to take care of your creation.
Amen.

Christian Aid

287. Prayer of confession

God our Father,
we confess our negligence in caring for your creation.
Lord, have mercy.
Lord, have mercy.
We confess our reluctance to say thank you to you when we enjoy the
    fruits of the harvest.
Lord, have mercy.
Christ, have mercy.
We confess our greediness in storing up material things, and our
    failure to share with our sisters and brothers.
Lord, have mercy.
Lord, have mercy.

Jessie Anand

288. Standing in solidarity

God of solidarity,
you entrusted the earth and its resources
to the stewardship of humankind.

Yet the goods of creation,
destined for the whole human race,
are enjoyed by a privileged few.

For the producers of our consumer goods
there are no privileges;
working long hours for little pay.

For us, who benefit from unfair trade,
we take for granted the toils of men and women
who maintain our standard of living.

Inspired by Jesus who brought good news to the poor,
show us how we may stand in solidarity with people
who suffer through unjust trading rules.

May they soon experience the joy of the vineyard workers
who were called to be the first among the last,
and were included as equal inheritors of your Kingdom.

Tony Singleton

289. Praise
(Based on Psalm 8)

God, when we think about your creation, we're amazed;
we walk through a masterpiece every day.
Your imagination has created such beauty.
We can never come to the end of your wonders.
How incredible it is that you've trusted us to take care
of your prized possession!
You've shown us how to sustain life:
help us to use this knowledge for the good of your world,
the benefit of your people and the glory of your name.
We praise you, painter of creation's harvests!

Christian Aid

290. A prayer seeking God's blessing

Accept, Lord God, this, our offering of the fruits of our labours, the work of our hands, and the devotion of our hearts which we now present unto you. Bless them for your glory; use them for the building up of your church and the relief of those in need. This we ask through Jesus Christ our Lord.
Amen.

Jessie Anand

291. Prayer from South India

Lord God Almighty, the Creator and Father of all, you crown the year with your goodness. We thank you that you have ordained for humankind both seed-time and harvest, and bestow upon us the fruits of the earth in their season. For these and all other mercies, we praise and magnify your glorious name, through Christ our Lord.
Amen.

translated by Sister Kasthuri Manickam,
Church of South India

292.

As you have set the moon in the sky to be the poor person's lantern, so let your light shine in my dark life and lighten my path.

As the rice is sown in the water and brings forth grain in great abundance, so let your word be sown among us that the harvest may be great.

And as the banyan tree sends forth its branches to take root in the soil, so let your life take root in our lives.
Amen.

adapted from *Another Day: Prayers of the Human Family*

293.

Lord,
I believe that I can make a positive difference in the world
by my attitudes and my interventions.
Help me to become more aware of the wonder, beauty and vulnerability of your creation
and to make every effort to cherish and protect it.
Amen.

Imelda Davidson
South Africa

294.

Bless our beautiful land, O Lord,
with its wonderful variety of people,
of races, cultures and languages.
May we be a nation
of laughter and joy,
of justice and reconciliation,
of peace and unity,
of compassion, caring and sharing.

We pray this prayer for a true patriotism,
in the powerful name of Jesus our Lord.

Archbishop Desmond Tutu

295. To you, Creator of nature and humanity, of truth and beauty, I pray:

Hear my voice, for it is the voice of the victims of all wars and violence among individuals and nations.

Hear my voice, for it is the voice of all children who suffer and will suffer when people put their faith in weapons and war.

Hear my voice when I beg you to instil into the hearts of all human beings the wisdom of peace, the strength of justice and the joy of fellowship.

Hear my voice and grant insight and strength so that we may always respond to hatred with love, to injustice with total dedication to justice, to need with the sharing of self, to war with peace.

O God, hear my voice, and grant unto the world your everlasting peace.

Pope John Paul II

Sources and Acknowledgements

Permission to use the reflections and prayers in *Just One Year* has been kindly granted by the copyright holders, to whom any requests to reproduce individual items should be directed. We have made very effort to trace the sources of the material used, but would be happy to rectify any omissions or errors in future printings.

ADVENT
Reflections
1. Wendy Bray, *Christian Aid Lent Book 2004*.
2. Sean Healey SMA, specially written for this book.
3. Kevin Toomey OP, specially written for this book.
4. Sheila Provender, letter.
5. Henri Nouwen.
6. Oscar Romero.

Prayers
7. Wendy Bray, *Christian Aid Lent Book 2004*.
8. Gray Featherstone, *Roots for Churches*.
9. Annabel Shilson-Thomas, CAFOD.
10. Bernadette Farrell, OCP Publications.
11. Linda Jones, CAFOD.
12. Annabel Shilson-Thomas, CAFOD.
13. Lesley G. Anderson, specially written for this book.
14. Alan and Clare Amos, specially written for this book.
15. Marjory Macaskill, specially written for this book.
16. Marjory Macaskill. specially written for this book.
17. Lala Winkley, CTBI.
18. Pamela Turner, CTBI.
19. Linda Jones, CAFOD.
20. Annabel Shilson-Thomas, CAFOD.
21. Annabel Shilson-Thomas, CAFOD.
22. Linda Jones, CAFOD.
23. Annabel Shilson-Thomas, CAFOD.
24. Kate McIlhagga, from *Shine on, Star of Bethlehem*, ed. Geoffrey Duncan (Canterbury Press, 2004).
25. Grace Sheppard, specially written for this book.
26. Clare Amos, specially written for this book.
27. Gerardo Oberman, World Council of Churches website.

28. After St Anselm, from *The Book of a Thousand Prayers*, ed. Angela Ashwin (Zondervan, 2002).
29. Ephraem the Syrian.
30. Bede.
31. Unknown.
32. Clementina Naita, CAFOD.

CHRISTMAS AND EPIPHANY
Reflections
33. Joseph Donders.
34. Mary Britt OP, specially written for this book.
35. Naim Ateek, Sabeel website.
36. Christian Aid.

Prayers
37. Dorothy Day.
38. Harry Wiggett.
39. Annabel Shilson-Thomas, CAFOD.
40. Graham Kings, specially written for this book.
41. Annabel Shilson-Thomas, CAFOD.
42. Christian Aid.
43. Clare McBeath, *Roots for Churches*.
44. Jan Grimwood, CTBI.
45. Fiona Liddell, CTBI.
46. Gray Featherstone, *Roots for Churches*.
47. Vivienne Lassetter, specially written for this book.
48. Vivienne Lassetter, specially written for this book.
49. Peter Rose and Anne Conlon, CAFOD.
50. Laurentia Johns OSB, CAFOD.
51. Christian Aid.
52. South African Council of Churches, Christian Aid website.
53. Mary Cotes, *Roots for Churches*.
54. Stephen J. Brown, *Roots for Churches*.
55. Ann Lewin, *Candles and Kingfishers: Reflections on the Journey* (Foundery Press, 1997).
56. Lesley G. Anderson, specially written for this book.
57. Rebecca Dudley, Christian Aid.
58. Martin E. Leckebusch, Christian Aid.
59. Annabel Shilson-Thomas, CAFOD.
60. Annabel Shilson-Thomas, CAFOD.
61. Annabel Shilson-Thomas, CAFOD.
62. Ann Lewin, *Candles and Kingfishers: Reflections on the Journey* (Foundery Press, 1997).

JESUS BEGINS HIS MINISTRY: Ordinary Time 1
Reflections
63. Margaret Hebblethwaite, specially written for this book.
64. Margaret Atkins, specially written for this book.
65. Chris Chivers, specially written for this book.
66. Imelda Davidson, *CAFOD/DLT Lent Book 2001*.

Prayers
67. *Common Worship: Christian Initiation* (Church House Publishing, 2006) copyright © The Archbishops' Council 2006.
68. Maranatha Community.
69. Imelda Davidson, *CAFOD/DLT Lent Book 2001*.
70. Christian Aid.
71. Tony Singleton, CAFOD.
72. *Hunger for Justice*, Christian Aid.
73. Terry Oakley, *Roots for Churches*.
74. Sheila Cassidy.
75. Roy Jenkins.
76. Janet Wootton, *Christian Aid Lent Book 2002*.
77. Jan Grimwood, CTBI.
78. CAFOD, *Celebrating One World*.
79. John Bell, Christian Aid.
80. Garth Hewitt, *Hunger for Justice*, Christian Aid.
81. Diakonia Council of Churches, South Africa, Christian Aid.
82. Brazilian Youth Group, CAFOD.
83. Mary Cotes, *Roots for Churches*.
84. Timothy Woods, *Roots for Churches*.
85. Rabindrath Tagore, Andhra Christian College.
86. Christian Conference of Asia.
87. White Fathers of the Sahara, CAFOD.
88. World Council of Churches.
89. World Council of Churches.
90. Anon.
91. From Zimbabwe.
92. Clement of Rome.
93. Erasmus.
94. Mozarabic Sacramentary, *Great Souls at Prayer*, ed. Mary Tileston (Keats Publishing, 1983).
95. Eugene Bersier, *Great Souls at Prayer*, ed. Mary Tileston (Keats Publishing, 1983).
96. Earl of Shaftesbury, *Great Souls at Prayer*, ed. Mary Tileston (Keats Publishing, 1983).

LENT
Reflections
97. Andrew McLellan.
98. Jon Sobrino SJ, *CAFOD/DLT Lent Book 1998*.

99. Bishop Kallistos of Diokleia, *The Lenten Journey* (St Stephen's Press, 2003), pp. 1, 16.
100. *Christian Aid Lent Book 2003.*
101. Imelda Davidson, *CAFOD/DLT Lent Book 2001.*
102. Mercy Amba Oduyoye, *CAFOD Lent Book 2000.*
103. Henri Nouwen.

Prayers
104. N. Ndungane, *Christian Aid Lent Book 2004.*
105. © Jan Berry from *Dancing on Slaves* compiled by Geoffrey Duncan and Martin Hazell © compilation, The United Reformed Church, 2005. Used by permission.
106. Annabel Shilson-Thomas, CAFOD.
107. Annabel Shilson-Thomas, CAFOD.
108. Peter Graystone, Christian Aid.
109. Maggie Hindley, *Roots for Churches.*
110. Christian Conference of Asia.
111. AIDS Sunday, Christian Conference of Asia.
112. Linda Jones, CAFOD.
113. St Anselm.
114. © Neil Thorogood from the worship material written for The United Reformed Church Assembly, Warwick, 2005. Used by permission.
115. Timothy Woods, *Roots for Churches.*
116. Mary Bradford, Christian Aid.
117. Christian Conference of Asia.
118. Norma P. Dollaga, www-e-alliance.ch/gwa_resources.jsp. © 2004 Norma P. Dollaga.
119. Irene Sayer, www-e-alliance.ch/gwa_resources.jsp/Traidcraft. © 2004 World Alliance of Reformed Churches, www.warc.ch.
120. Colin Gibson, Dunedin Methodist Church.
121. Evan Lewis, Dunedin Methodist Church.
122. World Alliance of Reformed Churches, www-e-alliance.ch/gwa_resources.jsp. © 2004 World Alliance of Reformed Churches, www.warc.ch.
123. World Alliance of Reformed Churches, www-e-alliance.ch/gwa_resources.jsp. © 2004 World Alliance of Reformed Churches, www.warc.ch.
124. David Adam.
125. Mother Teresa.
126. St Francis.
127. Johann Arndt, *Great Souls at Prayer* ed. Mary Tileston (Keats Publishing, 1983).

HOLY WEEK
Reflections
128. Sandra Winton OP, specially written for this book.
129. Daniel B. Das, specially written for this book.

130. Kathy Galloway, *Christian Aid Lent Book 2002*.
131. Jean Vanier, France, the founder of the L'Arche community. From *Drawn into the Mystery of Jesus through the Gospel of John* (DLT, 2004), pp. 235–6.
132. Peter Graystone, Christian Aid website.
133. Oliver McTernan, USA, specially written for this book.
134. Brian Pierce OP, specially written for this book.
135. Oliver Rafferty, specially written for this book.

Prayers
136. Joyce Karuri, specially written for this book.
137. Clare McBeath, *Roots for Churches*.
138. Bishop Jacob, CSI.
139. Caroline Ainger/Methodist Relief and Development Fund.
140. Roy Jenkins.
141. Brian Hudson, CTBI.
142. David Coleman.
143. Lesley Husselbee, *Roots for Churches*.
144. Jan Berry.
145. Janet Morley, *All Desires Known* (SPCK, 2005).
146. Thomas Cullinan OSB, specially written for this book.
147. Richard Carter, specially written for this book.
148. Hugo Slim, specially written for this book.
149. Indian Christian, USPG website.
150. Clare Amos, specially written for this book.
151. Grace Sheppard, specially written for this book.
152. Ann Lewin, *Candles and Kingfishers: Reflections on the Journey* (Foundery Press, 1997).
153. Janet Morley, *All Desires Known* (SPCK, 2005).
154. Kathy Galloway, *Christian Aid Lent Book 2002*.
155. Mary Cotes, *Roots for Churches*.
156. Kathy Galloway.
157. World Council of Churches.
158. Michael Ramsey, *Prayers of our Faith*, ed. Douglas Dales (Canterbury Press, 2003).

EASTER
Reflections
159. Lavinia Byrne, *Christian Aid Lent Book 2004*.
160. Henri Burin des Roziers OP, Brazil, specially written for this book.
161. Jean Vanier, France, founder of the L'Arche community. *Drawn into the Mystery of Jesus through the Gospel of John* (DLT, 2004), pp. 329–30.
162. Phumzile Zondi-Mabizela, an Elder in the Uniting Presbyterian Church of Southern Africa and Coordinator of the Women and Gender Programme at the Institute for the Study of the Bible, University of Natal, South Africa, *CAFOD/DLT Lent Book 2004*.

Prayers
163. Clare McBeath, *Roots for Churches.*
164. Clare McBeath, *Roots for Churches.*
165. Clare McBeath, *Roots for Churches.*
166. Richard Carter, specially written for this book.
167. Donald Macaskill, CTBI.
168. Annabel Shilson-Thomas, CAFOD.
169. Annabel Shilson-Thomas, CAFOD.
170. Annabel Shilson-Thomas, CAFOD.
171. Ana and Tod Gobledale, specially written for this book.
172. Ana Gobledale, specially written for this book.
173. Frances Makower, RSCJ.
174. Pam Macnaughton, specially written for this book.
175. Iris Perez, *Maryknoll Book of Prayers*. Copyright © by Orbis Books. Used by permission of the publisher.
176. Christine Odell, *Open with God* (Methodist Publishing House, 2004).

PENTECOST AND TRINITY SUNDAY
Reflections
177. Gabrielle Kelly OP, specially written for this book.
178. Anil Netto, specially written for this book.
179. Esther Mombo, specially written for this book.
180. Jean Vanier, *Befriending the Stranger* (DLT, 2005), p. 110.

Prayers
181. Janet Morley, *All Desires Known* (SPCK, 2005).
182. Margaret McNulty, CAFOD.
183. Albert Nolan OP, specially written for this book.
184. Sue Cooper, CAFOD.
185. Aruna Gnanadasan, specially written for this book.
186. Elizabeth Tapia, specially written for this book.
187. Elizabeth Tapia, specially written for this book.
188. Tony Singleton, CAFOD.
189. June Boyce-Tilman, CTBI.
190. Kathy Galloway, ACTS/CTBI.
191. Diakonia Council of Churches, South Africa. Christian Aid website.
192. Ann Smith, CAFOD.
193. From *Catch the Vision* © The United Reformed Church. Used by permission.
194. Gray Featherstone, *Roots for Churches.*
195. Terry Oakley, *Roots for Churches.*
196. Vince Gilbert, ACTS/CTBI.
197. Allan Boesak, World Council of Churches/Wild Goose.
198. Maggie Hindley, *Roots for Churches.*
199. Barry Vendy, *Roots for Churches.*
200. Beverley Humphries, *Roots for Churches.*
201. Annabel Shilson-Thomas, CAFOD.
202. Janet Morley, *All Desires Known.*

203. St Augustine.
204. Bishop Munib Younan, Christian Aid website.
205. World Council of Churches.
206. World Council of Churches.
207. Brother Roger of Taizé, *Book of a Thousand Prayers*, ed. Angela Ashwin (Zondervan, 2002).
208. Alan Paton.
209. Mary Cotes, *Roots for Churches*.
210. St Benedict.
211. St Thomas Aquinas.
212. Bunsen's Collection, *Great Souls at Prayer*, ed. Mary Tileston (Keats Publishing, 1983).

JESUS CONTINUES HIS MINISTRY: Ordinary Time 2
Reflections

213. Frank Turner SJ, specially written for this book.
214. Cherie Booth QC, human rights lawyer, specially written for this book.
215. Carla Grosch-Miller from *Dancing on Slaves* compiled by Geoffrey Duncan and Martin Hazell © compilation, The United Reformed Church, 2005. Used by permission.
216. David Adam, *CAFOD/DLT Lent Book 2001*.
217. Dr Anthony G. Reddie, specially written for this book.
218. Tina Beattie, specially written for this book.
219. Frank Regan SSC, specially written for this book.
220. Eildon Dyer, *Christian Aid Lent Book 2002*.
221. Inderjit Bhogal, *Christian Aid Lent Book 2002*.
222. Njongonkulu Ndungane, Archbishop of Cape Town and former prisoner on Robben Island, *Christian Aid Lent book 2004*.
223. Margaret Silf, *CAFOD/DLT Lent Book 2002*.
224. Ian Smith, *All Year Round* (CBTI, 2004), p. 198.
225. Wendy M. Wright, specially written for this book.
226. Philippe Denis OP, South Africa, specially written for this book.
227. Dr Sarojini Nadar, School of Religion and Theology, University of Kwa-Zulu Natal, South Africa, specially written for this book.
228. Phumsile Zondi-Mabizela, an Elder in the Uniting Presbyterian Church of Southern Africa and Coordinator of the Women and Gender Programme at the Institute for the Study of the Bible, University of Natal, South Africa, *CAFOD/DLT Lent Book 2004*.
229. St John Chrysostom.

Prayers

230. Janet Morley, *All Desires Known* (SPCK, 2005).
231. Eildon Dyer, *Christian Aid Lent Book 2002*.
232. Inderjit Bhogal, *Christian Aid Lent Book 2002*.
233. David Adam, *CAFOD Lent Book 2001*.
234. Jill Thornton and Clare McBeath, *Roots for Churches*.
235. *Voices from the South*, ACTS/CTBI.

236. *Voices from the South*, ACTS/CTBI.
237. Tod and Ana Gobledale, specially written for this book.
238. David Mowbray, Christian Aid.
239. Eduardo P. Hontiveros, Christian Aid.
240. Diakonia Council of Churches, South Africa.
241. Ingrid Shelley, *Roots for Churches*.
242. Yashoda Sutton, CTBI.
243. Judy Bainbridge, *Roots for Churches*.
244. Judy Bainbridge, *Roots for Churches*.
245. Rachel Poolman, *Roots for Churches*.
246. Andrew Roberts, *Roots for Churches*.
247. Maggie Hindley, *Roots for Churches*.
248. Deborah. McVey, *Roots for Churches*.
249. Annabel Shilson-Thomas, CAFOD.
250. World AIDS Day 2003.
251. Roots, *Roots for Churches*.
252. Peter Privett, *Roots for Churches*.
253. Roots, *Roots for Churches*.
254. Richard Bowers.
255. Lala Winkley, CTBI. Originally written for WOW (Women's Ordination Worldwide), 2001.
256. Grace Sheppard, specially written for this book.
257. Grace Sheppard, specially written for this book.
258. World Council of Churches.
259. Martin Luther, *Book of a Thousand Prayers*, ed. Angela Ashwin (Zondervan, 2002).
260. Joyce Karuri.
261. Evelyn Underhill, *Prayers of our Faith*, ed. Douglas Dales (Canterbury Press, 2003).
262. George Dawson, *Great Souls at Prayer*, ed. Mary Tileston (Keats Publishing, 1983).
263. Thomas Wilson, *Great Souls at Prayer*, ed. Mary Tileston (Keats Publishing, 1983).
264. Christina Rossetti, *Great Souls at Prayer*, ed. Mary Tileston (Keats Publishing, 1983).

HARVEST
Reflections

265. Mary Grey, specially written for this book.
266. Martin Hazell, from *Dancing on Slaves* complied by Geoffrey Duncan and Martin Hazell © compilation, The United Reformed Church, 2005. Used by permission.
267. Christian Aid week material.
268. Christian Conference of Asia.

Prayers

269. Linda Jones, CAFOD.

270. Richard Carter, specially written for this book.
271. Richard Carter, specially written for this book.
272. Christian Meeting Point, CTBI.
273. John Coutts, CTBI.
274. David Mowbray, *Hunger for Justice*, Christian Aid.
275. Alison Blenkinsop, *Hunger for Justice*, Christian Aid.
276. Daphne Fraser, CTBI.
277. Christian Aid.
278. www.ecocongregation.org.
279. Stella Bristow, *Roots for Churches*.
280. Christian Conference of Asia.
281. Christian Aid.
282. Fiona Ritchie Walker, www.e-alliance.ch/gwa_resources.jsp/Traidcraft.
283. Dorothy McRae-McMahon, www.e-alliance.ch/gwa_resources.jsp. © 2004 Dorothy McRae-McMahon/Ecumenical Advocacy Alliance, www.e-alliance.ch.
284. Christian Aid.
285. Christian Aid.
286. Christian Aid.
287. Jessie Anand, USPG.
288. Tony Singleton, CAFOD.
289. Christian Aid.
290. Jessie Anand, USPG.
291. Church of South India.
292. *Another Day: Prayers of the Human Family*, Triangle.
293. Imelda Davidson, *CAFOD/DLT Lent Book 2001*.
294. Desmond Tutu, *Book of a Thousand Prayers*, ed. Angela Ashwin (Zondervan, 2002).
295. Pope John Paul II.

Index of Authors